DARE TO DREAM

The Dukes hold up the championship trophy after winning the 1981 ECAC Tournament. Photograph courtesy of James Madison University Athletics.

DARE TO DREAM

How James Madison University Became Coed
and Shocked the Basketball World

by Lou Campanelli
with Dave Newhouse

FOREWORD BY RONALD E. CARRIER

George F. Thompson Publishing

To my wife, Dawn, and my children, Kyle, Brooke and Racelle,
for their love and support.
To my grandchildren, Luciana, Grant, Sterling, Caprice and Ava,
who keep me smiling.
To my dad and best teacher, John J. Campanelli.
To my mom, Josephine, a tender heart.
To my brother, John Jr. ("Bear"); we've always been there for each other.

—L.C.

To Callan and Campbell,
a grandfather's legacy.

—D.N.

Charles Fisher brings the ball down court in JMU's first-round game against Georgetown in the 1981 NCAA East Regional. The Dukes defeated the Hoyas 61–55 in a game that brought JMU to the nation's attention. Photograph courtesy of James Madison University Athletics.

CONTENTS

With or without a shovel, Dr. Ronald E. Carrier knew groundbreaking. During his first decade as the fourth president of James Madison University, he brought new buildings throughout campus: Godwin, Miller, and Chandler halls; Greek Row; Madison (now Bridgeforth) Stadium; Grafton-Stovall Theatre; and an addition to the Carrier Library. At the latter's groundbreaking, pictured here, Board of Visitors member Dick Strauss happily watched fellow board member Nell Long and Director of Libraries Mary Haban indent the ground while Dr. Carrier offered support. By 1983, JMU was ranked by *U.S. News & World Report* as one of "America's best colleges and universities," a legacy that continues today. Photograph courtesy of James Madison University Libraries: Special Collections.

FOREWORD

Dr. Ronald E. Carrier
PRESIDENT EMERITUS, JAMES MADISON UNIVERSITY

When I first visited Madison College in October 1970, I found a small-town school that was primarily a teachers' college for women with around 3,000 students (400 men). At the time, I was a vice president and provost at Memphis State University, a campus approaching 20,000 students in the midst of a turbulent period, with all the excitement of a sprawling urban institution: Athletic programs, cultural events, and academic challenges.

My wife, Edith, and I were part of a very satisfying social life in Memphis. Why would I trade my position at Memphis State for the presidency of Madison College? Higher education had just left the most challenging time in the history of higher education. The transformation of institutions and the sense of empowering students were forces in changing the college campus scene. This was an environment of racial issues and the Vietnam War. I believed that there was potential for this emerging college in Harrisonburg, Virginia, to move with these challenging times into a new era of education and that it could carry unlimited changes into the future.

I realized that Madison College was a place where I could have an impact. So, in January 1971, I began twenty-nine years as its president—a great journey, a wonderful challenge, and a broadband of opportunities. Five stages of transformation had to be undertaken. First: Curriculum and growth in student diversity and enrollment. Second: Cultural and curriculum expansion and change in social rules. Third: Construction of new buildings. Fourth: Enhancement of faculty and the student body. Fifth: Graduate studies and research.

The immediate task was to increase enrollment so that the funds generated by that increase would diversify the curriculum. Many forces were at play that brought about the change and the transformation. One of the important activities that I implemented, and which I felt was important to the transformation of a college into a university, was to build an athletic program that served both men and women.

Madison College had a long history of very fine and competitive women's programs. They weren't, however, members of the National Collegiate Athletic Association, or NCAA. And the men's program at that level was just starting upon my arrival. The new intercollegiate program was to play a very important role in the transformation of our institution into its present status as a nationally known, and highly respected, major university.

But, back in 1971, we had to find a niche that would allow us to compete successfully, academically and athletically, with other Virginia institutions. That niche was defined by placing a great emphasis on the undergraduate program, social life, athletic programs, and many other clubs and organizations that allowed students to reach their full potential.

Athletically, that potential required growth on the field of play, because we were lacking in sports facilities. We played baseball at Simms School, which today is a continuing education center for the City of Harrisonburg. We played basketball at the old Keezell Gym before shifting to Harrisonburg High School. When we started football, we also played at Harrisonburg High until a facility could be built on our campus.

Gradually, we began to look like a major university in terms of our sports programs. We built Godwin Hall, which served as a physical education facility and basketball arena, while also housing programs for gymnastics, swimming, and volleyball. We built a baseball field on property purchased on the back of campus. We built a football stadium and a track and field facility adjacent to Godwin Hall.

We advanced, within a four-year period, from Division III to Division II to Division I, thanks to the guidance of our fine athletic director, Dean Ehlers, who also coached men's basketball during the first year of that transformation. Then we turned to a new person, Lou Campanelli, to lead our men's basketball program, which became one of the main athletic endeavors of the university. Partly through our success in basketball, Madison College evolved into James Madison University in 1976.

Lou's record of achievement at JMU was extraordinary. His passion and enthusiasm for the game and for his players was reflected in various ways. He had a perfect graduation rate. His winning seasons led, eventually, to the building of the new, larger Convocation Center. And he achieved with players who were

This aerial photo of Madison College from 1951 shows the original and intimate 1908 campus layout, designed by Richmond architect Charles M. Robinson, and the bucolic Shenandoah Valley landscape to the east, with the base of Massanutten Mountain at the top. U.S. 11 (the old Valley Pike) is at the bottom. Fast forward only a few decades and that undeveloped land east of the campus will be divided by Interstate 81 and filled in with large-scale commericial development, including Valley Mall beside U.S. 33, as well as new student housing, the future campus for the College of the Applied Science and Technology, and Edith J. Carrier Aboretum that were developed under Dr. Carrier's presidency. Photograph courtesy of the 1951 *Schoolma'am*, the school's yearbook.

This aerial view from 1999 shows the expanded JMU campus that reflects Dr. Carrier's vision for the university. Following Dr. Carrier's official retirement, Dr. Linwood H. Rose became JMU's fifth president in 1998. U.S. 11 is at the bottom of the photograph, and Interstate 81 (top diagonal) parallels the Norfolk and Southern railroad track (center diagonal). The JMU campus is unique because tens of thousands of drivers on I-81 pass through it every day. Godwin Hall (center right, adjacent to Bridgeforth Stadium) was home to Coach Lou's initial teams; the Convocation Center (top right, east of I-81) is where the Dukes later played and still play today. Photograph courtesy of the Edith J. Carrier Aboretum at James Madison University.

overlooked or passed over by the major basketball powers. Lou produced two NCAA Division II tournament teams and then three consecutive NCAA Division I tournament teams, scoring some significant upsets. Lou's young men fought highly ranked teams from Virginia and North Carolina down to the wire. That one specific period, 1981 to 1983, remains a special time in JMU's athletic history.

Besides Lou's accomplishments, there were achievements throughout the athletic department, such as our beating the University of Virginia in football in 1982 and our baseball team qualifying for the College World Series, also in 1982. My vision of transforming the institution by providing opportunities for student growth and development was realized, in part, through the importance of athletic competition.

I made the correct choice in coming to Madison in 1971, and I made the correct choice in hiring Lou Campanelli to help guide the institution through a most important transition. And may I say, Go Dukes!

This book gives the reader a close-up view of Lou's basketball program, with his wonderful cast of overachievers. The book also reveals Lou's own personal transition, which is a book in itself. We are grateful to Coach Campanelli for recording these memories for us.

"It all started out as 'Dolley' Madison College, a largely all-girls' school, when a decision was made by President Ronald E. Carrier to go co-ed, build a mens' sports program, and eventually change the name to James Madison University. Lou Campanelli, one of the most innovative college basketball coaches, took on the challenge with the help of Dr. Carrier. Four years later, Madison College was in the NCAA Division II Tournament for the first time; and, only five years later, the newly named JMU was not only in the NCAA Division I Tournament, but it was knocking off Georgetown, Ohio State, and West Virginia in big upsets and playing eventual 1982 national-champion North Carolina to a classic two-point game. Coach Lou's commitment to his players and institution, along with his cutting-edge basketball defenses and flex offenses, were light years ahead of his time."

—ROLLIE MASSIMINO, *Head Basketball Coach, Villanova University, 1973–1992, who won the 1985 NCAA national championship and was inducted into the National Collegiate Basketball Hall of Fame in 2013*

"I lived this great adventure with Lou Campanelli from the beginning, and to watch the program grow and develop over the years was truly amazing. When it came to basketball, Lou was the most fundamentally sound coach I've ever been associated with. No shortcuts, no cheating, just integrity, keeping things simple with great execution—these guiding principles were integral to his recipe for success."

—MIKE FRATELLO, *NBA analyst and NBA Coach of the Year*

"Lou was very passionate and enthusiastic about the game, even as a high school coach. He knew in his heart he wanted to be a college coach, and he achieved his goals with great success."

—HUBIE BROWN, *NBA analyst, two-time NBA Coach of the Year, and 2005 inductee into the Naismith Memorial Basketball Hall of Fame*

DARE TO DREAM

This aerial photo from 2011 shows the original JMU campus between Interstate 81 (top) and U.S. 11 (bottom). This is the campus that greeted Coach Lou and some of his original players on their homecoming to campus on January 25, 2014. Dr. Jonathan R. Alger became JMU's sixth president on July 1, 2012, following the presidency of Dr. Rose who, along with generous alumnae, was instrumental in building the new world-class, state-of-the-art Forbes Center for the Performing Arts (bottom center), which opened in 2011 and overlooks the historic 1908 quad, expanding Bridgeforth Stadium (top right), and renovating Duke Hall and its distinguished Gallery of Fine Art (bottom left). Photograph (original in color) courtesy of the James Madison University Marketing Photography Department.

INTRODUCTION :
Homecoming

Dave Newhouse

T**he red van crawled unnoticed** through the James Madison University campus on a chilly Saturday morning, in January 2014, motoring past three-story buildings that populate former fields and hills. Academic majors offered inside these buildings mostly weren't available when the school opened its doors in 1908. There were no male students then, no intercollegiate sports, no typical campus life. The school even lacked a name that stuck. Philosophically and architecturally, few universities in the country would change so dramatically.

Six passengers in the red van are largely responsible for this unique transformation. The driver, Lou Campanelli, built a winning basketball program that brought national recognition to this once rural college in Harrisonburg, in the beautiful Shenandoah Valley of Virginia. Five players whom he recruited during the 1970s, and who forged James Madison University's greatest basketball success, joined him on this campus tour in January 2014.

Sardined into their seats, 6-foot-8 Dan Ruland, 6-foot-7 Linton Townes, 6-foot-4 David Dupont, 6-foot-3 1/2 Pat Dosh, and 6-foot Joe Pfahler sat crammed behind Campanelli and his memoir collaborator. Their knee-squeezing discomfort was eased by their eagerness to explore a campus that had undergone a radical change since their undergraduate days.

"The campus TV station was the only building that was right there," said Pfahler, pointing out the window as the van approached Newman Lake, occupied this day by some fifty ducks, flapping their wings in twenty-degree weather. "There were no fraternities and sororities around either."

Campanelli drove past the newly expanded 25,000-seat football stadium. When Pfahler was recruited as Campanelli's first scholarship player in 1972, football hadn't yet arrived at Madison College. Dosh arrived three years later, by which time a small, high school-like stadium had been constructed.

"There were only bleachers on one side," said Dosh. "It didn't really make any difference, because no one went inside to watch football games. The best party every week was on the hill outside the stadium."

Campanelli drove on as Dosh's attention shifted elsewhere.

"The bookstore and the parking lot weren't there," Dosh said, noting further change. "All the school buildings were close together on the quad. My only time spent down campus was for practice and games. Except for Godwin Hall and a few dorms, everything else was above campus."

After Dosh graduated, the college expanded from one campus into two, upper and lower levels, divided by Interstate 81. Dining choices expanded as well after he picked up his degree.

"The round building we just passed," said Dupont, "had the dining hall, Dukes Grill, and a salad and hot dog bar. That was it for eating choices. The student union was an intersection where everyone traveled through. It was a place to hang out, to visit with your friends, and to sight-see."

To sight-see, indeed, as there were plenty of girls to ogle. The school was founded as an all-girls institution to produce elementary school teachers. Initially known as the Normal and Industrial School for Women at Harrisonburg, the school underwent several name changes, becoming, in order, Harrisonburg Teachers College, Madison College, and, finally, James Madison University. The school didn't become fully coed until incoming president Dr. Ronald E. Carrier sanctioned the move in 1971. He changed the name to James Madison University in 1976, in effect, one president saluting another.

"Dr. Carrier lived on campus, right there," said Dosh, pointing to a house by Carrier Library, yet another campus manifestation. "There used to be a road here. Now it's a sidewalk. And there was a small gym, Keezell Hall."

Small edifices, over time, became larger structures, which the players gazed at before Campanelli, mistakenly, steered the red van onto a sidewalk—all because the campus he once knew no longer looked the same.

Dupont espied one building that brought back memories. "I had an anatomy class there," he said, "that had a cadaver."

"You lifted that cadaver's arm without a glove," Ruland reminded him.

Romance developed in that anatomy class. "That's where I met my wife," said Dupont. "I pinned one of her sorority buttons on the cadaver."

Dosh recognized a familiar building. "We just rode past my second home, the (today's Carrier) Library," he said. "That's where I spent most of my time here at JMU."

"The library has a wing named after him," chuckled Pfahler.

Others in the red van joined in the laughter at Dosh's expense.

"The percentage of girls to boys was seventy to thirty," Dosh continued. "Even a guy like me could get a girl. This quad was the place to be on a warm April afternoon. They'd all come out in their bathing suits, lying on the quad. We'd throw Frisbees to make it seem like we weren't looking at the girls *all* the time. The quad also is where we had our graduation, right there on the lawn. Now, with all its students, JMU probably has its graduation in….how many different locations?"

"Three, at least," Pfahler speculated.

From the mud, metaphorically, grew the lotus.

"Basically, all the buildings you see with gray stones were the ones that were here when we were," said Dosh. "The ones without the gray stones have been added." The gray limestone matched the gray skies that January day.

Campanelli guided the van around a statue of James Madison, the nation's fourth President and a native Virginian. Someone mused: "Shouldn't the school's nickname be Presidents instead of Dukes?" Someone else imagined a 1770s-like mascot with a musket and white wig. JMU's actual mascot is a bulldog with a royal crown atop its canine head.

"These dorms on the upper campus had a lot of parties," said Dosh, who seemed to know about such things. "But when we went to school, we were on campus for four years. So this was your town, your life. Nowadays, kids live on campus the first year and then move off-campus for their last three years. They don't have our same sense of community."

The red van proceeded past Hoffman Hall, where Ruland and Dupont roomed together as seniors in the best of all campus living situations. "At that time, it was a coed dorm," said Ruland, "when there weren't many coed dorms on campus. In fact, that might have been the only one."

One was plenty, given Virginia's academic social mores in the 1970s. "The third floor was all male," said Dupont. "The girls were on the second floor. But we were bookish guys, especially Dan."

Nobody laughed this time. All of Campanelli's JMU players graduated.

"Dan was very self-conscious about his feet, size sixteen," Dupont said. "One night in study hall, someone stared at his feet as he walked in the room. Dan got up on the table and walked across the guy's books and said, 'What in the heck are you looking at?' That was the end of *that* conversation."

With Townes's small-town upbringing, JMU looked "big city" to him as a wide-eyed freshman. "Now it looks twice as large," he said, shaking his head.

Townes relived those frosty days in the snow when he and other students used food trays from the dining hall as "sleds" to slide down campus hills.

Even during basketball's infancy at JMU, there were sellout crowds of 5,000 at Godwin Hall, where Campanelli's early teams played. "Basketball was all we had," said Dosh. "Most schools are football-driven, but football wasn't even on the map back then at JMU."

"The growth here has been extraordinary," noted Townes. "My son now is a freshman at JMU. He's among the 4,000 to 5,000 who were accepted."

When Townes, the father, attended JMU, enrollment was 8,700. Current enrollment has climbed to more than 20,000, much to Pfahler's chagrin. "I didn't want Madison to turn into a Virginia Tech," he said. "That didn't stop Dr. Carrier."

Dr. Carrier was equal parts president, visionary, and official greeter. "He would stop and talk to us on campus, like he was one of our buddies, and it was genuine," said Townes. "Even today, people are so much nicer here, because it feels more like a family."Added Ruland, "Dr. Carrier was universally loved by everyone on campus, I never heard anyone say a bad word about the guy."

Without Dr. Carrier, everyone in the van agreed, JMU wouldn't have its present-day enrollment or academic stature. "He was the catalyst," said Dupont.

Credit for JMU's emergence as a first-rate university also belongs to Lou Campanelli's gang of basketball overachievers, snubbed by the big-time college programs. "I'm proud," said Ruland, "that what we did here was partly responsible for the growth of the school as well as its reputation as a great place to go to school. I feel great about that."

"The influence we had, though, is like a ghost," noted Townes. "When I come back for a game, someone will say, 'We could use you.' But that pride will always be there."

Dupont reflected fondly on those early basketball days at brand-new James Madison University and on the character of those JMU players. "People remember the 'Electric Zoo' atmosphere at our games," he said, "and that we were good guys who, by and large, went to class and stayed out of trouble." "And," said Pfahler, "who were smart enough not to get caught."

Good feelings filled the van as it slipped through campus. Campanelli stopped to ask some students for directions to some building he recalled from another time. The students were fuzzy about the building's location. With good reason, for, as time passes, buildings change and not everything is where it once was. But who were those guys in the red van, anyway?

"We were the foundation," Pfahler said with pride. "We got the program going. But to see this growth on campus, it's inevitable."

Campanelli steered the van toward the alumni center—yet another campus addition since he created a basketball legacy at JMU.

"I guess you have to look back at the beginning," Dosh said of his own college experience. "I attended high school in the Washington, DC, area. My friends asked me where I was going to college. I told them, 'Madison.' They asked me why I wanted to go to school in Wisconsin."

The University of Wisconsin's primary campus is located in the state capital of Madison, while Harrisonburg is situated three hours from Dosh's boyhood home. But none of his friends had ever heard of Madison College.

"I lived three hours in the other direction," said Dupont, a North Carolina native. "When I told people that I was going to James Madison, they said, 'That's a girls school, right?'"

By then, James Madison University had been fully coed for seven years.

Pfahler had his own nostalgic story. "Before I came here, I was recruited by George Washington University," he said. "I had my choice of two flights to get there on a recruiting trip. The earlier one I didn't take was hijacked to Cuba. Coach (Campanelli) would have needed a new point guard."

Campanelli grinned. He loved listening to his former players, whom he was enjoying now more than ever. Their coach-player bond remains endless as they shared something unique—a basketball journey like no other.

"It's awesome now, really impressive," Campanelli said of the campus setting, drastically altered since his arrival in 1972. "I was looking for a small college where I could walk from my home to my job. At that time, in basketball, there was a university level and a college level. We became Division I so soon that I no longer had this cozy little job. Once we were on national TV, people saw James Madison University in a different light."

That era illuminated James Madison University basketball like no era since, for Campanelli took his Dukes to five NCAA tournaments. In sharp contrast, the 2013–2014 Dukes had a 6–13 record on Saturday, January 25, when the old coach, then seventy-five, pulled into the parking lot of the Convocation Center, a much larger basketball facility than any he had experienced on campus.

Joining a pre-game function inside the arena, Campanelli and his players were recognized instantly, even though thrity-plus years had passed since JMU's hoops heyday. The five players were received as ageless heroes.

"People came up to me and said, 'Wish you still were here. We sure could use you.'" Dupont said later. "It's amazing."

Their imprint on JMU basketball seems eternal. It's naturally hard for others to let go of the best of times, that is, until something better comes along. Such a future might be wishful thinking at JMU.

The 2013–2014 Dukes hung on that afternoon for a gritty 58–56 victory over College of Charleston. Campanelli was introduced during the game to loud applause. He did a halftime radio show with legendary JMU game announcer Mike Schikman, who was the play-by-play man when Campanelli coached the Dukes. Campanelli, with his unerring coaching eye, projected a JMU freshman guard, Jackson Kent, as a future star.

Campanelli dropped off the five players at a Marriott prior to their dinner engagement that evening, which he would host. As the red van pulled away, he mused on how it all came together so many years ago: A girls' school turning coed, a bunch of non-recruited players shaking up the basketball universe, a small college becoming a major university—all of that remarkable change occurred in the short span of nine basketball seasons. A miracle, of sorts, like no other to be found anywhere in academia.

"Dr. Carrier was this energetic, dynamic president," said Campanelli, "who had a vision of what he wanted a college to look like. We helped him achieve that vision through basketball by increasing enrollment and, really, by enhancing the image of the school."

Together, Dr. Ronald E. Carrier and Lou Campanelli lifted a largely unknown regional college onto the national map. Now, in this book, Campanelli recaptures this one-of-a-kind evolution in season-by-season, crossroad-by-crossroad detail.

Ride along.

CHAPTER 1
Tar Heel Titanic

Michael Jordan!

My game plan must contain Michael Jordan, simply the greatest basketball player who ever lived?

James Worthy!

My game plan also must contain Worthy, who's recognized as basketball's prototype power forward?

Sam Perkins!

My game plan must contain him, too? Perkins is 6-foot-9 with the arm span of a 7-foot-3 player. His arms look as long as a giraffe's neck.

Hey, I'm just a basketball coach, not some magician like David Copperfield.

Those three superstars played on the same University of North Carolina team. And my feisty bunch of James Madison University upstarts must beat Jordan, Worthy, *and* Perkins? All right, but, first, how do we guard them?

I thought this was basketball, not "Mission Impossible."

Incredibly, that was my mission, which I accepted because I had no other choice. I needed to come up with a game plan that would defeat the greatest North Carolina basketball team ever in the 1982 NCAA Tournament.

How would I define greatness? NBA teams drafted twelve of the fourteen players on that North Carolina roster. During my thirteen years at James Madison, the NBA drafted only five of my players, the earliest of which was Linton Townes, the first pick of the second round by the Portland Trail Blazers in 1982.

Conversely, Worthy was the NBA's first overall pick in 1982, while Jordan and Perkins were the third and fourth overall picks in 1984. Jordan and Worthy won a combined nine NBA titles and three Olympic gold medals. Perkins played in two NBA finals. Jordan and Worthy were selected among the NBA's fifty greatest players, and deserved to be in the top twenty.

Townes was my only JMU player to *make* an NBA roster. Mama mia!

So are you getting a complete picture of what my gritty James Madison guys were up against? North Carolina recruited McDonald's High School All-Americans—James Madison's players ate at McDonald's.

In my unbiased opinion, North Carolina is still America's team. But the odds makers saw my James Madison Dukes as a bunch of half-baked potatoes. So, I guess, while North Carolina had studs, we had spuds. Nice odds.

And here I was, Lou Campanelli, having to match wits with Dean Smith, the most respected of college hoops coaches, who was in his sixteenth year of operating North Carolina's elite program. When Smith took over at UNC, James Madison was a women's college!

As if my mission wasn't difficult enough, this second-round game of the 1982 Eastern Regionals was being played at the Charlotte Coliseum, a ninety-minute bus ride from the UNC campus in Chapel Hill. So it was like a home game for the Tar Heels. And of the available 11,000 seats, 10,000 went to UNC fans. JMU fans received the other 1,000, a mere sprinkling of purple and gold Madison colors amidst all that Carolina baby blue.

Yet one more obstacle: The Tar Heels were ranked No. 1 in the country, a ranking they also held before the season in both the Associated Press and UPI Coaches Top-20 polls. James Madison wasn't listed in either pre-season poll. But, hey, none of those twenty schools are named after a president.

With the improbable task of playing North Carolina in North Carolina before basically North Carolina fans, it felt as if my dark horse bunch of Dukes were taking on the entire Tar Heel State. Talk about March Madness!

And, to top it off, we kept hearing "JM Who?" (as in J-M-U). The prevailing attitude: Did JMU even belong on the same basketball court with North Carolina?

So when I awoke that morning, March 13, 1982, I was scared—scared that North Carolina might thrash us by twenty points. My game plan was designed, specifically, to prevent such a thrashing. Crazy as it sounds, if my players executed the game plan the way I drew it on the blackboard, I felt that we could win the game. But only if our execution was nearly perfect.

Unlike their Nervous Nelly coach, JMU's players eagerly awaited the chance to confront those terrifying Tar Heels. My Dukes had such supreme confidence. They saw themselves as David in sneakers, facing Goliath in the low post, and using smartness and togetherness as our proverbial slingshot. JM Who? My Dukes felt they'd show UNC who they were, all right.

It's amazing, though, that we were even in a position to play North Carolina. Just look at the huge mountain we had to climb to reach this point. No other college basketball program was like us. Not even close.

Only ten years earlier had our school, then known as Madison College, turned fully coed through the vision of our new president, Dr. Ronald E. Carrier, whose purpose was to give the school a national name, partly through his inclusion of intercollegiate athletics. Dr. Carrier hired me to fulfill his purpose. Then, after we started out at the Division II level, Dr. Carrier decided, in 1976, to re-name Madison College as James Madison University and move us up to Division I. Dr. Carrier always thought big. Thus, an upset victory over the ultra-talented Tar Heels would give our little school, hidden away in the Shenandoah Valley, its first coast-to-coast recognition.

But I'm getting ahead of myself, because North Carolina wasn't our first opponent in that NCAA Tournament. We had to get past a rugged Ohio State team in an opening-round game that was personally scouted by Dean Smith as North Carolina had a bye. If you're North Carolina, you get byes.

So I'd better have a solid game plan against Ohio State; otherwise, my game plan for North Carolina was meaningless. The Buckeyes were from the vaunted Big Ten, which instantly made them the favorite against JMU, from the relatively unknown Eastern College Athletic Conference.

Tradition and exposure were on Ohio State's side. They had previous Final Four experience and were NCAA champions in 1960. The Buckeyes were used to nationally televised games and front-page coverage. JMU, to the typical hoops fan, was back-page fodder.

But my fearless Dukes, unimpressed by often misleading conference reputations, believed we matched up well against the Buckeyes. Though we lost to Old Dominion in the finals of the ECAC South, which earned ODU an automatic berth in the NCAA Tournament, we were 23–5. Thus, we earned the first-ever at-large invitation for a mid-major school in the NCAA's forty-eight-team field, plus a No. 9 seed. Ohio State, 21–10 and the Big Ten runnerup behind Minnesota, was a No. 8 seed.

Big Ten? Big deal. Let's jump ball and see who's best.

Preparing for the Buckeyes, I watched a tape of their late-season game with Minnesota. I was awed by Ohio State's athletic ability. The Big Ten recruits great players; they're not getting no-names. The Buckeyes had the cream of the crop compared to my guys, the crop.

But our twenty three wins were achieved with a take-no-prisoners style, playing tough defense, and forcing teams into a half-court game. We had intelligent kids who worked for good shots. Remember, this was the era before the shot clock and three-point shot, so we could set the tempo offensively. We also controlled the tempo defensively through multiple schemes: Man-to-man, two-three zones, two-two-one press, one-three-one zone. This mixed bag of confusion made teams adjust to us; we didn't adjust to them. Thus, we always had a chance.

That's not to say Ohio State would be easy. Hardly. Like I said, they had great athletes. Clark Kellogg was their star, the Big Ten's Player of the Year. He was known as "Special K," and he was special—a former high school All-American who averaged 16.1 points and 10.0 rebounds that season. Kellogg was strong and active at 6-foot-7, 225 pounds. If he got the ball inside fifteen, sixteen feet, he was hellacious. We had to find a way to deny him the ball. Ohio State had balanced scoring, but you always schemed to contain the team's best player, to prevent him from doing a one-man highlight film against you. If Kellogg went for twenty-five, thirty points, we were done.

Ohio State wasn't a one-man show by any means. Tony Campbell, also 6-foot-7, was a guy you couldn't neglect, because he averaged 12.8 points. We didn't recruit special players like Special K; therefore to win, we had to play good position defense, deny the ball, and block out on rebounds.

Without our executing fundamentals properly, we stood no chance of advancing. We also had to disallow second shots, limit transition baskets, and keep the score in the fifty-five to sixty-point range. Ohio State, of course, wanted to run the score up higher. If you didn't guard the Buckeyes, they'd get it up into the eighties or nineties. If it got up that high, we truly were half-baked potatoes.

Ohio State did have a big man, 6-foot-11 Granville Waiters, though he wasn't a go-to player. He averaged seven points that season. He primarily was a shot-blocker, a complementary player. The Buckeyes had three quick guards in the six-foot range. Troy Taylor and Larry Huggins averaged 7.7 points, and Ron Stokes 6.5. Taylor was the team leader in assists at 3.5 per game.

Though they were Ohio State and we were the underdog, I didn't make any radical changes. Technically, we would play them like we played everyone else. We felt assured and confident with our winning style of play. My players bought into it and felt they could control just about anybody. Our motto: We respected everybody and feared no one.

Ohio State had no weaknesses, but what bothered them was switching defenses. By playing in the gaps, we felt we could disrupt their passing game. So we put Townes in the passing lane between their guards, and we converged in the paint. We didn't double-team as much as we fronted them, and we frustrated them. Without the ball, Kellogg couldn't score.

Only a special group of kids can play this way, by buying into the team concept. Everyone wants to score, but not everyone wants to play defense. We needed to do both to survive. Townes, the ECAC South Player of the Year, led us with 16.3 points a game and 5.9 rebounds, followed by Dan Ruland's 12.7 points and 6.3 rebounds. After that, we were pretty balanced—Charles Fisher's 8.9 points, David Dupont's 6.7, Darrell Jackson's 4.9, and top reserves Derek Steele's 4.6 and Keith Bradley's 2.2.

Statistics aside, in all my years of coaching, I never had a group of players who were as close on the court and off the court. They were a unified group. They even quadruple dated! That's the beauty of camaraderie.

Thus, our main asset was team play. We looked for the open guy to take the shot. We were resilient, bending but never breaking. It was a team of twelve players thinking as one: If I care about you, I won't let you down. That was the crux of our team, the dirty dozen Dukes.

It's not easy to get players—especially in today's era of self-importance, where it's all about "I" and "me," with players pointing fingers and leaving early for the NBA—to buy into a team concept. If it's not about "we," players don't give themselves up as readily for the betterment of the team. They're worried about scoring enough points to be drafted. JMU's players, unlike North Carolina's, weren't leaving school early for the NBA. Thus, players' agents congregated on campuses other than JMU's.

A coach must be a salesman. And I've never had a team that bought into what I was selling—togetherness, unselfishness, defense—like those 1982 JMU kids, who also were skilled players.

Townes, a 6-foot-7 senior, had a velvety smooth jump shot; he was accurate out to eighteen feet. Our other starting forward, Jackson, was a 6-foot-6 freshman, an athletic kid and a good defender, though not much of a shooter. Ruland, a junior center, was our tallest player at 6-foot-8. He had a deadly jump shot from twelve to fifteen feet. If the opposing center didn't come out to guard him, we had an advantage. Bradley, a 6-foot-6 sophomore, was our best reserve forward, a good passer and defender. His scoring range was four feet in, mainly using a one-dribble power move. He split playing time with Jackson.

Ruland was assigned to Waiters, giving up three inches. Townes would defend against Campbell at small forward. Jackson and Bradley had the biggest assignment: Kellogg. We had bigger starting guards in 6-foot-4 junior Dupont and 6-foot-1 junior Fisher, both accurate shooters. Dupont also rebounded well, and Fisher was as quick as a cat. Our top reserve guard was sophomore Steele, who was only 5-foot-7 but tough as iron. A little scooter bug, he played so low to the court that he could break through any defensive press. And he penetrated like a halfback on drives to the basket.

Fisher was a gamer. He broke his left thumb against Navy. In fact, he was injured a lot. But even banged up, you couldn't keep him off the court. He wore a soft cast on his left arm nearly up to his elbow to protect the fractured thumb. That cast was a deciding factor in a tournament game to remember.

If we had one weakness or cause for concern, it was if another team pressed us early and forced us into a game of up and down. That meant we were in trouble, because our tempo would be affected. The worst thing was to play too fast, even if we were scoring, because that meant we were out of control. I've said this a thousand times at coaching clinics: The tempo of a game is set in the first five minutes. That is absolute gospel in my mind.

And, so, wouldn't you know it? We ran into problems from the start against Ohio State. It wasn't so much our tempo but allowing Kellogg and Campbell to take charge early. We held their guards in check, and Waiters wasn't much of a factor, but those two forwards were killing us.

We had trouble getting untracked. With eleven minutes left in the game, we trailed 42–34. I called a time out, searching for some strategy to slow their momentum. I decided on a 1-3-1 half-trap zone to prevent their smallish guards from getting the ball into Kellogg and Campbell.

"Let's tighten up the defense another notch," I encouraged my team. "We can beat these guys. Bradley, I really need you to play Kellogg tough."

We responded instantly, chipping away at their lead. We didn't want to be a one-and-done team. Still, we needed a turning point to shake Ohio State's confidence and to show the Buckeyes—not to mention the nation, the NCAA Selection Committee, and those formidable North Carolina Tar Heels—that JMU was a team to be reckoned with.

JMU's 1-3-1 Half-Trap Zone Defense in Its 1982 NCAA Game versus Ohio State

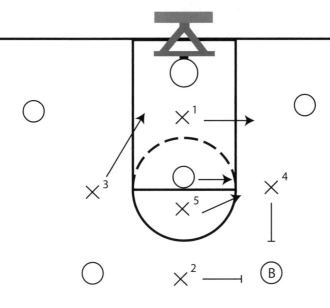

Designed by Morgan Pfaelzer for Coach Lou Campanelli. © George F. Thompson Publishing.

This is how Coach Lou drew up the JMU 1-3-1 half-trap zone defense:

- The half-trap defense puts defenders X^2 and X^4 five to six feet away from the offensive player. (Taller players make this very effective.)

- All of the defenders' hands are up. Their goal is to force a lob pass or bounce pass.

- The defender at the high post (X^5) must deny any pass to that area.

- As X^4 covers the wing, X^3 protects the interior.

B = basketball   O = OSU's offensive player   X = JMU's defensive player

Guard David Dupont scores the game-tying basket in the Dukes' big 55–48 win versus favored Ohio State in the first round of the East Regional of the 1982 NCAA tournament. Photograph courtesy of James Madison University Athletics.

David Dupont provided that turning point with a decisive flourish. Playing at the top of the 1-3-1 zone, he picked off a cross-court pass and flashed down the floor for a sensational breakaway dunk. That defining moment tied the score and seemed to deflate Ohio State. The Buckeyes already had lost their offensive composure due to our 1-3-1 zone, which denied their penetrating passes. Then we shifted between the 1-3-1 zone and a man-to-man defense to rattle them. They hadn't faced a multiple defensive scheme like ours. We showed our true character by outscoring them, 14–0, down the stretch. They couldn't knock us out, and we had delivered the haymaker—Dupont's dunk, which clearly broke their spirit.

But I couldn't overlook Keith Bradley's impact on the game. Though a role player, he was a wiry, strong kid and our best interior defender. He played lockdown defense on Kellogg over the last eight minutes, checking him with two points over that span by fronting him, denying him the ball, blocking him off the boards. Ohio State scored six points over the final eleven minutes. Man, we could defend.

Once we got up by four, five points against anyone, we felt we could win the game because we had such good free-throw shooters. We used that advantage all season, and Ohio State, obligingly, put us on the line. And we won going away, 55–48.

We succeeded in keeping the score under sixty points. Our defense held Ohio State to .388 field-goal shooting (19 for 49), while we shot .500 (21 of 42). We averaged in that 49–50 percent range all season, and we were among the nation's best defensive teams in points allowed. It was no fluke that we won.

Ruland had a season-high eighteen points. Townes added twelve points. Bradley came up big with eight points and five rebounds. Dupont had six points, seven rebounds, and four assists. Fisher scored five points, and Steele hounded the Buckeyes' guards like a junkyard dog. We had balance, like the team we were.

Kellogg ended up with fourteen points and twelve rebounds. Campbell matched Kellogg's fourteen points, but Waiters was their next-highest scorer with six. True character reveals itself toward the end of battle, and James Madison's character shown brightly that day. Virginia's Blue Ridge Mountains, I heard, had a radiant glow after we stunned the Buckeyes, a glow that could be seen as far away as Columbus, Ohio.

We were confident, minus swagger. Fisher was a little yappy, because he was the point guard. But you couldn't find quieter kids than Townes, Ruland, and Dupont. Dupont's wife told me later on at a reunion that she wouldn't date him in college because he didn't talk to anybody. She thought he was arrogant. I had to tell her he was shy.

Our kids didn't pull out their jerseys with their thumbs and strut around the court after a win, like you see nowadays. They stayed within themselves and played for one another. We weren't a Dream Team, but those JMU kids were a coach's dream, believe me.

And Dr. Carrier was a dream of a college president. He came into the locker room after every game, win or lose, to cheer on the players. After we beat Ohio State, he came in and led the cheers. No college coach ever had a finer president or a finer athletic director in Dean Ehlers. Dean was a man of few words. After a win, he'd slap me on the back and say, "Way to go, man." Dr. Carrier, Dean, and I were together for thirteen years at JMU. My assistant coach, John Thurston, called our Dukes teams "the perfect storm." Can't argue, but that assessment also included Dr. Carrier and Dean Ehlers. We were one big team.

Dean Smith was a great coach and a dignified man. After watching us beat Ohio State, he told the media: "If you had changed the lettering on the shirt, you'd have thought James Madison was Ohio State. If they played again on Saturday, James Madison would beat Ohio State again. They're just a better team." Obviously, he said that for his players' enlightenment, as if they needed enlightening, but I believed he meant what he said.

Clark Kellogg, who later played in the NBA, is a top college basketball analyst today. Every time I see him, I say, "Clark, how are you doing? What was the name of that little Virginia school that knocked you guys out of the NCAA Tournament?" I kill him every time, but he's a good sport.

Although Ohio State was a staunch opponent, North Carolina was a notch above. Make it two notches. We had no time to savor our victory, because the Tar Heels—Smith, Jordan, Worthy, Perkins—were forty hours away.

North Carolina, with *three* superstars, was a rarity in college basketball. And UNC had no weaknesses; Matt Doherty and Jimmy Black were good role players. Worthy averaged 15.6 points, Perkins 14.3, Jordan 13.5, Doherty 9.3, and Black 7.6. Few shots were left for the other Tar Heels. In my thirty-two years of coaching, I never faced a team that had three players of the caliber of Worthy, Perkins,

President Ronald E. Carrier and his wife, Edith, cheer on the Dukes at the 1982
NCAA game with Ohio State. The Dukes' victory further propelled JMU onto the
national scene as a basketball program and university on the rise. Just as Dr. Carrier
had envisioned when he and Athletic Director Dean Ehlers hired Coach Lou.
Photograph courtesy of James Madison University Athletics.

Coach Lou signals a defensive call against North Carolina in NCAA play in Charlotte, March 1982. The Dukes nearly beat the eventual national-champion Tar Heels in a game everyone—including Michael Jordan, James Worthy, Sam Perkins, and Matt Doherty—remembers to this day. Photograph courtesy of James Madison University Athletics.

and Jordan. No other coach I can think of has either. Where's that slingshot, David? Goliath just got a whole lot bigger.

After arriving in Madison in 1972, not in my wildest dreams did I ever envision playing North Carolina. They were on another level, playing on television every Wednesday and Saturday. And I had grown to admire Coach Smith, who had been very gracious to me.

After my first year at Madison, Mike Fratello, my assistant, and I drove down to Duke, Clemson, and North Carolina to learn from their systems. We were no threat at that time to all three. Coach Smith opened his door and shared information with us. He couldn't have been nicer. I always admired how Coach Smith ran his program. His players graduated. Even those Tar Heel players who left early for the NBA returned to complete their degrees. I wanted that same kind of student-athlete to play for me.

And then to play a team like North Carolina and in the NCAA Tournament, it was just mind-blowing. But not mind-crippling. Charles Fisher told me the night before the UNC game, "We can beat this team, because we're a team of destiny."

Destiny's darlings? Well, if you watch the tape of that JMU-UNC game, tell me that we didn't play with poise. We had a few breakdowns, sure, but don't forget who was harassing us. Our mindset was to hang with North Carolina the best we could, then hope to make something happen at the end like we did against Ohio State.

I always wanted to measure my teams against the best and measure myself against the best coaches. When I looked into my players' eyes before meeting North Carolina, I saw nothing but confidence. They were ready for the biggest game of their lives. When I looked in the mirror that same morning, I saw a renewed confidence in spite of my earlier apprehension.

Before tipoff, I met with Coach Smith for the customary coaches' handshake at half-court. He said, "Lou, you've got a very good team. This is going to be a tough game. The score will be something like 55–50. I hope we have the 55."

My jaw dropped. "Aw, c'mon, Coach," I said, not sure how to react. Was he being honest or setting me up?

"No, I'm serious," he emphasized. "You guys have a good team."

Stunned, I walked back to our bench. But I had instructed my star-less team to play star-ladened North Carolina the same way we had played all season—determined, together, defensive-minded, smart. That's all we knew.

Here was JMU's once-in-a-lifetime opportunity, to play the nation's No. 1 team with the entire country watching. It hasn't happened since at JMU.

The tension was awesome. I loved being in that moment, even with all the Pepto-Bismol I swallowed the past few days to quiet a nervous stomach. If you are a competitor, this is the kind of challenge you wanted. Remember, ten years before, we were playing teams like Bridgewater and Eastern Mennonite. This biggest of stages was like a coach's dream.

I felt the tension reverberating throughout the arena that day. Though there were only 1,000 JMU fans in attendance, they sounded like 5,000 when their spunky Dukes took the floor. We ingested our fans' passion, plus the electricity in the air. At times that afternoon, our 1,000 would sound louder than North Carolina's 10,000. With the school bands playing and the cheerleaders' groups cheering, I saw, once again, why no basketball atmosphere is as genuine and exciting as the college game. And absolutely nothing in sports can match March Madness for the unexpected, especially the first week of competition, where colossal upsets occur with regularity.

I wore a maroon sport coat for the North Carolina game after donning a three-piece suit for Ohio State. I couldn't guarantee that the three-piece suit would bring good luck again. The sport coat felt lucky, regardless, as we controlled the tempo early and jumped out to a 12–6 lead. North Carolina, the No. 1 team in the land, was playing at *our* tempo.

Our strategy was working. We showed the Tar Heels three different defenses in the first five minutes while maintaining our lead at 15–10. Smith pulled Michael Jordan from the game, even though he was....Michael Jordan! But, at the time, Smith didn't lose much by benching Jordan. He was a freshman and not yet Air Jordan. Worthy, a junior, was a consensus All-American. Perkins was a second-team All-American. Only at North Carolina could Michael Jordan be a third option.

Jordan was unpolished at that time, missing shots that he would make routinely in the NBA. He developed his shooting touch over time. Still, you sensed his potential greatness. His first step was unreal. But, I must admit, I liked him best sitting on the bench.

We knew North Carolina could react in a heartbeat, and the Tar Heels pulled ahead, 16–15, on Black's jumper, his fourth field goal in four attempts. Even their complementary players could burn you. Jordan returned with a dazzling

JMU's Rotation-On-the-Pass-to-the-Corner Offense in Its 1982 NCAA Game versus North Carolina

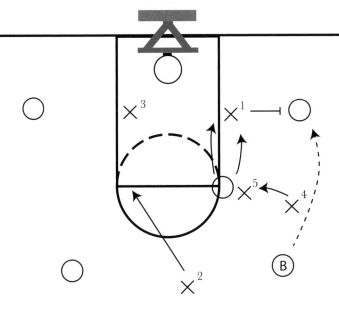

Designed by Morgan Pfaelzer for Coach Lou Campanelli. © George F. Thompson Publishing.

This is how Coach Lou drew up JMU's rotation offense:

- X^1 covers the pass to the corner.
- X^5 fronts the ballside block.
- X^4 dives to the ballside elbow.
- X^2 covers the opposite elbow.
- X^3 defends the basket.

B = basketball   O = JMU's offensive player   X = UNC's defensive player

JMU's Charles Fisher, even with a broken left arm, works hard against North Carolina's Michael Jordan (#23) and Matt Doherty in the classic second-round 1982 NCAA East Regional game. Following their down-to-the-wire two-point win against the ninth-seeded Dukes, the Tar Heels went on the win the national championship, a 63–62 win against Georgetown and its star center, Patrick Ewing. A year earlier, JMU beat Georgetown, 61–55, in the first-round game of the 1981 NCAA East Regional. Photograph courtesy of James Madison University Athletics.

baseline move, but his basket was disallowed because he stepped out of bounds. Quickly, he was back on the bench. Dean Smith had a learning curve, even for Michael Jordan.

North Carolina led at halftime, 31–28. I sensed another fifty-point game, ideal for us. Maybe Dean Smith was right. Both teams had eight turnovers at intermission, but we were shooting sixty-one percent to the Tar Heels' fifty-nine percent. They realized that we weren't mesmerized, that we weren't going to fold up our tent and disappear. We didn't feel subservient to them.

Townes told me later on: "You know, Coach, we were more or less just happy to be there. But once the game got started and the game wore on, we felt pretty good about our chances. We knew they were a strong team. We just wanted to be close at the end, and maybe we could pull it out."

The night before, I envisioned Worthy and Perkins dunking on us, with their getting into the open court freely and with Jordan scoring, too. As it turned out, the three superstars had two dunks all day. Jordan wound up with, imagine, only six points. Our kids battled them tough; it was nip-and-tuck all the way.

North Carolina got its biggest lead, 37–30, after Perkins floated in a jumper from the baseline. Fisher gave us inspiration by using his unbroken right arm to make his first four shots from the field. What a competitor!

The Tar Heels played the game cleanly, which is more than I can say for the Naval Academy, which took some hard fouls on Fisher, breaking his left thumb, which meant he would play in a cast the rest of the season. Charles is a tough kid, but I confronted the Navy coach and said, "The next hard foul you take, I'm coming after you." That was the last hard foul they took. Listen, I always protected my players. I'm a competitor, and I've got that edge. I'm from New Jersey, which is an edgy state.

UNC planned to trap Townes, but he kept escaping and popping in that smooth-looking jumper. My Dukes hung with them. Then Worthy stole a pass and broke away for UNC's one and only "Showtime" dunk that day.

Jordan subsequently was fouled, but he missed both free throws. North Carolina gave us chances, and we took advantage. Ruland kept burying mid-range jumpers as the Tar Heels left him alone. Thus, we stayed within six points. Carolina felt the pressure building because they couldn't pull away. Perkins threw an elbow at Steele's jaw in tight coverage and was charged with a foul. It wasn't an intentional act, but you sensed their growing angst.

Townes swished another fifteen-footer to narrow Carolina's lead to 44–40. The Tar Heels slowed it down, but Fisher nailed a clutch jumper from behind the key to make it 47–44 with two minutes left. It was anybody's game. Where did I put Cinderella's slipper? Bradley then made a big-time inside power move on Worthy to cut the lead to 47–46 with 1:38 left.

I'm thinking, "We're right there." We were one point down to America's Team with a minute-and-a-half left. Coach Smith's strategy? What else but his signature four-corner delay game? We had put *him* on the defensive. Little ol' JMU had *North Carolina* worried.

Smith spread the court with a guard and two wings, placing Perkins and Worthy in the corners. With no college shot clock at the time, the Tar Heels moved the ball from corner to corner and then back around again. Something, or somebody, was needed to disrupt this clock-eating strategy.

Using a counter strategy, I placed two big men near the key, trying to direct the ball into the corner. Our strategy was to double-team their man in the corner if he drove the baseline. With a minute left, the strategy worked as Perkins got the ball. We put two guys on him right away. He drove the baseline and ran smack over Ruland before somehow making the basket.

There it was, a golden opportunity, clearly an offensive foul. Wave off the basket, ref. It's JMU ball, our chance to take the lead. Wait a second, what did he call? A block? No way, ref. Perkins to the line? You can't be serious. Ruland had position, ref. He got there first, was firmly planted, and he was run over. I threw down my program in disgust.

I felt cheated until Ruland told me afterward that he got there a hair late and that he actually committed the foul. Perkins's basket counted, and his ensuing free throw made it 50–46.

Then came the play that still feels like a Rocky Marciano punch to my solar plexus every time I see it on tape. I will see that play until the moment I take my last breath and maybe beyond if heaven has instant replay. Here was Charles Fisher, with the basketball in his good right hand, driving toward the hoop, trying to make something historic happen, like destiny.

And there was Worthy, jumping straight up in the air, his arms extended above his head, as Fisher split him and Perkins with clear aim at the hoop. Worthy made no effort whatsoever to block the shot; he hoped, somehow, to draw a foul. Just as Fisher released the ball, he lifted his left arm, the one in a cast, and pushed it against Worthy.

I saw it clearly: A nudge, a no-call, for sure. You saw it, too, ref, right? What, an offensive foul? Not a second time! I couldn't believe it. It was the damn *cast*, not Fisher, that precipitated the call. Irate at seeing a historic upset drifting away over another questionable call, my competitiveness revealed itself, and I made a choking sign. I should have received a technical foul, but nobody saw it, except on television.

A nervous Worthy rattled home both free throws to push North Carolina's lead to 52–46 with fifty seconds left. From there, it got a little hazy. Fisher flashed down the court and hit a basket to make it 52–48. Then bodies came together in a corner, and, as Dupont reached in to pry loose the ball, he was hit with an intentional foul. *Intentional?* Dupont wasn't that kind of player. C'mon, ref, not a third time! Are we getting hosed or what?

I lost it again and made two quick choking signs, which were again seen on television but, thankfully, missed once more by the officials. Frustration and North Carolina had wrung me dry emotionally, and I reacted twice totally out of character. Never before that game and never again after that game did I make a choking sign on a basketball court. I could apologize a hundred times for my actions, but does destiny even care?

Carolina failed to score again, and Townes banked in a jumper at the buzzer to make the final score 52–50. I congratulated Dean Smith and wished him luck the rest of the tournament. He was as gracious as always. I walked off the floor—without my maroon sport coat, which I had discarded in the second half. Our team manager, I think, retrieved it for me.

I've relived that game a thousand times. In my head, I see Townes hitting that banker, and we're running off the court as the winner. If we had gotten three more points against North Carolina, could we have gone on and beaten Arkansas, the next opponent? Yes! Could we have made the Sweet Sixteen? You bet! Thus, it was a heartbreaking loss.

When I got to the locker room, some of my Dukes were crying. They were as emotionally spent as I was. What a courageous effort; they had showed the country that they could play with the best. "Until the day I die," I told them, "I will never forget how you competed. You should feel proud about how you played."

Dr. Carrier spoke next. He told the team, "You brought much honor and glory to the university." They had done precisely that. But, as our school's president spoke, I thought of Dean Smith's pre-game prediction. He was off by three points. He may have missed another true calling as a market analyst.

Though we didn't beat the Tar Heels, we showed them that the ECAC could play with the ACC (Atlantic Coast Conference). We out-shot them, .568 (21 of 37) to .526 (20 of 38). We out-rebounded them, 21–19. Perkins led Carolina with seventeen points and ten rebounds, while Worthy added fifteen points. Ruland, Townes, and Fisher each had twelve points for JMU, with Dupont contributing five rebounds and four assists.

That game meant everything to Dupont. Hailing from North Carolina, he dreamed of being a Tar Heel but wasn't even offered a walk-on spot. He was crushed. Dean Smith later acknowledged his mistake, saying that, if he had to do it over again, Dupont would be a Tar Heel. Over my dead body!

While Smith and his Tar Heels were interviewed in the pressroom, I wept uncontrollably for ten minutes on the shoulder of JMU's sports information director, Rich Murray, in the bathroom. Losing finally got to me. We came so close. My tears were about losing, not about how we lost. The refs didn't screw us. The Tar Heels won because they did enough to win, and we didn't, even though we gave them the scare of their lives.

Then Rich said, "Coach, it's time to go to the pressroom." I heard some noise in the hallway and, opening the locker room door, saw a couple hundred fans dressed in purple and gold chanting, "JMU! JMU! JMU!" Typical of our school spirit, they saluted their Dukes for a great effort. Pushing through the crowd, I slapped hands with a number of these supporters. I loved coaching for them and for JMU.

I learned later on that the Tar Heels were very complimentary. "James Madison is a really excellent team," said Dean Smith. "I wanted our players to respect them. I don't care what the fans think about them. I certainly don't want to take away from the game that James Madison played. We didn't play a bad game."

Worthy echoed his coach, saying, "It's one of the toughest games we've had all year. They are so smart, so disciplined, one of the best teams in the country today. We didn't overlook them. We were aware."

North Carolina was all class. They didn't try to alibi and say, "Well, we just had an off game." They were sincere. They gave us their best, and we gave them our best. Hey, if they had played badly, we would have won.

The Tar Heels went on to win that 1982 NCAA Tournament, beating George-town, 63–62, on a Jordan shot and an ensuing errant pass from a Hoya, Fred Brown, to Worthy. It was Dean Smith's first NCAA championship after three previous losses in NCAA title games, including the year before to Indiana.

I like to think that we had a hand in preparing Smith and his Tar Heels for that title run. He had other great teams, but that team really played together. Then his three superstars became even greater at the next level.

After drying my tears, I made it to the interview room with some of our players. We handled ourselves with composure and dignity. I showed great respect for North Carolina in my comments, even though I was dying inside. We lost by two points—two tantalizing points.

Sunday morning, as we bused back from Charlotte to Harrisonburg, the majority of the players slept. I sat in the front seat with my wife, Dawn, and our three children, replaying the game in my head. We still lost at the end.

I expected an impromptu pep rally on campus to lift our dejected spirits. That was the case the previous year after we beat Georgetown and then lost to Notre Dame in the second round of March Madness. But when our bus pulled up in front of Godwin Hall, our 5,000-seat basketball facility, nobody was there to greet us. The campus looked deserted.

One car was in the parking lot, belonging to Rich Murray. He boarded the bus and told me that a few local reporters were waiting inside the gym, wanting to interview the players and me.

"Rich, the kids are exhausted," I argued. "Let them get back to their dorms."

"Coach, it will only take a few minutes," he pleaded.

OK, then, a few minutes. We headed up the steps to the gym. Then the doors swung open, the pep band started playing, and we saw 5,000 people inside, roaring for us. I lost control and shed a few more tears. What a scene!

They were there for us, win or lose. That's why James Madison University always will have a special place in my heart. President Carrier, Rich Murray, and the cheerleaders hastily pulled this celebration together. JMU was the greatest working environment—anywhere. Go Dukes!

After the emotional high of that weekend, I experienced a down period. I couldn't get that North Carolina game off my mind. Depression set in over the next two weeks. I was an emotional mess. Finally, Dawn said to me, "Snap out of it. You had a great season. Feel good and happy about what you accomplished." She was exactly right.

It's funny how some things become preserved over time. That loss to North Carolina remains, thirty-three years later, the most famous basketball game ever played by James Madison University. And it's still talked about in North Carolina, where Dupont lives.

"It's just strange," Dupont told me, "how that game, out of the blue, will pop up in people's conversations. It's amazing how many people remember that game, whether they were a Carolina fan or anybody but a Carolina fan—how close the game was and what it meant to our program."

It meant *everything* to our program. We had a remarkable team, without one of our players recruited by a major power. Those same underrated kids came to James Madison and created something special. They competed against the best in the land and didn't give an inch. There is no substitute for heart, strong will, and determination. When it came to intangibles, those kids had it all.

CHAPTER 2
Petticoat Junction

The job was Bobby Watson's. He only had to agree. Madison College coveted him as its men's basketball coach. He was a hot commodity, having built Ferrum Junior College into a national juco power. Plus he would be a local hire—Ferrum, Virginia, is two hours south of Harrisonburg—which made even more sense. Me? I was an unknown college assistant coach.

Madison made Watson an offer that, it turned out, he could refuse. His sights were set higher, on an established program. He eventually accepted the head-coaching job at the University of Evansville in Indiana. Evansville, a member of the Missouri Valley Conference, was a mid-major school with a solid basketball background. And it wasn't a former girls' school.

I was ready for a college head coach's job—anywhere. I would have sacrificed anything for such an opportunity. In fact, I already had sacrificed. Leaving high school coaching to become a college assistant, I took a $1,500 pay cut. My wife cried, "We'll never be able to buy a house."

She meant her first house as a college head coach's wife. We had a house at the University of Rhode Island, but not the dream house Dawn envisioned. Still, it was fancier than the faculty apartment we lived in at Bridgeport, while I slowly moved up the coaching ladder, one rung at a time.

I would have leased a house to become a college head coach, though I didn't tell Dawn. I was chomping at the bit to succeed at the next level.

If I sounded desperate, well, I was at that point. I had paid my dues. Besides coaching, I had attended clinics all over the East Coast. Basketball camps. Those, too, sometimes for free. I did anything to build contacts. I even flew to Halifax, Nova Scotia, to do one camp, though the camp director, Les Goodwin, who was my coach when I played at Panzer College, told me beforehand, "I can't pay you, but I'll give you an airline ticket." I told Dawn, "Don't worry, honey, it's for the future." I think she understood.

After returning from Canada, I drove to Allentown, Pennsylvania, to do yet another camp. Then I came back home from Allentown, washed my clothes, and drove to Vermont for still another camp run by my coaching mentor, Rollie Massimino. I now thought of myself as Camper Campanelli.

Dawn was wondering if she had married a traveling salesman instead of a basketball coach. "It's OK, honey," I said, "I'm getting somewhere." She'd give me a kiss and send me off.

In Allentown, I picked up Henry Iba, the legendary coach, at the local airport. Iba had won an NCAA title with Oklahoma A&M, and then he was an Olympic coach. I'm Lou from New Jersey, but I asked the great man a favor.

"Coach Iba," I said, "at night the guest coach usually stays up and talks basketball with the high school coaches. Would that be a possibility?"

He replied, "Coach, if you get me a bottle of bourbon, we'll talk 'til the sun comes up." His forte was man-to-man defense, and we picked his brain until the wee hours. Just a wonderful man. You gotta love it, basketball 24–7.

The man-to-man defense that Coach Iba lectured us on was, in fact, how I got the freshman coach's job at the University of Bridgeport in Connecticut. Bruce Webster, the Bridgeport varsity coach, liked the way I taught that defense, and so he hired me.

I was no longer a high school coach. I was on my way, I thought, but not even success at the college level guaranteed advancement. The varsity and freshman teams at Bridgeport were winning big, but I couldn't even get an interview for the head coach's job at the Coast Guard Academy, possibly the worst Division III program in the country. I drove up to New London, Connecticut, and they refused to see me. A blessing, as it turned out.

Patience is a virtue, even for coaches. As Abraham Lincoln supposedly said as a younger man: "I will study, work hard, and prepare myself, and some day my chance will come." As proof, Honest Abe lost his share of elections before finally getting his big chance as our President. So who was I to hurry progress?

Progress then beckoned. Tom Carmody, the coach at Rhode Island, offered me the varsity assistant's job. I stayed there three years, learning a lot, but I still wanted to run the show my way.

Meanwhile, time was ticking. College coaching jobs become available every year, but there were any number of Lou Campanellis out there, eager to land them. It was supply and demand, and supply exceeds demand. Getting ahead isn't all that easy.

Sometimes a break, even an unforeseen consequence, must happen to take that next important step. That's what happened to me. Carmody called me into his office to say that Watson, one of his former high school players, had just interviewed at Madison College but was looking elsewhere.

Madison College? I hadn't heard of the school. Where is it? What NCAA division? Do I need a map to locate it?

"Lou, sit down," Carmody said. "What I'm about to tell you will sound weird, but you're looking for an opportunity, and I've learned of an interesting possibility. Madison College is a girls' school . . ."

"Tom, I don't want to coach at a girls' school."

"Wait, Lou, let me finish. It is a girls' school, but it's going fully coed. They have a new president with big plans. He's instituting a college athletic program, and he has big plans for Madison. They need coaches and . . ."

"Where did you say it was?"

Carmody instructed me to call Dean Ehlers, the Madison College athletic director. I phoned right away, and Ehlers confirmed that the basketball coaching position was open, and would I like to send him an application and a resume? Would I?

I complied immediately. But two weeks went by without a response. I figured they had chosen somebody else. I was bummed out.

One night, after a recruiting trip, Carmody, freshman coach Mike Fratello, and I stopped for a nightcap. My frustrations came spilling out.

"Five years as an assistant coach," I groused, "and I can't even get an interview at a girls' school."

Feeling sorry for me, Carmody said, "Oh, it probably wasn't a good job anyway."

I left them at the bar and headed home, feeling even more downcast. I found a note taped to the refrigerator: "Call Dean Ehlers in A.M."

Bingo!

Things happened fast. The very next day, I flew to Washington, DC, and grabbed a commuter flight to the Shenandoah Valley Airport. I couldn't believe what I was seeing: Paradise painted blue—the Blue Ridge Mountains—and a rolling countryside with farms. Here was rural America in rustic splendor. What a gorgeous landscape. But where is the college?

Ehlers and Dr. Ray Sonner, President of the Madison College Foundation, met me at the airport. The school was twenty minutes away, and I loved the campus right away, with its blue limestone buildings and Spanish tile roofing. There was room to grow on campus as far as the eye could see, even a lake, and the campus was so clean. Ehlers informed me that Godwin Hall, a brand-new basketball facility, would be dedicated on May 15, 1972.

It was almost too much to absorb at once. "I can build a program here," I told myself, excitedly. "It's a perfect fit."

Ehlers took me over and introduced me to Dr. Carrier. After some light conversation, he asked point blank: "Coach, do you think you can build a program like Old Dominion University in four or five years?"

Old Dominion was a Division II power, and Madison College was moving from Division III to Division II. I hadn't ever seen Old Dominion play, but I didn't tell that to Dr. Carrier or let it dampen my enthusiasm.

"Yes, sir," I said emphatically. "I can build the same kind of program as Old Dominion."

This college president had his own game plan, I discovered, and he wanted the right man to execute that game plan. I had to show Dr. Carrier that I was his man. My father always told me, "You never get a second chance to make a first impression."

I felt I had interviewed adequately. Dr. Carrier seemed pleased, but I still couldn't be sure if I was his man. I sensed that this was a feeling-out session. So I headed back to Rhode Island without a job offer.

I was pumped-up, regardless, believing Madison was the right place for me and for my family. I felt I could do something meaningful there, something historic, turning a women's college into a men's basketball power. As good as Old Dominion? We'll outdo Old Dominion, Dr. Carrier.

He made me wait for an answer. During that nerve-wracking time, I researched Madison College's background, so that I would sound fully knowledgeable about the school, should I be asked about its history. And what an interesting history, I discovered—socially, economically, academically. It had transitioned like few other colleges in America.

The school was founded in 1908 as the Normal and Industrial School for Women at Harrisonburg. Has there ever been a longer college name?

Harrisonburg, the county seat of Rockingham County, busted its buttons over being awarded the state's first Normal school, winning out over a dozen applicants. The hometown newspaper, *The Daily News*, was so overwhelmed that it waxed poetic: "The Normal's come to Harrisonburg, and Oh! My lawdy daisy. All the folks around this town are just a-running crazy."

O. B. Roller, the town's mayor, called it, "The proudest moment in Harrisonburg's history." Julian A. Burruss, the school's first president and

After the formation of clubs with regional geographic bounds such as Roanoke and the Tidewater region of Virginia, young women from different states formed the Ramblers Club at Harrisonburg State Teacher's College. This dapper group of students proudly marked their luggage with their respective state initials, ranging from South Carolina to New York. Photograph courtesy of the 1922 *Schoolma'am*, the school's yearbook.

only thirty-three, thanked Senator George B. Keezell for securing the college for Harrisonburg. Keezell stood 6-foot-7, a power forward before his time. The school's first gymnasium was located in Maury Hall, then later in Ashby Hall's basement, just enough room for a half-court basketball game.

A Normal was a two-year institution that trained elementary school teachers, mostly women in 1908. Men of that era apparently disliked cleaning blackboards. This particular Normal was Virginia's first college to set up a four-quarter system and to give complete courses in industrial education.

The school set down strict rules of etiquette: Students couldn't marry or even date, there was no loitering at the local ice-cream parlor, and smoking and dressing in bright colors were not permitted. Students had to wear two petticoats—yes, petticoats—and their dresses extended to six inches from the ground. Was this Normal a women's school or a women's prison?

When one student had the audacity to elope, this bit of news even made the front page of *The Washington Post*. But the *Schoolma'am*, the college's matronly-named yearbook, omitted this juicy tidbit.

In 1914, the school's official name was shortened, just a tad, to the State Normal School for Women at Harrisonburg. This change was greeted with a hip saying of the time: "Oh, it's the essence of bug juice." Yes, bug juice.

Red Cross-sponsored First Aid classes appeared on campus during World War I. Teachers dealt with students' minor scrapes, such as floor burns from skidding after basketballs or bloody noses from playing field hockey.

After Burruss left to become the president of his alma mater, Virginia Polytechnic Institute (now Virginia Tech), his replacement was Samuel P. Duke, thirty-three, who remained in charge from 1919 to 1948. His own rigid code of conduct: No lollipops, no public dancing, no joy riding, no cutting classes, no electrical curling irons, and no hot plates. No college fun?

Duke, however, did relax the school's dating policy. Students could date one night a week in addition to Friday and Saturday nights. Seniors could practice basketball two nights a week. Bobbed hair was forbidden. Flapper!

Another name change occurred in 1924: Harrisonburg Teachers College. During the Roaring Twenties, dresses also grew shorter on campus.

The Great Depression of 1929 didn't prevent the school from building Wilson Hall, named posthumously for President Woodrow Wilson, who hailed from nearby Staunton. The $200,000 hall was dedicated in 1931, and Wilson's widow attended the ceremony.

The 1930s brought campus dances to good ol' H.T.C., but students were warned to stay "a hymn book's distance apart from their partners." Otherwise, God might set fire to their corsages. But President Duke did manage to bring "normalcy" to old-maidish Normal.

The school newspaper took on a new name, *The Breeze*, in a run-off vote against the "Campus Cat." *The Breeze* reported the school's basketball success— undefeated seasons in 1929, 1930, 1934, and 1935. H.T.C. girls obviously could hoop it.

In 1938, the school became Madison College, named for James Madison, a Virginian who was the shortest of U.S. Presidents at 5-foot-4—like having Muggsy Bogues, the famous 5-foot-3 point guard, in the White House.

A new campus curriculum no longer focused solely on training teachers. A liberal arts degree was available. And the school's sports teams became the Dukes, named after President Duke, with the hope that he would fund the teams' uniforms, equipment, and travel. He refused, then consented, and now he's forever immortalized on campus as the mascot man.

When World War II arrived, students volunteered for airplane spotting. They made thousands of bandages for injured servicemen, and they entertained soldiers in local churches. Dancing, by now, had eliminated the hymn book's distance between partners, without evoking heaven's wrath.

By war's end, enough men had enrolled on campus to form their own basketball team. During the 1946–1947 season, the male Dukes, mostly military veterans, posted a 4–3 record, defeating two high school teams, the Mary Washington Boys and Shenandoah Boys, and topping the Bridgewater College freshmen. This makeshift scheduling continued until 1968–1969, when a full varsity men's basketball schedule was implemented.

In 1949, Madison College had its first male graduates, even though men couldn't live on campus. Dr. Duke had a stroke in 1948 and was tended to by his wife until his death in 1954. By this time, there were fourteen buildings on campus, eight of them constructed on Duke's twenty-nine-year watch. And the campus had expanded from forty-nine to sixty-nine acres, with still more room to grow.

George Tyler Miller replaced Duke as the school's president during a time of considerable change. Miller was a man of action, adding 240 more acres to the campus, introducing post-graduate programs, and revising the school's entrance standards, which meant more male students—and possible integration. This raised havoc with segregationists, as this was a Southern school in a Southern town in a Southern state. For the time being, integration was shelved.

The school was evolving, regardless, but some old rules held fast. Curfew was at 11 p.m. Dresses and skirts, not pants, remained the classroom attire. Outside of class, raincoats covered up shorts and jeans, even when the sun was shining. First-year Madison College females weren't allowed to go home at Thanksgiving because, the rumor went, they might not return.

More change was afoot: Dormitories for men; housing for student mothers whose children came with them; the first master's degree in 1956; the "School-ma'am" yearbook was renamed "Bluestone", and campus protests arrived in the 1960s. Even actress Jane Fonda showed up on Madison's campus to stir anti-war sentiment over Vietnam. Faculty members and students clashed over her negative nickname, "Hanoi Jane," which stemmed from her support of North Vietnam. Madison students defied school policy by letting their hair grow long and by dressing as hippies. They even dared to walk across campus lawns, a no-no. Students who rebelled faced expulsion. Protestors were thrown in jail. Times, indeed, were a-changing. Miller was a progressive, but the social revolution was too overwhelming even for him. And so he retired as president after twenty-two years.

Dr. Carrier arrived in 1971 with a fresh set of relaxed rules. Students now could walk across the grass, lie on the grass, picnic on the grass. This was their campus, too, Dr. Carrier reasoned. Dress codes were thrown out. You could wear your hair long, and you could wear pants or shorts. Also, no more curfew. And integration arrived to the chagrin of segregationists.

The last remaining vestige of vintage campus life—a May Day tradition of women students circling the May pole—ended its promenade in 1971. And May Day queens, who dated back to 1924, were discontinued as well. Modernism had come to the Madison College campus, like it or not.

By 1970–1971, males made up 25.1 percent of the school's student body. By 1974–1975, that figure increased to 40.5 percent. Overall enrollment jumped from 4,041 to 7,000 in just four years.

Now that I was fully educated on the school's history, I thought, how could they pick anyone but me? I knew I was the right man for the job, but would I even hear back from the school? As each agonizing day passed without a phone call, I figured they had found someone else.

Increasing the diversity of JMU's student body was a key theme in Dr. Carrier's presidency. By 1990, the date of this photograph, the percentage of male students had steadily increased to 44.4 percent, and one in four students now came from out of state. Photograph courtesy of James Madison University Libraries: Special Collections.

Then Dean Ehlers phoned. He asked if I would come down for a second interview. I said yes, but could I bring my wife? He said, "Certainly." If I was offered the job, I wanted Dawn there to be a part of it. We were a team. I knew she wanted this as much as I did, for the two of us and also for our two children at the time. As we packed for the trip, I was really optimistic. "I'm going to get this job," I told her.

Returning to the Madison College campus, I met some new people, we took a tour of the downtown, and we even checked on real estate. The housing market was limited, I was told, and interest rates were as high as eighteen percent. But I was getting ahead of myself: The job wasn't yet mine.

I didn't meet with Dr. Carrier until the second day. Once again, he got right down to business. "Coach," he said, "we are going to make you an offer of $13,000 to be the head basketball coach at Madison College."

I paused. I wanted this job so badly but not at $13,000. I was making that same figure as an assistant at Rhode Island. I explained this to Dr. Carrier. "I felt that, when I got a head coaching position," I said, "I would get an increase in salary." I held my breath.

"Well," he said, "what are we talking about for a salary?"

"I'd want $15,000." I don't know why I picked that figure, but I was sincere.

"Coach," he said, "would you step outside and wait in the hall? We are going to discuss this." He meant Dr. Sonner and Dean Ehlers, who were present in the room.

I waited in the hall, perspiring, for fifteen minutes. Had I presented a deal-breaker? I thought of running back in there and saying, "I'll take the $13,000." But it was important to stick to my guns. I was worth $15,000.

Finally, Dr. Sonner opened the door and invited me back inside. I stood in front of Dr. Carrier, who said, "Coach, I hope you can coach and recruit as well as you can negotiate. We are going to offer you $15,000 and a four-year contract—$13,000 from Madison College and $2,000 from the Madison Foundation. Congratulations."

Wow! I was a college head coach. I shook Dr. Carrier's hand, and then I shook Dr. Sonner's and Ehlers's hands. I couldn't wait to tell Dawn the good news. She was outside, waiting nervously on a park bench. Ehlers asked to see me, first, in his office. He wanted, I discovered, to mark his turf.

He looked at me straight and said, bluntly, "I want to have a say in this. It's a three-year contract, not a four-year contract." As the athletic director, he felt he hadn't a final say in my hiring, and now he was speaking up.

I didn't hesitate. "That's fine," I said. I knew, deep inside, that, after three years, I would be getting a new contract. I didn't pursue this job to fail.

I ran down the stairs to find Dawn, who was on pins and needles. She took one look at my face and knew we had found our new home. We hugged. But now we needed a place to live—the dream home. "Let's go find a house," I said. "We have five hours before our plane departs from DC."

I had no realtor, and I had no leads. I just drove around neighborhoods, looking for "For Sale" signs. We went past an elementary school, made a few turns. Then we spotted a house under construction. A man was working on the site. We approached him, hoping against hope. "Excuse me, sir," I said, "is this house for sale?"

"Why, yes, it is." He turned out to be the contractor. We sat down with him and made some changes, picking out different paints and wallpaper. I gave him a deposit check of $1,500—Boom! Bam!—and we had our house for $38,000.

"What did we just do?" Dawn asked on the drive to the airport.

"Honey," I said, "you're not coming back here until we move. So we had to get this done. And we just got lucky."

Lucky, indeed. I got a head coaching job and a house in a couple of hours. We were on a roll. We couldn't wait to get back to tell the kids.

I got the Madison job strictly by accident, only because Bobby Watson didn't want it. But fate is so fickle. While at Evansville, Watson and his basketball team were traveling by private charter to an away game when the plane crashed upon landing, and everyone aboard perished.

When I read that tragic news, I was stunned. It was an eye-opener about cruel misfortune. I couldn't stop thinking that, if Watson had taken the Madison job, he would be alive today, and where would I be? Had I stayed at Rhode Island, I would have been a victim of bad timing. Tom Carmody was fired the following December, and his entire staff was fired, too.

What would I have done then? Where would I have gone, with a wife and two kids? Coaching is such a transitory existence to begin with.

Though it's sad to say, I had little time to dwell on Watson's and Evansville's misfortune. I had to build a basketball program in a hurry.

The Dukes were 16–7 the previous year with Dean Ehlers as their coach.

Three of those wins were over Luther Rice, and two were over Millersville. But Madison lost twice to Shepherd, with single defeats to Federal City and Christopher Newport. Christopher Newport?

I could see the pushover schedule that Madison was playing, though it lost by thirty-one points to Old Dominion, the same school that Dr. Carrier used as the guidepost in hiring me. Old Dominion was four hours east of us in Norfolk, but it felt much closer and more personal to Dr. Carrier.

Some of these patsies would be eliminated from my first schedule, but my feet didn't touch the ground for weeks. I felt like I was going ninety miles an hour. Some coaching colleagues tried to slow me down, in a negative way.

"A girls' school, Lou?" they said. "What are you doing?" In the back of their minds, they were thinking, "We may never hear from Lou again."

I assured these colleagues that Madison College now was fully coed. "I'm building a winning program," I added. And I wasn't blowing smoke.

Though the Harrisonburg community was excited about my coming, it was a tempered excitement. They didn't know me or my coaching style. I brought along Mike Fratello, another Jersey guy from north of the Mason-Dixon line. Now south of that line, we had to watch our Ps and Qs.

I was allowed only one assistant, which was Mike. To say he was nervy and blunt was putting it mildly. But I knew he would get the job done. He was creative. Then I found out exactly how creative was Mike.

When we started bringing in recruits for campus visits, there was an immediate problem: My office had only one desk, with no couch for recruits to sit on. Mike swung into action.

His office was located on the second floor, with the physical education instructors, while I was on the first floor. Nothing stopped Mike. A few days before some recruits visited campus, I saw Mike and Phil Deane, the head maintenance man, coming down the hall with a big couch sitting on a platform with wheels. I asked Mike where he was going with the couch.

"We're going to put it in your office," he said. "We need a couch, right?"

"Mike," I asked, "where did you get the couch?"

"I borrowed it from the P.E. instructors' lounge."

"Mike, we're going to get in trouble for this."

"Don't worry, Lou. We'll be fine."

The couch went missing, and nobody knew where it went. Somehow, we kept the couch for at least a month until our new couch arrived. Mike felt we needed the couch more than the P.E. instructors. So he borrowed it.

Then early one morning, Mike and Phil returned the couch to the P.E. instructors' lounge, without anyone catching on. Somehow, we dodged a bullet. Like I said, Mike was nervy.

From the very start, Mike and I wrote to every basketball coach in Virginia as a means of introducing ourselves. That spread some good will, but the rest was up to us. If we didn't produce, good will turns to bad will.

I had come to Madison College to build its image and to create my own image—even with the unheard-of challenge I faced in educating a former girls' school on how to play hoops with the big boys. Though they wore petticoats on this campus back in the day, I wasn't interested in a "Petticoat Junction" image or formal dances. We were headed for the Big Dance, the NCAA Tournament.

Madison College's 1972–1973 Men's Basketball Roster

Name	Year	Position	Height	Weight	Hometown	High School
Richard Bailey	Fr.	G	5-9	158	Spring Lake Heights, NJ	Manasquan
Gary Butler	Sr.	F	6-4	200	Fredericksburg, VA	King George
David Carnavale	So.	F	6-4	185	Williamsburg, VA	St. Thomas
David Correll	Fr.	F	6-6	190	Roanoke, VA	Jefferson Senior
Joe Frye	Jr.	C	6-6	200	Colonial Beach, VA	Colonial Beach
Tim Meyers	So.	F	6-3	195	Roanoke, VA	Patrick Henry
Wilbert Mills	Fr.	G	5-11	160	Pocomoke, MD	Pocomoke
Lennie Mosser	Jr.	G	6-3	185	Roanoke, VA	Patrick Henry
Joe Pfahler	Fr.	G	6-0	163	Allentown, PA	Central Catholic
Jim Phillips	Fr.	G	6-4	190	Annandale, VA	Annandale
Mike Slivinski	Fr.	C	6-6	195	Reston, VA	Herndon
Jack Snead	Fr.	F	6-8	200	Fairfax, VA	Woodson
Rich Sumpter	Fr.	F	6-4	190	Arlington, VA	Yorktown
George Toliver	Sr.	G	6-1	173	King George, VA	King George
Jerry Tutt	Jr.	G	5-9	155	Luray, VA	Luray

This is the official roster of players who were part of Coach Lou's first team at Madison College. The foundation for the future success of basketball at Madison College and JMU under Coach Lou began with this first group of players, eight of them freshmen who were "unwanted" by traditional basketball powers. Compiled by Mikki Soroczak for Coach Campanelli.

CHAPTER 3
The Unwanteds

Having my own college basketball team realized a life's dream, but I faced a major obstacle from Day One: How to improve our roster so that we could compete with the strengthened 1972–1973 schedule I had inherited? Luther Rice now was Rice-a-Roni. Arrividercci. Clinch Valley and D.C. Teacher's were two more schools removed from our schedule.

Nonetheless, I had to be honest about my recruiting chances. Madison College, in stature, wasn't North Carolina, Kentucky, Kansas, or UCLA. Big-time high school stars weren't flocking to our gym door. We had to go out and find the sleepers, and some of them were tucked away in remote places.

With the blue-chippers, naturally, gravitating toward the major powers, I realized that blue-collar guys would be the backbone of our unknown program. I wasn't even sure about the players I had inherited from the previous Madison College team. I had to learn their names first.

Dean Ehlers wrote an evaluation of the returnees to help me out. During his interim year as coach, finishing 16–7, he signed four players to letters of intent. I asked Dean what else was needed. He emphasized: Point guard.

Checking my recruiting lists from Rhode Island, I remembered a kid from Allentown, Pennsylvania, Joe Pfahler. We had backed off him because he was waiting for St. Joseph's of Philadelphia to offer him a scholarship. He liked St. Joe's because his brother played there. I took a chance and phoned him. He said the St. Joe's offer didn't come through.

Opportunity awaited. Could this be my first significant recruit?

"Joe, how would you like to take a visit to Madison College?" I asked, fingers crossed. "We're going to build a top Division II program. We have a beautiful campus and a brand-new 5,000-seat gym. Nobody has heard of us yet, but, believe me, they will. I have big plans."

Joe seemed excited. He flew down to Virginia for a look-see. As it happened, our returning guys were playing a pick-up game in the old Keezell Gym. I asked Joe if he had brought along his sneakers. He had, indeed, so he scrimmaged with our guys. This was an NCAA no-no, but Madison College wasn't yet an NCAA member, so it couldn't be a violation.

Ehlers watched that scrimmage, then elbowed me. "Pretty good player, Coach," he said. Though a man of few words, Dean was a good evaluator. He was right: Joe could play. Before he returned home, I offered him a scholarship. He didn't hesitate before accepting.

One down. More quality players were needed before my Madison College Dukes could hold our own with the improved competition. As it turned out, we were the only school to offer Joe Pfahler a scholarship. He was that proverbial apple at the bottom of the barrel but a real pippin, as it turned out.

Joe started for me three and a half years. He played on two NCAA Division II tournament teams. He was a steady, solid player, one of those guys who came to play every night. He was a good shooter, though his primary job was getting the ball to others.

I won't ever forget Joe's becoming my first scholarship player at Madison. Eight or nine guys were coming back in 1972–1973, mostly seniors. I needed to plan for the future. A year later, Sherman Dillard, Van Snowdon, John Cadman, and David Van Alstyne became my first recruiting class, based strictly on their potential. Potential was our only hope.

Sherman Dillard would become our first star. He gave us twenty points a game for four years. He was from Bassett, Virginia—6-foot-2, a deadeye shooter and excellent student. Richmond, a Division I school, also was recruiting him. How we got him was interesting.

I interviewed six different candidates for an assistant's job. One of the six was Ernie Nestor, Dillard's high school coach. I was unaware of Sherman until Ernie gave me his name—Ernie did so regardless of whether I picked him as my assistant. I didn't pick Ernie, not then anyway, but, in the process, he demonstrated his integrity as well as his ability to judge talent. I sent Mike Fratello down to scout Sherman. Mike said he wasn't much of a dribbler or passer, but he was an excellent shooter. You never can have enough shooters, so we recruited him hard.

It came down to Richmond and us. Sherman's dad passed away when he was thirteen, but his mom liked what I had to say. I told her that I would look after him like he was one of my own. I couldn't promise her that he would play at the next level, but I promised her that he would graduate.

I made that very same promise to the parents of every kid I recruited. And I followed through: Of the forty-two kids who played for me at Madison, all forty-two graduated, although the forty-second, Steve Stielper, needed to come back much later to finish up his degree.

Sherman's mom believed me, and so he signed with us. He then grew to 6-foot-4, moved from guard to small forward, and became JMU's No. 2 all-time scorer with 2,065 points as a 52.1 percent career shooter. And he was the definitive student-athlete, an Academic All-American.

Sherman Dillard was our first quasi blue-chipper. Our under-the-radar thinking was: "Let's not look at what he can't do; let's focus on what he can do." Sherman was a pure shooter. He couldn't pass the ball or dribble, so we got him the ball in the open court. Twenty points a game was the result.

I had recruiting adventures that Bobby Knight and Dean Smith never experienced. Shortly after becoming Madison's coach, I drove to eastern Pennsylvania to attend a 5-Star Camp. Mike, my assistant, was at the camp, and he wanted me to evaluate some of the college prospects there.

On the way up, I committed to speaking at a camp in Culpepper, Virginia, without knowing how long it would take to get there, other than it involved an overnight stay. All I saw along the roads were motels with "No Vacancy" signs. Finally, I found one that didn't, and a light was on inside the office. But, as I pulled in the gravel driveway, the light went off. Exhausted, I knocked on the door anyway.

A woman opened it. "We just sold the last room," she said.

"I'm dead tired," I said. "Do you have a couch I could sleep on?"

"Oh, no, my husband wouldn't like that."

Frustrated, I turned around to leave.

"Wait a minute," she said, grabbing a flashlight. "Come with me."

There was a popup camper in the backyard. "You can sleep here," she said. "I'll let you have it for $6.50."

"Can I have a 7:30 a.m. wakeup call?"

"The rooster will wake you up at 6 a.m."

I woke up with the rooster's crowing in my ear. That's when I looked around the camper, which was a pigsty. Beer cans, cracker boxes, and soda bottles were strewn everywhere. I couldn't get out of there fast enough. That lady had a lot of nerve charging me $6.50.

Driving away, I thought, "How will I ever be a big-time college recruiter, bunking down in some crummy camper?" I knew it would take plenty of determination to get ahead in my world, not to mention an imaginative mind, but I never imagined I would need backwoods lingo to recruit.

I pursued a player from Big Stone Gap, Virginia, right there in the heart of Appalachia. I told Dr. Carrier that I was planning to make a home visit. He had kept abreast of how I was progressing on the job, probably to make sure he had hired the right man.

"Coach, you can't go down there alone," he cautioned.

"Why not?"

"They talk mountain talk."

"What's that?"

"Here, brush up on this."

He handed me a book titled *Mountain Talk*, which looked like a foreign language to a guy from Joisey. Dr. Carrier was from Bluff City, Tennessee, so he had a hankerin' for Appalachian speech patterns.

I thought I'd better do what the good president suggested, so I started reading. "Fer git hit" meant "forget it." A "caliption fit" described a "very angry" Appalachian. "Grinnin' like a mule eatin' briars" was a "big smile," while "Hittin' caty-wompus" was something "crooked, out of alignment."

I wasn't clear how mountain lingo would impact recruiting, but I read on. "I'm as tard and far'n twice as hot" was someone who was "very tired." "Well, I swan!" is a "surprised individual." I tried a couple more. "Kocsis Army" was "a lot of anything." "A fine kittle of fish" meant "what a mess." "Like as not, I'll be agoen" suggested that "Maybe it's time to leave."

It came time to stop this caty-wompus translating.

"Dr. Carrier," I said, "I don't know if I can handle this."

"Better yet," he reconsidered, "I better go with you on this trip. You're going to need an interpreter. By the way, is he a pretty good player?"

"Yes, sir."

"I'll see if I can get us a private plane. My friend, Ray Carr, has a plane. I'll give him a call."

I pinched myself. Here was a school president about to accompany a coach on a recruiting trip. That didn't happen at Duke, North Carolina, or anywhere else. I started to believe that Dr. Carrier walked on water.

The borrowed plane was available, a single-engine aircraft that sat four people, a new kind of air travel for me. I thought, "If the pilot has a heart attack, we're going down." Unless, I told myself, "I bet Dr. Carrier probably knows how to land a plane." Still, I was more than a bit apprehensive.

We flew to some place called Lonesome Pine, a small airstrip up in the mountains. We managed, mercifully, to land safely. Someone, thank heaven, had lit up the runway. Someone else drove twenty-six miles up the mountain with our rental car. We headed for a drugstore in the town of Norton, where our recruit, Barry Hamler, met us. Then we drove to his home in Big Stone Gap. If you don't love recruiting, and this was a major test, go find another job.

When we arrived at the house, Barry's grandfather, who was 103, was sitting in a rocking chair on the front porch, smoking a corncob pipe. We shook hands, and his gorilla-like grip buckled my knees. They make 'em strong in Appalachia, even at 103.

We went inside and met Hamler's mother and father. He was seventy-two and had worked in the coal mines forty-two years. Because of Dr. Carrier, the home visit went smoothly, though I wasn't always sure what was being said. Luckily, I wasn't asked to speak mountain talk. Finally, it came down to Marshall University and us, and Marshall won out on Barry Hamler. Now, it was the Marshall coaches who had to bone up on mountain speak.

That's how it is in recruiting: You don't always succeed. You just take a deep breath, suck in your gut, tighten your belt, and move on to the next home visit, still believing in what you have to say and hoping that you don't need to bring along a translator.

That wasn't the only plane we used for recruiting. Dr. Carrier had connections. He called me up one Saturday morning. "Coach," he said, "I'm going to pick you up in a few minutes."

"Where are we going?"

"We're going to take a ride to see a friend, Cletus Houff, who owns a trucking firm at the Shenandoah Valley Airport. He just bought a brand-new plane. Maybe he'll let us use it."

Shortly thereafter, we arrived at the airport.

"Ron, what can I do for you?" asked Cletus Houff.

"Cletus, we'd like to see if we could use your plane for recruiting."

"How many hours are we talking about?"

Dr. Carrier turned to me.

"Coach, how many hours do you think you might need?"

"About twenty-five hours," I guessed.

Cletus Houff pulled out a business card.

"Coach," he said, "here is the pilot's phone number. Call him, and, if we're not using the plane, you can borrow it."

It was a beauty, too, a twin-engine Aero Commander that sat six, and it greatly facilitated our recruiting. I was now convinced that Dr. Carrier walked on water.

But even without leaving the ground, recruiting elevates your emotions. Take the case of Pat Dosh, who became one of our best players. But, because of a gross error in judgment on my part, we almost missed out on him.

I first saw Pat play in the Jelleff Summer League of Washington, DC, before his junior year of high school. He was 6-foot-3 1/2, a wingman with a nose for the ball and a shooting range out to sixteen feet. He played hard, rebounded well, but he was a "tweener," someone who couldn't play guard and was too small, we thought, to be a forward. So we initially listed Dosh as a backup player. We were after the proverbial "better athlete."

One night, I happened to speak at a banquet. I told the audience that we wanted kids who played hard, who had good character, who could score regardless of position, and who wanted a good education. I brought along our team captain, Joe Frye, who did the driving.

On the way home, I blurted out, "What a jerk! The type of kid I was talking about at the banquet is Pat Dosh. He is exactly the young man our program is all about. Joe, pull into the next rest stop." I called Mike Fratello and told him to go up to DC in the morning and offer Dosh a scholarship.

"I thought he was a backup," Mike said.

"No," I said. "I want him. Stay up there until he commits."

Mike stayed up there the entire week and watched every baseball practice—Pat also was a first baseman—just to let the kid know that we really cared. His high school coach at St. John's, the legendary Joe Gallagher, instructed Pat to make us wait. I guess Joe wanted to bust our chops a little bit to show who was in charge there.

Pat committed to us, finally, and, thank God, we got him. He started every game for three and a half years and wound up as the school's No. 2 career rebounding leader and No. 6 scorer. He was a fun kid who came to play every game, and he was a winner. We made the NCAA Division II tournament twice with Pat Dosh.

Once in a while, though, it helps to have a little religion in order to win over a prospect. That was my experience with Linton Townes, someone we managed to land in a roundabout sort of way.

I had sent my graduate assistant, Gerry Vaillancourt, to see a particular player. The next morning, I asked, "How'd you like him?" He replied, "Not that much, but there was this skinny kid on the other team who can really shoot. You should check him out."

The skinny kid was Townes. So the following Friday, I went to see him play for Covington (VA) High School. I asked a student which player was Townes. She pointed to someone in the corner, a lean kid who then launched a pretty shot that hit nothing but net.

He was 6-foot-4, 164 pounds, but his shot was as smooth as silk. I looked around, didn't see any other college coaches, and couldn't wait for the game to end. I burst into the locker room and introduced myself to the coach, who said that Linton was a fine young man. I asked if he was being recruited. When the coach said "Yes," my heart sank. He added, "Roanoke College and Liberty Baptist have offered Linton financial aid." Financial aid isn't a full scholarship. My heart jumped back up.

"Coach," I said, "I'll offer him a full scholarship right now."

After Townes came out of the shower and dried himself, I introduced myself and told him of our scholarship offer. He was thrilled, like this was a gift straight from heaven. In his spiritual world, that made sense. We made a date for the following week, when he introduced me to his parents.

Linton's father was the Reverend Henry Townes. The reverend and his wife, lovely people, thanked me for offering their son a scholarship. The father explained that he had no money put away for their son's education, so a scholarship truly was a blessing.

The reverend then asked if I would join his family in a prayer of thanks. After the parents, Linton and his sister got off the couch, we knelt to pray. To myself, I said, "Dear Lord, Linton's got a sweet shot, but help him to grow and to get a stronger body. See what you can do."

Four years later, he was 6-foot-7, 194 pounds, and a valuable contributor on two NCAA Division I Tournament teams. Madison hasn't ever had a better perimeter shooter (.557) than Townes. After several years in the NBA, he played twelve years in Europe and then a few more years in Israel.

My prayer had been answered; never underestimate the power of prayer. We gave Townes an opportunity to play, the same opportunity we gave to other unheralded players. By playing a lot, a kid improves; that's how Townes became a star. We also gave our players a style of play at which they could succeed—based on toughness, defense, and discipline—with four years to perfect that style. That way, we gave the big-time programs all they wanted in terms of competition. And, sometimes, that was enough.

But if I had to single out one recruit based wholly on commitment to basketball, it would have to be Charles Fisher, the marathon dribbler.

Recruiting progressed slowly for us one year. We still needed two guards. We found out Fork Union Military Academy was bringing in high school players on a Saturday morning. Prep schools such as Fork Union are big on the East Coast, giving a player, basically, a fifth year of high school without disturbing his four years of college eligibility.

I sent Ernie Nestor, by then working for me, to Fork Union. From the gym, Ernie called to say, "Lou, there's a young man from Cape Charles, Virginia, who's about 6-foot-1, quick, a good shooter though not with his left hand. He's a combo guard, but he could be a point guard in the future."

"Forget the left hand, Ernie. Let's get him over here for a campus visit."

Fisher liked our campus, and our program, and he accepted our scholarship offer, the only one he received. That's when we learned of Fisher's fierce love of basketball. Talk about going the extra mile!

He lived in a farming community on Virginia's eastern shore, a six-hour drive from our campus. There was a dangerously high bridge to cross over Chesapeake Bay to get to Fisher's house. Recruiters may not have known where he lived or they were too scared to cross that bridge to recruit him. Even though I'm scared of heights, Fisher was worth the fear factor.

After finding his home, I asked him where his high school was located.

"About twenty-five miles down the road."

"How do you get to school?"

"A bus comes and picks me up."

"Right here where you live?"

"No, about five miles from here."

"How do you get to the bus?"

"I dribble my basketball there."

"Five miles?"

"It's no problem."

"Even when the weather's bad, like a snowstorm?"

"Yeah. No problem."

"What about after basketball practice?"

"The bus drops me off five miles from here, and I dribble home."

I had found my point guard.

There's this expression: "It's not the size of the dog in the fight, but the size of the fight in the dog." Let me tell you about Keith Bradley.

Remember when Mike Tyson bit off part of Evander Holyfield's ear? Well, Keith Bradley's dog took off part of his ear, too.

Bradley attended Lloyd C. Bird High School in Richmond, Virginia. His coach, Chuck Tester, recommended him to my assistant, Bill Leatherman, who drove over to check him out.

Bill's report was positive: Athletic kid, 6-foot-6, nice frame, wiry strong, jumps well, good passer, scores well around the basket, tough defender. No Division I schools recruited him either. We gave him a scholarship.

I found out about Bradley's toughness in another way.

He returned from Christmas break one year at JMU with a bandaged left ear. "Keith," I asked, "what happened?" He told me that he was wrestling with his aunt's German shepherd, and the dog bit off the tip of his left ear. Talk about a dog day afternoon!

The doctors cleared him for competition, but he had to keep the ear bandaged. He played the rest of the season, didn't complain, and helped us to another winning season. Cosmetic surgery waited until after the season.

Then there's Derek Steele, who went from carrying a football to dribbling a basketball, though he was skilled at both endeavors.

One night, I was at Archbishop Carroll High School in Washington, DC, watching the Virginia All-Stars scrimmage in preparation for the Virginia-Maryland Game at the Capitol Centre. A 5-foot-7 guard caught my eye. He was jet quick with the ball, and he had good court vision. I was standing next to Jack Kvancz, Catholic University's Athletic Director. I asked Jack, "Who is that little guy?"

"Derek Steele, from Mount Vernon (VA) High School," Jack replied. "He's going to your school but on a football scholarship. He prefers basketball, but nobody has offered him a scholarship."

I raced down to the locker room, introduced myself to Derek, and offered him a basketball scholarship on the spot. Madison lost a tough football player, but we gained an off-the-bench player who contributed to two NCAA Tournament teams and then started for us his last two years.

Every kid I've mentioned here was an unwanted player or a prospect barely wanted by the big-time programs. Roger Hughett was a different story. He was a prized recruit, an in-state kid from Radford. And we had out-recruited Virginia Polytechnic Institute to sign him. This was unusual for us, beating out a Division I school, as Madison College still was in Division II.

Hughett was a 6-foot-2 guard. He wasn't a blue-chipper, though he was very close. He lived ten miles from the VPI campus. He called me one day and said he was coming. We were elated. On signing day at his home, his father invited Mike Fratello and me to join him in a toast—a drink of moonshine in the storm cellar. Both of us gagged, it was so awful, but we wanted to make the father happy.

After only a few months on campus, Roger told us he was leaving. We were shocked, thinking he was enjoying Madison. Homesickness often is a freshmen affliction, which was the case with Roger. After I spoke to him twice, he changed his mind and decided to stay.

Well, the next thing I knew, one of my assistants rushed into the office to say, "Roger is out in front of Godwin Hall with his suitcases." I found Roger sitting on the curb. I didn't want to lose this kid—he was a player!

Calmly, I sat down next to him on the curb. We just talked. I inquired about what he wanted to do if he left. "I think I want to be a fireman," he said.

I had a heart-to-heart talk with him.

"Roger, when I was a freshman in college, I wanted to quit ten times," I told him. "I was living at home, commuting thirty miles each way. School was too hard, I was on the freshman basketball team, and it just felt overwhelming. But I decided to stick it out."

"What changed your mind, Coach?"

"By quitting, I would have broken my father's heart. He had taken $1,000 from his retirement money, which was a lot of money in 1956. My quitting school would have been like lighting a match to it. I just didn't want to disappoint my father. I loved him too much."

A long period of silence passed between us.

"Roger," I continued, "the first semester is hard for everyone. We all get homesick. Can you stick it out another month and see how things are then? Remember, a college degree is important for your future success."

Hughett thought it over. I held my breath.

"Coach, I'll give it another month," he said.

A month went by, and he still was there. Four years went by, and he graduated. Hughett was a three-year starter and a fan favorite. He was a key component as we laid the foundation for success at the Division I level.

There was another kid we recruited, but he wanted so badly to go some place else, and that was all he could think about. He dreamed of this place, but it didn't happen for him, and that's how we got David Dupont.

The school, of course, was North Carolina. Dean Smith's assistant, Eddie Fogler, phoned us to say there was a prospect in Greensboro who needed a school. Dupont was that prospect. Fogler said UNC had contemplated bringing him in as a non-scholarship player but opted for somebody else.

Ernie Nestor called Mac Morris, Dupont's coach at Page High School, and received a glowing recommendation on the kid. High school coaches, as a rule, tend to glamorize their players, perhaps for their own ego. For if one of their players gets a full scholarship at a marquee program, that high school coach can brag about that player for life.

That's why I talked to guidance counselors about a recruit, for a more balanced view. I also watched the kid in practice. Did he hustle? How did he react in the huddle? Were his eyes on the coach or on his girl friend up in the stands? Was he coachable? Did he work hard in the classroom? If the kid were a screw-off, I would find out by talking to enough people. I even asked the coach, "C'mon, be honest with me, what's the kid really like?" Most of the time, they were honest.

Our players, once we got them, loved the Madison campus environment. And our teachers loved the players, because they were good students. I always told the kids to sit in the front row and ask one question, to show the teacher you're interested. Madison is a caring place, but if you're a lazy dog in the classroom, you'll be a lazy dog on the basketball court.

We didn't tolerate troublemakers. If a recruit visited the campus and our players saw him abusing alcohol or drugs, those were red flags. Our players would tell us, and we thanked those kids and sent them away. But we screened the kids pretty well, so it wasn't a big problem.

I sent Ernie to Greensboro to watch Dupont in a scrimmage arranged by his coach. "Lou, I like him," Ernie phoned from the gym. "I think you should fly down tomorrow to see him play."

That's what I did, and I liked Dupont right away. He came up for a visit. Our prospects of getting him looked good. He didn't have another Division I school recruiting him, just a couple of small schools in North Carolina.

"Coach, I want to play D-I basketball," he said, almost pleading with his eyes. By that time, we had been D-I for two years.

"David," I said, "you can play for us."

Dupont wasn't chopped liver. His high school team defeated James Worthy's high school team in the playoffs. Maybe they would meet again one day, perhaps with David as a Duke. Who could say?

Dupont loved our campus and finally committed to JMU. The following week, we visited his family, and he signed the scholarship papers. The Duponts were Tar Heel fans, no doubt about it. David's bedroom was like a shrine to UNC. His parents told me that, ever since he was a little boy, he wanted to go to UNC. UNC and only UNC.

That following summer, David played in the North Carolina State All-Star Game. Ernie and I made the trip. David was our first recruit from that basketball-crazy state, and we had to be there. We were excited when he stole a pass in the first half and broke away for a slam dunk.

"Who the heck is that?" said Carl Tacy, the Wake Forest coach.

Ernie leaned over and said, "Coach, that's David Dupont from over in Greensboro. He's coming to JMU this fall." The look on Tacy's face said it all. Other coaches wore that same expression over the next four years, as Dupont found ways to beat them, sometimes with that same slam dunk.

Though Dupont was denied the opportunity to attend North Carolina, he faced them twice in the NCAA Tournament, including a game for the ages. In an ironic twist of fate, David's son made the North Carolina squad as a walk-on before the 2011–2012 season, which thrilled the entire Dupont family.

To our credit, we recognized the big-time potential in Dillard, Dupont, Townes, Fisher, and others who the big-time programs missed. But, in all honesty, it would be nearly impossible nowadays to duplicate our recruiting success. With the plethora of AAU teams existing today and the number of players needed to fill those rosters, it's harder than ever to go undiscovered. Those hidden bushes where we discovered overlooked players, hey, everyone's now looking behind those same bushes.

Regardless, there is a valuable lesson to be learned in recruiting when distinguishing between blue-chippers and blue-collar guys: One man's reject can be another man's gold.

The legendary "Buddy" Mills scores in his first-ever game at home in Godwin Hall versus Bridgewater College, December 2, 1972. The Dukes won 69–54 against the rival Eagles in Coach Lou's debut game at Madison College. Photograph courtesy of James Madison University Athletics.

CHAPTER 4
Holy Mennonite!

In my debut as Madison College's basketball coach, Deccember 2, 1972, we faced Bridgewater College, our rival at the time. Our gym was filled to capacity: 5,000 excited fans. But just before halftime, I lost my best player for the season. My first game!

Gary Butler went up for a rebound and landed wrong, requiring major knee surgery. He wasn't only done for the season—he was done. He was married, nearly finished with his degree, and he wasn't coming back. He let me know that right away. And I had him for all of fifteen minutes, my projected go-to player. How could a college head-coaching career start out any worse?

Butler had been Madison's captain twice. At 6-foot-4, he led the team in rebounding three years and in scoring once. His 11.2 career rebounding average remains the school record. Once Madison established an athletic hall of fame, he was inducted in 2008.

But what was I supposed to do? Call off the season? Dr. Carrier and Dean Ehlers hired me to build a program that would match Old Dominion's. Those two were interested in victories, not injury updates. My job was to make this former girls' school contend, not curtsy.

Contending would be done ethically. Before each season at Madison, Ehlers would bring in the coaching staff and have us read the NCAA manual. He wanted us to be knowledgeable about all the rules. There would be no cheating. Dean was a straight arrow and as honest as the day is long.

Anticipation of our first game was huge. The local paper even built it up. Bridgewater College was just seven miles from us. Coached by Mel "Shifty" Myers, the Eagles were a Division III school, meaning they could only give financial aid. We were in Division II and thus could award scholarships, a total of five our first year.

Though I never thought of failing, we faced pressure from the start. I hadn't ever seen Bridgewater play and didn't know any of their players. Dean handed me a scouting report from the year before. The Eagles weren't very athletic, so they played at their own pace and took only good shots.

Conversely, we weren't a fast-breaking team, because we didn't run well as a group. Our whole season, I projected, would be charting the great unknown. Besides Bridgewater, I had no idea what George Mason, Washington & Lee, and our other opponents looked like either.

So here I was, dressed in my new blue sport coat, pocket square, and plaid slacks—plaid was big back then—with the tie Dawn also had picked out—she was my wardrobe manager. And I'm wondering how my new team would respond with its best player headed for surgery.

Panic struck me momentarily, and then I put all negative thoughts behind me quickly. Injuries happen in competition. I needed to implement Plan B.

George Toliver was a proven player, too. He was a strong, silent-type leader and a solid captain my first year there. He had attended the same high school as Butler in northern Virginia. George was Madison's first 1,000-point scorer and a future school Hall of Famer himself.

So it wasn't like our team was decimated when Butler went down. Those Dukes showed me something by pulling together. Tim Meyers replaced Butler. Timmy, a future team captain, was smart with a decent shot. We put together a solid second half against Bridgewater to win comfortably, 69–54.

Not having Butler, though, reduced our scoring punch. We weren't going to put up as many points as I had envisioned even as Madison College had posted six 100-point games the year before. But we won our next three games rather easily against Eastern Mennonite, 67–52, Tusculum, 81–44, and George Mason, 78–69, before losing to Old Dominion, 69–55. The Monarchs were so much better than us at that point, but I was pleased—I just didn't want to get beat by twenty-five or thirty points.

We won our next five games against Southeastern, 93–40, Virginia Wesleyan, 87–56, Christopher Newport, 73–67, Southeastern again, 67–46, and St. Andrews, 73–57, to push our record to 9–1. My other Dukes stepped up in Butler's absence. Freshman forward David Correll would lead the team in scoring that season with a 13.2 average, followed by Toliver at 12.5, Wilbert "Buddy" Mills at 12.1, and forward Joe Frye at 11.1. We had good scoring balance, but we lacked that go-to guy, someone who could get us a quick score.

Nonetheless, I was proud of how the team responded. I brought passion, energy, and enthusiasm with me from Rhode Island, and the players bought into all three. I was in a unique position: Not many coaches get an opportunity to build a program from scratch, though Dean Ehlers laid the groundwork.

Not every Duke proved coachable during my first couple of years at Madison. Jack Snead was 6-foot-8 and a good prospect. He worked hard in practice and went to class, yet he was the first player to challenge my authority.

My etiquette rule for travel required jackets, ties, and dress shoes. The jackets would be blazers purchased by the school. Our entire team traveled in one van—fifteen people and luggage crammed into the van. That's when I noticed Snead was wearing orange Converse high-top sneakers. I immediately questioned his reasoning.

"I wore the sneakers to class today," he said. "They were comfortable, so I left them on."

"Really?" I said. "Stop the van."

Our trainer was the driver. He pulled over. and I ordered Snead to get off. "When you get properly dressed," I said, "you can come down to Hampden-Sydney for the game."

A state trooper was behind us, and he gave Snead a lift back to campus, fifteen miles away. Snead's safety made me feel better, but a rule is a rule. As I was giving my pre-game talk, Snead arrived. Some of our cheerleaders had given him a ride. He played off the bench that night, and we won, 83–71.

Snead played only his freshman year for us before giving up on basketball and school. That was a rarity for me at Madison, kids quitting basketball and dropping out of school. I wished Jack the best, hoping he would find whatever he was looking for, wherever that might be.

My first few years at Madison required coaching not only the players, but also the student body. After a pre-season practice, I'd head over to the dormitories, fraternities, and sororities to meet with students. I explained how important they were to our building process. I told them that they were on our team— Madison College's sixth man—and that we needed an intimidating crowd to make the opposition feel uncomfortable.

I'd visit two buildings a night, which made for some late dinners, but the students responded. Opposing teams feared coming into Godwin Hall, where we had capacity crowds of 5,000 for every home game. Oh, did I mention the students and I shared a few beers while I was recruiting them? I'm sure the statute of limitations has run out by now on possible campus infractions.

We chose an honorary coach to sit at the end of our bench during home games. He listened to our pre- and post-game talks, a different person every night, perhaps a team sponsor, faculty member, or a friend of the program. One faculty member was even in tears after a loss. But this concept of an honorary coach created a lot of good will on campus.

After we split with George Mason that first year—another positive sign—we came up against Eastern Mennonite, a college that was across town from us. As I understood it, the Mennonites dressed plainly, lived simply, and worshipped devoutly. They were peaceful people who didn't believe in war, swearing under oath, or holding offices that required the use of force. I saw quite a few Old Order Mennonites riding around town in a horse and buggy.

We beat them at home, 67–52, in my second game. We played them later that season at Eastern Mennonite in their tiny gym, which held maybe 250 people. We lost at the end, on a foul call at midcourt. They hit two free throws to beat us, 72–71. It was a big setback and a bigger blow to my pride.

Holy Mennonite!

I went home after that game, depressed. While sitting in the living room with Dawn and drinking a beer, I started to cry. "How am I going to build a program," I asked, "if we can't even beat Eastern Mennonite?"

We hadn't come to play, we lost our focus, and we got upset. There were stories in the paper the next day, noting that we gave out scholarships and Eastern Mennonite didn't. But the bold reality was that they out-shot us and out-scrapped us. I told my kids: "You just learned a lesson. You have to play hard every night against everybody."

I was so embarrassed. I was hired to beat Old Dominion, not to lose to Eastern Mennonite. I felt like I had let everybody down, but, to his credit and to my great relief, Dr. Carrier never said a word.

We just played on. Losing that game didn't alter my coaching style, which remained passionate. I wasn't a yeller and screamer as a coach, just vocal. Listen, defense is hard to teach, and my players hadn't been around anybody with as much passion for the game as I had. After Eastern Mennonite, they would learn what I meant by consistency.

I let them know that anything the mind conceives and, if you believe in that conception strongly enough in your heart, you can achieve it. A little philosophy here and there can't hurt, especially if it works. In our situation, it worked. We finished 16–10, a good career start. With Gary Butler, we'd have won twenty games, and we wouldn't have lost to Eastern Mennonite!

I liked the way our team played. Correll had a good turnaround jump shot.

Pfahler was a distributor. Toliver had limited range, but was quick and could drive. Mills was solid in the backcourt. Frye was tough in the post. So we had scoring variety. And we competed well.

I enjoyed that first team. Toliver is a great guy who became my graduate assistant while working on his master's degree. He later became an NBA game official and then a supervisor of NBA officials.

Mills was another favorite. He wasn't a jet in terms of speed, but he had fifteen- to eighteen-foot scoring range. And he was a sweet man. He was black, Correll was white, and they roomed together for four years on campus. My players didn't want to live off-campus; it was too far from the dining hall. And Correll liked to sleep late before going to class.

If you didn't get along with Buddy Mills, something was wrong with you. He never said a bad word about anyone. He was just a special kid, a dependable player who averaged 7.8 points over his career, shooting 51.2 percent, and producing three assists per game. And he was coming back in 1973–1974 with some promising recruits, including Sherman Dillard.

Oh, man, could Sherman score! I recognized that right away when he was a freshman. He was the best overall shooter I would have at Madison. Steve Stielper was good from sixteen feet in, and Townes was my most accurate perimeter scorer. But Sherman really could hit those twenty-foot shots, plus he could run the court and get us easy baskets. He was the kind of player who brought us closer to the caliber of players that Old Dominion and Randolph Macon recruited. Sherman took us up another notch.

We were more athletic my second year and more competitive. Because Sherman could get down the floor, we were better in transition. That made us much tougher to guard. We lost to Old Dominion by ten, which I interpreted as progress. But the main thing was that, unlike the previous year, we beat the teams we were supposed to beat. We took down George Mason twice, and, when we came up against Eastern Mennonite, we dominated the Royals 92–66. I never wanted to hear "Holy Mennonite!" again.

One of my main goals from the start was to beat a Division I school. We got our first chance that second year against Virginia Military Institute, only to lose a close one at their place, 58–54. What a pit their gym was, a portable floor placed over dirt, with wooden bleachers, like basketball in 1916.

Nevertheless, a four-point loss was encouraging. We made further progress.

Dr. Carrier, Dean Ehlers, and Dr. Sonner, the director of JMU's foundation, had to like how quickly I had converted Petticoat Junction into a competitive Division II basketball program. That extra $2,000 I asked for on my initial contract already was paying dividends.

We were invited to a Florida Southern tournament, where we had a barnburner of a game against Valdosta State, a very good Division II team from South Georgia, though we showed that we were evenly matched against them. How evenly? Well, the game went into the first overtime, then the second overtime, the third overtime, and, finally, the fourth overtime. I had this rule with my players: If they were tired, they just had to raise a fist, and I would substitute for them. Well, that was the night Sherman Dillard went for thirty-nine points. Take him out? I wasn't that crazy.

It was a humid night in Florida, and our players were gasping. Sherman had the hot hand, so, when he raised his fist to come out, I ignored him. I kept looking in another direction. He raised his fist again, and I'd be talking to Mike Fratello, my assistant. I told Mike, "Don't look at him." I can't tell you how long I kept this up, but I wasn't about to give Sherman a breather. He hung in there, as did our team, but Valdosta won, 91–89. Both teams had left everything on the court for sixty minutes—a game and a half.

We had to play the very next night against the University of the South. We were completely exhausted. I didn't even have the customary shoot-around the morning of the game. I let my players have some pool time to cool off, but I told them to rest their bodies. Mike left to do some shopping, and he returned a few hours later with this sly grin.

"I bought something that's going to give us good luck tonight," he said. "We need a little extra incentive, and I found just the right thing."

"Whaddya got, Mike?"

From a bag he pulled out purple and gold underwear, with top and bottom pieces made of pure silk, real slinky stuff.

"What are you going to do with that?" I asked.

"We're going to wear it," he replied, "for luck."

"Look, Mike, I know purple and gold are our school colors, but I'm not going to wear *that*."

"Lou, nobody's going to see it. What's your worry?"

Mike talked me into it, and we won the game, 63–58, pushing our record to

9–3. Afterward, in the locker room, the Dukes were fatigued but happy.

"Let's show them what brought us good luck," Mike announced.

Mike peeled off his shirt, which gave me the courage to drop my drawers, showing off our school colors. The players got a big kick out of it. Silly things can make college basketball fun, but once is enough, Mike, with the lucky underwear.

We won our next five games, lost to Old Dominion, and then knocked off our next nine opponents. We went 14–1 to end the regular season at 20–4, a better sequel than the original.

Which school did we get that big twentieth victory against? The Citadel, 43–41, notching our first win against a Division I program, and we achieved it on the Keydets' home court in Charleston, South Carolina. Remarkably, it was the fewest points we had scored that season and the fewest we had given up. We were establishing that defensive presence I wanted and we needed, in order to win consistently. The Keydets wouldn't come out of their zone, and, without a shot clock, we patiently looked for the good shot. Their cadets booed as we continued to slow it down, without any defensive pressure from them. That win was a breakthrough, a turning point in our program, and it helped our power rating by playing two Division I teams in the same season.

Twenty wins in my second season was awesome. Dr. Carrier, Dean Ehlers, and the entire campus had to be ecstatic. I came to Madison to win, and we were winning—big! Thus, we were invited to an NCAA Division II Tournament. How's that for getting from nowhere to somewhere in a hurry? Mike and I were elated, and the players were excited. We were creating believers, even those on the NCAA Selection Committee. But, first, as Virginia College Athletic Association West champions, Madison had to play the East champion, Randolph-Macon, for the VCAA title the very next night after we won at The Citadel. Talk about pressure? Wow.

Well, the VCAA was a loosely organized conference. We lost, 79–65, at Randolph-Macon College, which is in Ashland, Virginia. We had to fly from Charleston to Richmond, then take a bus to Randolph-Macon fifteen minutes away. But the travel and the quick turnaround didn't beat us; Randolph-Macon had the better team. We couldn't match up with their strong front line.

Our next game was the NCAA tournament—a play-in contest at Fisk University, located in Nashville, Tennessee. Fisk was solid and beat us, 59–54. That made us 20–6, a truly milestone season. We had built a foundation. We also gained the respect of high school coaches. They now looked at Madison College differently. So now, when we recruited, we had their attention. They saw that we were building a strong program.

Sherman Dillard averaged 21.0 points and 7.3 rebounds as a freshman. He shot fifty-four percent from the field. After the season, I kicked myself. Sherman should have taken more shots! What was I thinking?

Sherman, to borrow that Reggie Jackson line, was the straw that stirred the drink. He became our brightest star right out of the chute as a freshman, and we had a complementary cast that accepted Sherman's instant stardom.

By scheduling VMI and The Citadel, I discovered that my Dukes enjoyed competing against the big boys. That's what I wanted to instill, this feeling that you can be whatever your mind perceives you to be. There is a fine line between confidence and cockiness. I felt pride in my team, and I wanted my players to feel that same pride while maintaining their hat sizes. Though confident, they didn't become fat-headed.

It's all about having the right mind-set. Mike and I didn't just have our players to work on in terms of getting people to think differently. Remember, we were two guys from the North, and life moves slower in the South. I'd hear, "Coach, if we don't get that camp brochure out tomorrow, we'll get it done next week." And I'd say, "Dammit, I want it tomorrow, not next week."

Folks in Harrisonburg were used to a sleepy college-town atmosphere, while Mike and I were raring to go. Their turtle-like pace took us aback, and our hare-like attitude startled them. After a year or two, we managed to move at the same comfortable pace. We had met in the middle, North and South. Plus folks knew we were excited to be there and that we had made dramatic strides in basketball: No more girls' school excuses. We were on our way.

CHAPTER 5
You Gotta Love It!

My third year at Madison was approaching, and we had made the NCAA Tournament in just two years, capturing lightning in a bottle. Now we needed something to symbolize what we were all about. We needed an inspiring motto, possibly a catchy slogan to show my players, recruits, students, faculty, and the basketball world the kind of program we were building from the ground floor at Madison College.

Then I hit upon an idea: You Gotta Love It! Basketball is all about commitment. You Gotta Love It! School requires that same commitment. You Gotta Love It! And coaching is a commitment, too. You Gotta Love It!

And so I had these "You Gotta Love It!" t-shirts made up. My players wore them, our students wore them, and, when I spoke at camps, I'd pass out those "You Gotta Love It!" t-shirts. So campers wore them, too. Then I painted a big "You Gotta Love It!" sign in the Dukes locker room. My players didn't need encouragement to play the game they loved, but some extra motivation never hurt, as we engaged a tougher schedule against those same schools that had snubbed my players.

You gotta love what you're doing in life, for life offers hills and valleys, and you gotta find a way to love it through all of its ascents and descents. Often it's passion that gets you through all the tough times.

I learned this passion early on, for I was fortunate to be around Rollie Massimino and Hubie Brown, two other New Jersey guys who were intensely passionate about the game of basketball. They were high school teachers as well as coaches, and both were a little older than me when I was coming out of college ready to teach and coach at the high-school level. Rollie and Hubie loved basketball 24–7. They passed that passion on to me.

And just as Rollie, mostly, mentored me, I mentored Mike Fratello, my assistant at Madison and yet another New Jersey guy. We worked together at Rhode Island, and, now as a head coach, Mike worked for me. He also had passion for the game, so I assigned him more responsibility. He scouted opponents, he recruited players, and he served like a second head coach.

As Easterners, we had energy to go with our passion. We were take-charge guys, even pushy. For Virginia people, I was a little too pushy. Mike already let me know he was ready to move up to Division I. So I knew I wouldn't have him for long. Therefore, I decided to get things done now.

We upped it from two to three Division I opponents for the 1974–1975 season, scheduling George Washington, East Tennessee State, and Western Kentucky, all three on the road. I took these games wherever I could get them, although I knew beforehand that they would likely be losses. We weren't ready to face those three schools; that's why they scheduled us. They needed us to pad their records, and we made it easy for them, losing by a collective forty-one points. Still, we did the right thing by toughening our schedule. You get nowhere by hiding. Strength of schedule, I figured, would benefit us down the road with tournament selection committees, and our players relished the challenge of taking on a more demanding schedule—You Gotta Love It!

Even with those three losses, we were 19–6 on the season and playing in our second consecutive VCAA title game. As Dean Ehlers and I planned, we were laying the foundation for something better. Dr. Carrier understood it as well, though he still had Old Dominion as my measuring stick. ODU was our fourth loss that season, 89–54, on the Monarchs' court. They had Division I-type players, a cut above ours, and were worthy VCAA champions.

We showed versatility that third season. Sherman Dillard gave us not only a good shooter, but more athleticism. Pat Dosh wasn't quick, but he was smart, an aggressive scorer, and rebounder. Joe Pfahler was a valuable distributor. We had some height in two 6-foot-8 guys, John Cadman and Van Snowden. Van gave us eleven important points one night against VMI. Defensively, though, those two were a liability. Unfortunately, we weren't going to get a 6-foot-8 guy with good speed who could jump out of the gym. Those types were going to the ACC or Big East or Big Ten.

It was difficult for us to recruit complete players, so we took what we could get from the backwoods, the boonies, and the Eastern shore. Players with shortcomings, we coached them up. Otherwise, you don't survive.

Sherman gave us twenty points a game once again. David Correll, at 6-foot-6, was a post-up guy with a turnaround jump shot who averaged just under ten rebounds. We had a little quick guy in Leon Baker, a New Jersey guy who Mike pushed for and who started twenty-one games for us before he left school. Madison just didn't work out for Leon.

Sherman Dillard displays his perfect shooting stroke versus Old Dominion in Norfolk on December 13, 1975. Photograph courtesy of James Madion University Athletics.

Our ideal lineup was Dosh and Dillard on the wings, Correll and Snowdon in the post, and the unselfish Pfahler at the point. That way, I could max out Dillard's and Dosh's skills, because they complemented each other. Tim Meyers was our captain, even though he was a reserve. Everyone in the program respected Timmy. He was a solid guy, a smart guy, who knew how to play. He maximized his ability as well as anyone on our team.

Sometimes, a coach misreads a player's capability; I was guilty of that with Correll. Dean Ehlers recruited David just before I arrived. Though he scored and rebounded as a freshman, I wasn't happy with his defensive play. So I played him off the bench as a sophomore. Then Dean pointed out that Correll was a pretty good scorer and rebounder. Dean was right. David started for us as a junior and senior.

Re-evaluating Correll helped me mature as a coach not only in terms of who should start, but how to substitute. Because I was a student of the game, asking myself every year what I could have done differently, it finally dawned on me that I needed to substitute more fairly. After all, I had been a substitute as a player, so I should have better understood that aspect of coaching. But I was more concerned early in my coaching career about who should start, because the starters are your best players. I didn't fully realize the importance of substitutes in winning games.

This might be true of all young coaches, figuring out the right way to work guys into the game. It's trial and error. Once a player is in the game, how long does he stay in? I learned that, if you pull him after he misses a shot or makes a mistake, his confidence goes down. I was yanking players too soon from the game. My assistants said, "Lou, you have to let them play through their mistakes, to give them confidence."

My assistants were right. Once I did that, I *became* a college coach. But it's a process to get there. I coached freshman basketball at the University of Bridgeport in Connecticut, where I had only four scholarship players. The other players were walk-ons, guys you picked out of the student body. We never had more than nine players, and it takes ten players to scrimmage.

I recruited my neighbor, Tim Samway, so we could scrimmage. Tim was in his thirties, a salesman for a paper company. He couldn't run, but we now had five guys a side. What else could I do? Tim just loved the game and probably last played in high school. During my two years there, Tim practiced with us. I

Coach Lou gets a big hug from his daugher, Brooke, following the 77–57 win versus Washington and Lee in 1975, three years after Lou's arrival at JMU. Photograph courtesy of James Madison University Athletics.

should have awarded him a block letter, but I paid him off in pizza and beer. Today, that would be a NCAA violation!

With only four guys on scholarship, I had to start one walk on. So you can see why I didn't worry about substituting back then; I merely was trying to get by. When I became a varsity assistant at the University of Rhode Island, I didn't have to substitute, because that was Tom Carmody's job.

Thus, it took me a few years at Madison to appreciate the role of substitutes. I learned to substitute on the game clock, working a rotation. That way, a player knew he would be in the game for a certain period of time and wouldn't have to worry about a missed shot or a mistake. Guys play better if the coach shows he believes in them. Even if one of my guys hit three jumpers in a row, he had to come out to keep a sub rotating. That's how you develop a bench.

I finally caught on my third year at Madison. We created a huge home-court advantage with our starters and reserves. We built up a seventeen-game home winning streak that started from the previous year and continued through the 1974–1975 season. The students really bought into the sixth-man philosophy I instilled. We built up fan excitement with our running game. Three times, we scored more than 100 points, all three at home. We surrendered more points, too, but, after committing to a certain style, I stayed with it, because we were winning.

We were on solid ground, becoming more credible. Sherman made it all happen; he could score against anyone. We repeated as VCAA West champions with a 6–0 record and then played Saint Paul's College, the East champ from Lawrenceville, Virginia, for the VCAA title at our place. With our fast break in high gear and the crowd going wild, we outlasted Saint Paul's 107–96, in a wild shootout, as Sherman scored forty-two points.

The NCAA Selection Committee then bypassed us for the postseason Division II tournament. If we hadn't played those three Division I teams, we might have been 22–3 instead of 19–6, and almost a certain tournament invitee. Still, the committee's shortsightedness cost us, though Dean Ehlers made the argument that there was a really good field from which to choose.

We had long-range plans, and so I looked at it as give and take. I got over the selection committee's snub quickly, focusing on bigger things up ahead. If those dissatisfied selection committee members demanded an even more imposing schedule from us, I wasn't about to deny them. I lined up five Division I schools for 1975–1976: Virginia Military Institute (VMI), East Tennessee State (Dr. Carrier's alma mater), George Washington, Memphis State (where Dr. Carrier worked prior to coming to JMU), and Florida State.

But I would face that upgraded lineup without Mike Fratello, who was hired by Rollie Massimino at Villanova, fulfilling Mike's ambition to coach at a Division I school. I paved the way for Mike by introducing him to Rollie. Mike then jumped from Villanova to the NBA as Hubie Brown's assistant with the Atlanta Hawks. Mike later became head coach of the Hawks and Cleveland Cavaliers before becoming an NBA television analyst. Rollie, Hubie, Mike, Lou….four Jersey boys. But, of the four, Rollie was the most special to me—my coaching mentor and a forever friend.

With a nucleus of good players returning for my fourth season, I was confident we would defeat a Division I team, and we knocked off two: VMI, 82–76, and East Tennessee State, 90–77. Both games were at Madison, where our home winning streak grew to twenty-five games before Randolph-Macon nudged us, 59–57. Old Dominion clipped us in overtime, 87–83, at Godwin Hall four days later. So close, yet those same old ODU blues continued. Our three Division I defeats were: 104–80 at Memphis State, 80–70 at George Washington, and 85–65 to Florida State in our gym. However, the Memphis State experience was something altogether different.

Dr. Carrier and Dean Ehlers arranged the game with Memphis. Dean had coached there, and Dr. Carrier had been a vice president there. But Memphis's coach, Wayne Yates, didn't want to play us, all because we were Division II. I never got to meet Yates. The day before the game, we arrived to practice at their gym as they were leaving the court, and Yates didn't wait around to meet me, eschewing customary courtesy.

Then, before the game when the two coaches shake hands at the scoring table, he didn't come down. Dean told me, "Coach, he isn't too happy to meet you." After the game, he didn't want to shake hands either, so I never met him. Their goal, I heard later, was to score 100. Even though we ran a delay game the last three minutes, they had big-time athletes and scored 104.

The next day, we stopped to get breakfast on our way to the airport. A Memphis booster entered the restaurant wearing a Memphis jacket and Memphis hat. He came by my table and said, "Coach, I was at the game last night, and you have a group of nice young men who conduct themselves very well." I said,

"Thank you." And he said, "Why can't we get players like that?" They had some pretty shady kids, though I didn't tell the booster that.

Dean Ehlers knew coach Hugh Durham at Florida State, and Durham agreed to play us home-and-home, the first year in Harrisonburg. I was hopeful our improved schedule would get us a better power rating, and this proved true. Even with a 18–7 record, slightly below our previous season's showing, we were chosen to play in the NCAA Division II Tournament. Those wins over VMI and East Tennessee State were the tipping point.

We certainly weren't lacking in star power. Dillard led us in scoring with a 22.4 average, Correll averaged 9.4 rebounds, and Joe Pfahler, our senior point guard, set a team record with 158 assists.

So which team did we draw for our opening game in the NCAA Regionals? Who else but Old Dominion? And the game was at their campus in Norfolk, Virginia. We gave it our best shot but lost, 86–77. Then we fell to Morgan State, and the talented Marvin Webster, the following day in the third-place game, 86–81. Thus, we finished the season 18–9. Once again, we traded away a twenty-win season for the purpose of recognition. And, to my utter surprise, that recognition was happening faster than I could have imagined.

In early May, I got a phone call from Dr. Carrier. "Coach, how are you doing?"

"Fine, Dr. Carrier, how are you?"

"Good, Lou. Can you come over to my office? I have something I need to talk to you about."

"Sure, Dr. Carrier. I'll be right over."

Having no idea what he had in mind, I got on my trusty moped, which I used around campus, and headed over to his office. Jean Barnard, Dr. Carrier's private secretary, said to go right in, that he was waiting to see me.

"Coach," he said, "I've been doing some thinking."

Dr. Carrier is every bit the thinker, but I noticed he was rubbing his chin. "What are you thinking about, Dr. Carrier?"

"Coach, I think it's time to make a move."

Make a move? I was feeling secure about my coaching. "Um, Dr. Carrier, what kind of move do you want to make?"

"I'm going to ask permission from the (school's) Board of Visitors to change our name from Madison College to James Madison University."

I breathed a huge sigh of relief.

"It would be JMU," he continued. "We'd fit right in with UVA (University of Virginia), VMI, ODU, VPI, all these schools in our state. What do you think?"

"Sounds good to me, Dr. Carrier."

Then he paused ten seconds. I sensed he was thinking up something else. "And I think," he said, "that we should apply for Division I status in basketball."

What did he just say? "Really, Dr. Carrier, D-I?"

"The time is right," he said. "Old Dominion has just declared for Division I status. I'll give you a new four-year contract. Now go out and get me a schedule."

It was all about keeping up with Old Dominion. I received that four-year contract without Dean Ehlers's approval this time, although Dean added another year after my original three-year contract had run out.

"But, Dr. Carrier," I said, "We'll have to increase the budget by going Division I."

"I'll take care of that," he said.

We already had reached the maximum amount of scholarships at twelve. I got a small raise, maybe three percent, though I wasn't the greedy type. I had a radio show and a summer basketball camp that augmented my contract. My biggest contract at Madison, right before I left in 1985, topped off at $35,000. But with radio, TV, Nike, and my basketball camps, that pushed it to $90,000.

With a new contract, with our going Division I, and with a new name for the school, my head was spinning. It was about to spin some more.

"Coach, this calls for a toast," Dr. Carrier announced.

He went to his bookcase, moved some books around, and pulled out a brown paper bag with a bottle inside.

"What do you have there, Dr. Carrier?"

"My buddy from Bluff City, Tennessee, sent me up some good stuff."

"What kind of stuff?"

"Moonshine."

I remembered the terrible moonshine I drank with Roger Hughett's father in his storm cellar the day we signed Roger. So I tried to deflect Dr. Carrier. "We don't have much moonshine in New Jersey, Dr. Carrier."

"We'll just have a little toast."

Reaching inside his desk, he pulled out two Dixie cups. He unscrewed the bottle top and poured some of its liquor into the cups. Then we toasted the Division I Dukes of brand-new James Madison University. I have the greatest respect for Dr. Carrier, but his friend's moonshine wasn't any better than Mr. Hughett's.

Phil Chenier, star of the Washington Bullets, visits the 1975 JMU basketball camp with Coach Lou and his son, Kyle (six years old). It was Kyle's first basketball camp. Photograph courtesy of James Madison University Athletics.

"Good stuff, huh, Coach?"

"Oh, yeah, Dr. Carrier, good stuff."

I took another sip, gagged, and set down the cup. Returning across campus on my moped, I thought, "I took this job four years earlier because I was looking for a nice small, cozy college job. Now I have a different job."

I knew Dosh and Dillard could play against Division I teams, but I needed to find out if I had enough other pieces to make this work. I went down and told my assistants, John Thurston and Ernie Nestor, about all the changes. They were surprised, but excited.

Change was happening fast at Madison. I had to improve our schedule *and* roster for 1976–1977. I was able to increase the schedule to nineteen Division I teams in order to be eligible for the NCAA Tournament.

During this transitory time, I thought about my father and how he had sacrificed for years, drawing out his retirement money so I could go to college. I wouldn't have been in this coaching position without that sweet man. I know the success I had achieved at Madison in the shortest amount of time made him proud. Dad also had a sense of humor. He came to see me at Rhode Island when I was interviewing for the Madison job. A strong Catholic, he told me, "There are a lot of Baptists down there" in Virginia.

My first year at Madison, Dad and Mom came down for a game. I had my dad sit at the end of the bench. Dr. Carrier met them both and told me a few days later, "Your dad really loves you, and he believes in you. He told me, 'Give my boy a chance, and he will win for you.'"

In this team photo for the 1955 Springfield (New Jersey) Regional High School basketball team, Coach Lou (#23, top row, third from the left) crouches over Ron Golcher (#19), Lou's best buddy and the team's star guard. Coach Lou learned a lot about the importance of balancing academic and athletic achievement from Coach DeRosa. Photograph courtesy of Lou Campanelli.

CHAPTER 6
Kid in the Attic

My basketball life didn't start out so hot. I was cut from the freshman team at Springfield Regional High School. Looking back at that fourteen-year-old kid through the eyes of this old coach, would I have cut him, too? Truthfully, I'd have to say yes. I was a skinny kid, weak, slow, and only 5-foot-6. I was hoping against hope that I would make the team, but, being honest, I wasn't as good as the other guys. I was average, but I was already fascinated with the game.

That fascination started in the seventh grade. I would go to the local community center, which had an outdoor court with those chain nets. I loved the sound of outside shots going through the net. Ka-ching! "String music!," as coach and analyst Joe Dean Sr. later called it.

Older high-school guys would be playing. I was hoping they would pick me. Finally, someone would say, "Hey, kid, you wanna play?" So I'd run out there. Then they'd say, "Hey, kid, don't shoot the ball." No ka-chinging for me, but I didn't care, I was playing basketball.

Other kids my age had given up waiting to play with these older guys. They'd go pitch horseshoes, but I wanted to be in the game. It was important to me. So I waited for my chance, as long as it took.

I was a tweener, not a guard and not a forward. When the list was posted in the gym of the players who made the freshman team and my name wasn't on it, I cried. I loved basketball, and basketball didn't love me back.

So I worked even harder on my game, playing in Catholic Youth Association contests, where I was the best player on the court. When I went out for the junior varsity as a sophomore, I had shot up to nearly 6-foot-1, but I was cut once again. I cried even harder this time.

Would I have cut myself that second time? No way. I felt I was good enough to make the team. The JV coach put his arm around me and said, "I'm sorry, Lou, you were the last guy cut." That made it even worse in a way. I was thinking, "Which guy did he pick ahead of me?"

I lacked self-confidence as a kid. My ears stuck out, I stuttered a little bit, and I was quiet and shy. The girls didn't give me a tumble, not even a second look, and getting cut twice wasn't helping my confidence any.

My friend John Zappula, a wrestler, talked me into joining the wrestling squad. He said, "It will make you stronger and more aggressive, and they don't cut anyone in wrestling." John might have been saying, "They'll take even you," though I know he didn't mean it that way.

On the JV wrestling squad, I didn't have to beat anyone out. I weighed 150 pounds. The wrestling room smelled of armpits, but we had good coaches, and they taught me some escape moves. I wasn't strong, but I used quickness and smarts to win five of my seven matches. I started to feel good about myself, though basketball remained my primary goal.

I went out for the sport again as a junior, this time on the varsity, after punishing myself with offseason workouts. My good friend Ronnie Golcher kept encouraging me, though I felt like I was getting better. Some guys discouraged me, saying things like, "Why are you still working out? Coach isn't going to keep someone who hasn't played in the program."

I avoided the naysayers. I even went to church with my mom for eight consecutive Monday evenings. I'm not sure what she was praying for, but I was asking the Man Above for special intentions, through a novena, to help me make the basketball team.

My prayer was answered: I made it! I deserved it, too, believing I was as good as a couple of guys who made the team the previous year. There was no way I would have cut myself this time, and I'm not being biased.

I was the happiest guy in school. It was like Christmas Day, seeing my name on that list. Our first game was against the alumni, and I scored six points coming off the bench. But my happiness was short-lived. After the game, as I was coming out of the shower, the athletic director, Mike Suchena, pulled me off to the side. He told me I wasn't eligible to play, because I had flunked algebra and biology my sophomore year.

He asked why I didn't go to summer school to make up those credits. I explained that my mother was very sick over the summer and bed-ridden, and it would have been inhuman to show her my terrible report card. So those grades made me ineligible until February 1. It felt like a prison lockup.

The team manager, Red Tyjewski, advised me to tell the basketball coach, Lou DeRosa, about my academic situation. I dreaded doing that and replied, "He'll kill me."

Red said, "Tell him that you want to remain a part of the team, that you'll practice every day, and you'll sit on the bench in uniform during games. Just don't put your name in the scorebook."

So I approached Coach DeRosa, a tough, no-nonsense guy from western Pennsylvania's coal region. I told him about my mother's health situation, and could I stay on the team while making up those credits? He looked me over and said, "OK." I was shocked.

By February, through hard work, I was eligible again. With two strikes against me—having been cut twice—I finally realized how important school was, and I told myself that there would be no third strike.

I was a backup as a junior, but we had a heckuva team, advancing all the way to the New Jersey Group Three championship game against Cliffside Park, which had won thirty-nine in a row. They barely beat us, 58–53.

My senior season began oddly. I moved up to sixth man. Then a strange thing happened. Our best player, Les Lawn, had his arm in a sling all week long before the first game. So Coach DeRosa named me as a starter. I was so excited that I convinced my parents to come to the game. Although they were supportive of me, they hardly ever watched me play. As we dressed for the game, Les Lawn walked in, without the sling. "I'm ready to play, Coach," he said. "The arm feels great." Mr. Hollywood! So he got to start over me. I scored five or six points, but I was embarrassed with my parents sitting there, expecting me to start. And it was my only chance to start.

We had a strong team once again, but, in the county tournament, we lost to Plainfield, a school we had beaten twice that year, by twenty-five and twelve points. And our getting upset happened on the same night as our senior ball.

After the game, a buddy brought me my tuxedo and my date, Adrienne Napholz, a cheerleader. We dated for a few months. She, actually, was my only date in high school. Her locker was across the hall from mine, but it took me weeks to get up the courage to ask her out, though the guys told me she wanted to go out with me. She was a sweet girl. We'd park in front of her house, necking, and her parents would start blinking the porch light, informing her that it was time to come inside. Yo, Adrienne!

Though we lost in the county tournament, we still qualified for the state tournament. I played big against Hillside High, scoring twelve points. But we lost to Cranford, which went on to become State Group 3 champion.

Years later, I was reminded twice about my high school basketball days. Remember Les Lawn? Well, he went on to play college ball at Florida Southern. And remember that four-overtime game Madison had with Valdosta State in 1973–1974? Well, during the shoot-around the day of that game, who shows up but Les Lawn? He was excited to see me, and he told me how proud he was that I had become a college coach. I introduced him to the team and then asked him to sit at the end of our bench during the game.

He was delighted, and he sweated as much as my players during that basketball marathon. We shook hands afterwards, and I never saw Les again. But he turned out to be a good guy, not the Hollywood guy I pictured him as in high school. I realized it takes a while to get to know somebody really well.

Then, twenty-five years after I graduated from Springfield High, I got together with my coach, Lou DeRosa. I took him out for breakfast. He now was eighty-two, but I needed to know why he kept me on the team as a junior after I had been cut twice. His answer? "I saw a sparkle in your eye." I could tell how proud he was of me.

My high school teachers failed to see that same sparkle in the classroom. I graduated 246th out of a class of 312. I was an indifferent student, not the least likely to succeed in my class, but close enough.

I met with my guidance counselor, Helen Crawford, who said, "Lou, I don't think you are college material. Maybe you should consider joining the Army." Academically, I was a work in progress, but I wasn't anxious to salute others and march at sunrise.

What's odd is that I was a perfectly good student in grade school. When I reached puberty, everything went haywire. I couldn't concentrate. I was thinking about basketball or some girl I wanted to ask out. My academic focus was awful.

I felt badly about disappointing my parents, who were always so supportive of my brother, John, and me. Mom and Dad were such loving people. When I was ten, I was stricken with rheumatic fever and was bed-ridden for three months. My mother gave me penicillin around the clock. My father called her "Nervous Nellie." To me, she was Florence Nightengale.

John was three and a half years younger than me and much bigger. We called him "Bear." Playing middle guard on the high school football team, the Bear always was injured. Our dad wondered why; he didn't really understand football.

My first love wasn't basketball but baseball. I listened to New York Yankees games on my small Motorola radio. I couldn't wait for my hero, Joe DiMaggio, to come to bat. I'd sit there until my father came home from his pipefitting job, so we could play pepper behind the house. As soon as he walked in the door, I'd say, "Dad, let's go play." He never turned me down.

On Thursday nights during the college basketball season, after Mom put us to bed, I'd wait for Bear to go to sleep. Then I'd get my Motorola from the dresser, put it under the covers, and listen to Marty Glickman broadcast college double-headers from Madison Square Garden. My basketball heroes were Tom Gola of LaSalle, a great shooter who scored "Gola goals," and Bill Mlkvy of the Temple Owls, another big scorer. Mlkvy was known as "The Owl without a Vowel."

Backing up my story, I was born Louis Paul Campanelli on August 11, 1938, the son of John J. and Josephine Campanelli. We were a typical blue-collar family. Bear and I slept in the same bed until I was in the eighth grade, when we moved from Elizabeth to Kenilworth, New Jersey. We didn't have much money, but there was love inside our home and a strong sense of family.

Dad worked for Esso Standard Oil. He went to the YMCA three days a week to exercise. He was into fitness before it was fashionable. He was a pipefitter, and a proud man. When I was ten, I asked him why he always wore a jacket and tie to work. He replied that, when he drove up to the security gate at Esso, he showed the guard his badge, which read, "John J. Campanelli, Employee, Esso Standard Oil."

"The guard," he told me, "doesn't know if I'm a pipefitter or a vice-president. I want him to look upon me with respect. It makes me feel good."

My dad's example stayed with me forever. As a coach, I always wore a coat and tie. I loved my dad and wanted to be just like him, which made *me* feel good.

The post-World War II years were a happy time for us. Everyone in our neighborhood lived in apartments. Behind our apartment was a junkyard with, yes, a junkyard dog. Believe it or not, we carved out a small ballfield in that junkyard and made our own games. Times were tough, but Mom and Dad were good at saving money. Dad told me that he saved for seventeen years to buy our house in Kenilworth.

On Saturday mornings, Bear and I collected newspapers and rags. We'd bring them to the junkyard so they could be weighed. One Saturday, we were paid $2.10 for our load. Dad was all smiles.

"We're going to bring this home to Mom, so she can put it toward groceries," he said.

Depression folks understood the value of a buck. Bear and I learned those same values from our parents. No one in my family had gone to college; my father's education had ended in the eighth grade.

"Lou," he advised me wisely, "do you want to work with your back or your head?"

I already had worked with my back. I was a caddy at Echo Lake Country Club, five miles away. I caddied during high school and college. I carried double bags in the morning and double bags in the afternoon, adding up to thirty-six holes. I made four dollars a bag or sixteen dollars plus tips for the whole day, which was a ton of money at that time.

But I made the mistake of getting too much sun on a day off at the Jersey shore. I had a date with a girl I really wanted to go out with, which meant I had to caddy that same day, as I was short of money. But I couldn't put the golf bags on my shoulders, which were burned too badly. So I carried the bags with my arms hanging straight down, though each bag weighed twenty pounds. When the golfers asked what I was doing, I told them that I was building up my arms for basketball. They said, "Don't drag those bags. Don't let them touch the ground." I said, "Yes, sir." And I didn't, even while walking over rolling hills. Charles Atlas built his arms up with "dynamic tension." My arms didn't look like his, but I knew what he meant.

I didn't have a car, so I thumbed rides. One day, while having breakfast at home, I picked up the newspaper, and read this front-page story about a guy who had just murdered his mother. I was shocked, because that same guy gave me a ride the previous week. But I kept on hitchhiking.

My caddy money helped pay for tolls and gas when I'd get rides to college with John Zappula. I did have a car one year, but it was a wreck. I never forgot where I came from, and caddying helped shaped me into a man.

Boyhood friendships were instrumental in my life. Take Robby Hunter. Our mothers used to push us in baby carriages, side by side, in Elizabeth. After our family moved to Kenilworth, Robby's high school knocked my school out of the basketball tournament. Robby was a very good guard, and his team won the Group 3 state championship. But we continued as friends.

Ronnie Golcher was a standout high school basketball guard. We became friends along with Joe Hepworth, a knuckleball relief pitcher. Robby, Ronnie, and Joe were my Three Amigos. After I became a coach, we stayed friends. They came to watch my teams play, from high school through college. For thirteen straight years during my time in Virginia, they made a pilgrimage once a year, bringing their wives and kids. The Three Amigos even followed me out to California, when I coached at Cal. You couldn't find more loyal friends.

Joe was the nervy one in our group. How nervy? He wouldn't buy a ticket for a game; he'd figure out some way to crash the gate. We left a ticket for Joe at some event, but he convinced a band member to let him hold the tuba, and that's how he got in. Another time, he passed himself off as a team doctor and got inside the arena. Joe certainly had a gift of gab.

After finally realizing my goal of making the high school team, I figured out my life's goal: I wanted to be a teacher and coach. But my chances of going to college were bleak at best after graduating from high school.

Dad could have gotten me into the military reserves, if I wanted. I didn't want it. I got a summer job instead with a wholesale drug company called Ketchum. It was office work, and I hated it, but it sure beat reveille. Then, with the end of summer approaching, I didn't know what to do next.

I recalled my wrestling buddy, John Zappula, saying that he had been accepted at this private physical education college in East Orange, New Jersey, called Panzer College, which trained students to be health and physical education teachers, grades one through twelve, in the state of New Jersey. Panzer's enrollment was 500 students. I decided to check it out.

I got my high school transcript and told Mom to call Ketchum to tell them I was sick and wouldn't be coming that day. Then I drove up to East Orange.

I couldn't find the college, even though I had the address. I kept driving up and down the street until a woman pushing a baby carriage pointed it out, right in front of me: A Victorian home with a small sign by the driveway that said "Panzer College." Behind the home was a gym you couldn't see from the road. There was a laboratory, I later discovered, under the gym.

When I entered the registrar's office of Dr. Hazel Wacker, it was the last week of August, with school about to start. I asked her if there was any room in the freshman class. She asked to see my transcript, and I handed it to her nervously. I told her that I could do better and that I needed to learn how to study, because I was determined to become a teacher and coach.

She showed my transcript to the dean, Dr. Peter Stapay, then left his office looking distraught. She asked if I was involved in any extra curricular activities in high school. I told her that I played basketball. She said she would talk to the Panzer basketball coach, Les Goodwin, who then called the house to schedule a visit.

He showed up with a big book about the school. Except for the gym, most of the athletic pursuits at the college took place in an adjacent park. He mentioned my poor grades, but I told him I was motivated to do better. He mentioned the $1,000 tuition. Dad was paying off our house but said he could take $1,000 out of his Esso retirement plan. Dad was a saint, but I still didn't know if Panzer would admit me.

A few days later, a letter arrived from Panzer. I had been accepted, though on academic probation. I needed a 1.75 grade point average—a C minus—to remain in school. I was a *college man*. At Panzer, this meant attending class in coat and tie. My father, thrilled about this next important step in my life, spent another $90 on my physical education uniform.

Dad then created a study room in the attic. I holed up there seven days a week, teaching myself how to study, with zero social life. I made the freshman basketball team. John Zappula drove me to school, thirty miles away, every day. After practice, I hitchhiked home through rain and snow. I was *that* determined to come off probation, to make something of myself.

After my first semester, my grade point average was 1.73. Was I finished as a college student? A note arrived requesting my appearance before a faculty board, stating my case as to why I should be retained as a student. I faced a review board of six people, telling them that I had maintained a rigorous study schedule and that, if they gave me a second chance, they wouldn't ever see me before them again.

I poured out my heart, because, if I failed, I was either going into the Army or my dad would get me work as a pipefitter. I was asked to go outside and sit on a bench while the board debated my precarious situation.

I waited ten minutes and was called back inside. "Mr. Campanelli, we're going to give you one more semester," I was informed. "We like your professional attitude and your desire to teach and coach." That second semester, I got a 2.4 grade point average (G.P.A.). The board never saw me again.

I played on the freshman basketball team with some guys who were four years older. They had been in the military, including the Korean War. One non-military teammate was Jack Bicknell, who later coached football at Boston College when Doug Flutie won the Heisman Trophy in 1984. I wasn't a go-to player, as I came off the bench, but I scored thirteen points one game. Then, in trying out for the varsity as a sophomore, I tore ligaments in the same ankle twice. Suddenly, my basketball playing days were over.

I managed, though, to play four years of tennis in college. I was fourth or fifth man in singles, and I also played doubles. I needed to have my weak ankle wrapped every day in order to play. I was as good in tennis as I was in wrestling, which was good enough to win more often than I lost.

After my sophomore year, Panzer College merged into Montclair State Teachers College. Only students with a 2.75 grade point average could transfer. Those below that mark would be dismissed. I had a cumulative 2.78 G.P.A., so I just slid by. I still was a *college man*. There's something to say for grit and refusing to quit on one's self.

I still was that kid in the attic, grinding away, transforming myself into a legitimate student. My grade point average climbed to a 3.0—or a solid B. I had surpassed my one-time low expectations of what I might become and the low expectations others had projected for me.

Those last two years of college were like heaven and not just academically, for there were lots of pretty girls at Montclair State. The campus was big, and it felt more like a college than at Panzer. Before exams, I'd invite guys to my house to study over the weekend. Mom would feed us pasta. My last semester, I had a 3.5 G.P.A., and made the Dean's List.

My confidence grew out of sight. I could even talk to girls. I took public speaking, where you gave extemporaneous talks. The teacher gave you a subject as you walked up in front of the class. He said to me, "Mozart."

Mozart? Who's he? I had to think of something fast, because these talks lasted three minutes. "Mozart," I said, "was a beautiful artist who developed these famous paintings." The class knew I screwed up and started chuckling. The teacher didn't say anything, but I had to keep going to get to three minutes. I made it somehow. Walking back to my seat, the teacher said, "Mr. Campanelli, I admired the way you bluffed your way through this. Mozart, by the way, was a musician." Still, he gave me a B for the speech, mainly because I spoke for three minutes without losing my poise.

The day I graduated from college, my parents and the Bear sat in the first row. I don't know how early they arrived to get those seats, but my dad, who was wearing a suit and bow tie, was the proudest guy in the place. I wouldn't have been there that day without him. I loved him so very much.

My ambition to teach and coach was realized in the spring of my senior year. I signed a contract to be a roving elementary physical education teacher in Hillside, New Jersey, covering three schools in town for $4,000. I also received $200 supplements to be an assistant freshman football and basketball coach at Hillside High.

My football experience was limited. I took this technique class in college, so I knew how to get down in a three-point stance. Well, my second year, I was promoted to head freshman football coach. I needed an assistant, so I called upon my brother. We've always had a special relationship; there's never been a cross word between us. The Bear helped me for three weeks, just before he left for Marine duty. He worked with the linemen, and I worked with the backs. We had such a good time, brother helping brother.

Well, here came the final game, and our team was 3–3. The Bear wrote me a letter from boot camp, talking about his tough life there. And I'm thinking of Knute Rockne's "Win one for the Gipper" speech. We gathered in our shed with the blackboard. I read the Bear's letter and then told the team, "Win one for the Bear." I got them so torqued I even had a tear in my eye. The team manager opened the shed door for the players to come roaring through. Instead, one guy tripped and fell, and suddenly there was a pileup of players at the door. It was the "Three Stooges" in cleats. There went my Gipper speech, but we still won 7–6 because of a missed extra point.

My friendship with Rollie Massimino began in Hillside at a swim club the summer before my senior year of college. Rollie was the pool director and Hubie Brown the athletic director. I was one of six lifeguards.

Rollie had this natural edge, like a Joe Pesci, which I discovered the first day of orientation. The pool water was freezing, and the deep end was fourteen feet. That meant to vacuum, you had to dive in with an oxygen mask and a weighted belt. Rollie chose me to demonstrate. I reached the bottom of the pool, and, suddenly, I had no air. I took off the weighted belt and got back to the surface. There was Rollie, pinching the air hose and saying, "Welcome to the club, schmuck." He was a practical joker, and I was his guinea pig.

Rollie became a successful coach, but, like me, he wasn't that good an athlete. He was 5-foot-8, 170 pounds. He played basketball and football—he was a line-man—at the University of Vermont. I teased him: "You only played at Vermont

Coach Lou's first head-coaching job at any level was coaching basketball and baseball at Marist High School in Bayonne, New Jersey. The school had no gym, making it tough for the young basketball coach, but he learned how to persevere and not let any obstacles get in the way of improvement and performance for his players. Here, he poses with his 1964 baseball team. Photograph courtesy of Lou Campanelli.

because it was Division *Six*." Hubie, on the other hand, was a good athlete, playing basketball at Niagara University, a solid Division I program. Then, he thrived in the Eastern League against top talent.

Starting out at Hillside, I was the happiest guy in the state of New Jersey. And how fortunate I was to have Rollie as a friend. He was the varsity basketball coach at Hillside, and he brought me along to clinics. We watched eight-millimeter game films, and we always talked basketball. He was a wonderful role model and an excellent teacher of the game.

Besides teaching and coaching, I had other unexpected duties. On weekends, I baby-sat Rollie's children. The call could come any minute, say 5 p.m. on a Saturday as I was shaving before a date. Then, in the spring and fall, Rollie had either his wife, Mary Jane, or me putting up or taking down storm windows at their two-story house. Rollie was afraid of heights. A ball-buster, Rollie waited until I got to the top of the second story; then he'd shake the ladder. I'm shuddering, and he can't stop laughing.

After two years at Hillside, I got my first varsity head-coaching job at Marist High, a Catholic school of 500 boys in Bayonne, New Jersey. Even being a head coach has its shortcomings. There was no gym at Marist High. We practiced on the second floor of a firehouse, or in the basement of a junior high school, or in the Catholic Youth Organization center, or in the Jewish Community Center. Some days, it was an hour at one place until they kicked us out; then we'd go to another place for the second hour.

Talk about the big time! Well, high school basketball was big time for me back then, and I always found a place for us to practice. We did some pre-game walk-throughs, though, outside. I told the kids, "No excuses. Get it done." We lacked a trainer, so I taped ankles before practices and games.

Coaching friends warned me against taking the Marist job. "You can't win there, Lou. Besides no gym, they play in a tough city league. Wait for something better to come along." My second year at Marist, we went to the Catholic Class B Sectional Finals in the state tournament. This did even more wonders for my confidence.

After two years at Marist, I returned to my birthplace of Elizabeth to become a junior varsity head coach. It was a step back, and, once again, colleagues questioned my thinking. But I always had a plan inside my head. I hadn't ever coached inner-city kids, and I needed that experience if I wanted to become a college coach.

After that year, I was named head varsity coach at Levittown Division High School in Long Island. Levittown hadn't won in ten years, but, in just two years, we developed a winning program and went to the playoffs. I now believed I could turn around losing programs.

The consensus back then was that, if you weren't a good player, you couldn't be a successful coach. My department chairman, Bob Reggio, invited me to lunch. He asked me, "Lou, where do you want to be in 10 years?"

I responded that I wanted to coach at the college level. "You'll never be able to do that," he said. "You already told me that you weren't a good player. Lou Carnesecca wasn't a good player either, but he's an exception."

Reggio doubted me, but I wasn't about to let anyone belittle my ambition. I looked him square in the eye.

"Just watch me," I said.

He didn't have to watch too long. Bruce Webster, the head coach at the University of Bridgeport in Connecticut, recruited one of my players, Eddie Jerome. Webster came down to watch us play. He was so impressed with my man-to-man defense, he offered me the Bridgeport freshman coach's job.

I didn't tell Eddie, who also was being recruited by Seton Hall. Eddie did choose Bridgeport, because it was Division II, and he felt he would play more there. After he made his decision, I told Eddie he would have to put up with me for another year.

I was at Bridgeport two years before getting the job at Rhode Island, a step up to Division I. Hard work never goes unrewarded, but I will be forever grateful to Bruce Webster, who gave me the chance to coach at the college level. Bruce was a good man, and a good coach, but he couldn't get out of Bridgeport. When he retired, his son called to inform me about Bruce's retirement party and would I come? Would I? You bet I was there.

My life changed in another, permanent way as a high school coach. While coaching at Marist, I went to a local club where young people hung out, to grab a beer and to dance. Standing by the wall next to a jukebox. I had one arm around this one girl, and my other arm around this other girl. My confidence by now was off the charts. Just then, another girl walked by us on her way to the bar. I was bitten right away; she was beautiful. I made my way to the bar, where she said, "I saw you over there with those two other girls." And I said, "Once I saw you, I didn't want to talk to those girls."

That's how I met Dawn Luciano. We lived twenty-five miles apart while growing up; Dawn was from North Bergen, New Jersey. She worked at McGraw-Hill Publishing in New York City after attending the Fashion Institute of Technology there. She was sweet and shy, not someone to be at the front of a parade, but clearly the best thing in the parade, with or without a baton.

Like me, Dawn was from a typical Italian-American family. Her father also was a pipefitter. I had to be on my toes, because he was a former Golden Gloves middleweight boxing champion in New Jersey. He enjoyed lying on the couch and watching New York Giants football games. Dawn's mother was kind and loving. She loved to cook, like all Italian wives, and she enjoyed sports, especially basketball. Over time, she called herself "Lou's biggest fan." Dawn's brother, Bob, was over-protective of her, so I had to be on my best behavior with Dawn's family, which wasn't ever an issue, because I loved Dawn.

We dated three years before we wed in 1966. We lived at home until we got married. It was tough for her to leave the nest. I popped the question over dinner at a restaurant in New York. I had the waiter hide the engagement ring in a breadbasket. She dug in for a piece of bread, and there was the ring.

Then I had to announce my intentions to Dawn's family. While she hugged her mom in the dining room, both of them nervous, I approached Dawn's father in coat and tie, while he watched the Giants from the living room couch. I told him Dawn and I were in love and wanted to get married. He jumped off the couch and said, "Is that right?" I held my breath, but he gave us his blessing.

We wed in Our Lady of Libera, a Catholic church in North Bergen. Bear was my best man, while Rollie was in the wedding party. Rollie and I have been best friends for better than a half-century. I love him like a brother.

Dawn and I wanted a family. We have three lovely children—a son Kyle and daughters Brooke and Racelle—and five grandchildren.

Dawn completes me. She levels me out, puts things in perspective. She understands that losing is not the end of the world. There's always another day, another game. That's typical of a coach's wife. A coach looks at every game as a dramatic win or a dramatic loss. Most wives try to keep you on an even keel. Dawn did a great job of that.

On Sundays after Saturday night losses, our kids would bring out a game like Pictionary. They knew it would make me laugh, because I can't draw. They'd

Coach Lou, daughters Brooke and Racelle, wife Dawn, and son Kyle at home in Harrisonburg in 1979. Photograph courtesy of Lou Campanelli.

get hysterical. We'd build a fire and have a nice dinner. Those Sundays were soothing and brought me back down to Earth.

Having children fulfilled me as a man. To bring children into the world, to raise them, to teach them about life, to share with them the things that are important, to help them with self-esteem and to become the best people they can be….what else is there? The Campanellis always had a strong sense of family, in doing things together, like coming to NCAA tournaments.

We were, no doubt, a basketball family. Brooke, when she was three, became part of JMU's regular cheerleading squad, dressed in purple and gold. Kyle attended basketball camps from the time he was five. When he was six, he played with nine-year-olds and complained that they didn't pass him the ball. I said, "Kyle, if you were nine, would you pass the ball to a six-year-old?" Kyle loved coming to our practices and games. I had no idea back then that I would one day coach him in college.

Racelle was our only child born in Harrisonburg. Like her older brother and sister, I took her on our basketball trips to Williamsburg, Virginia, and Annapolis, Maryland, one child per trip. They'd sit with me on the front seat of the bus. After the morning shoot-around before a game, we'd tour the campuses and cities. I wanted them to be a part of my work.

Having grandchildren has been so gratifying. They come at a stage of your life where you're able to enjoy them. I didn't become a grandparent until my late sixties, as our children married late. Observing their parenting, it just warms my heart. Now it seems as if we've had those grandchildren forever. They're just so beautiful.

I learned from my parents that it pays to be a good role model. The love they showed me is the same love I've transferred to my own progeny.

It's been an amazing journey for me, mostly a self-made trip filled with purpose and drive. Cut twice in basketball in high school, I made the team on my third try. I almost didn't get into college; then after nearly being dismissed twice, I graduated on time and also earned a master's degree. I took over a girls' school after it had gone coed, and lifted its basketball team from Division II to Division I in four seasons.

All my life, I've been that kid in the attic, striving to make something better of myself, while showing the skeptics how wrong they were about me. I knew what was inside of me, once I discovered the true me.

CHAPTER 7

The "Greatest College President"

What can I say about Dr. Ronald E. Carrier? Better yet, what can't I say about this special man, because there is so much to tell? He is the most unique administrator I've ever come across. With Dr. Carrier, they threw the carbon copy away as a college president. That's because he was an original. He was a visionary. He knew the exact moment when to change Madison College into James Madison University. And he knew when to move from Division II to Division I in basketball, which happened at the same time.

He thought this whole thing out, and he constantly had a plan in mind. The difference with Dr. Carrier, compared to other academicians I've worked for, is that his plan *always* was the right plan. He was unfailing in his perspective.

I served under numerous administrators at the high school and college levels, many of them important figures in my career. So I've been blessed in that regard. But Dr. Carrier was something else and in so many different ways. In my humble opinion, he is the greatest college president ever.

I'm not alone in that evaluation. Just ask the people at James Madison who knew him, faculty and students alike. There simply was no one else like Dr. Carrier. He was everywhere on campus, relating to the students. They'd wave "hi" to him. They called him "Uncle Ron"—to his face. He even drank an occasional beer with them. How many other college presidents have that kind of relationship with students?

There was no pretense about the man. He was that down to Earth. The James Madison University campus had trashcans painted in purple and gold, the school's colors. If Dr. Carrier saw a soda can on the ground, he didn't ask anyone else to dispose of it. He'd pick up the can and put it in the trash. He didn't place himself above others; he was a man of the people.

Yet he was dynamic. He could capture an audience, whether it was speaking mountain talk in Appalachia or addressing a black-tie affair in Richmond or Washington, DC. He handled himself with incredible ease and composure. "He feels as comfortable talking to the governor as he does talking to a dock foreman," said a James Madison donor, appreciatively, of Dr. Carrier's smooth-as-warm-cognac speaking manner.

Dr. Carrier was extremely supportive of my teams. He was at every home game and spoke to the team afterwards, win or lose. Not many school presidents can say that. He went to our tournament games. The players knew he was with them all the way. Not many school presidents have that bond.

To say he was diverse is a gross understatement. He ran James Madison like no other president ran his or her university. And he did it as much with humor as hubris. Dr. Carrier was an absolute classic.

The stories about him seem hard to believe, and there are so many of them. He should write his own book. The first chapter could be titled "Bravado." Dr. Carrier was a school president who shot from the hip.

One of my favorite stories about him was a broken promise, which he almost never made. He had promised the Virginia General Assembly, after obtaining state funding for a new building, that he'd never return for additional funding. When he showed up the next year with a similar request, he was reminded of his promise. "I lied," he said. The legislators broke up, and he departed from Richmond with another appropriation.

Dr. Carrier knows how to size up a situation. In order to get the College of Applied Science and Technology (CAST) built, he didn't bother to ask the James Madison University Foundation to fund the project. He approached businesses and industries instead to finance the interest on a $1,000,000 loan that would get the building constructed. Of course, he was successful.

Dr. Carrier told me that, in trying to buy $4,000,000 worth of land across Interstate 81 for CAST from the main campus, he sealed the deal on the hood of a car and without a penny in his pocket. "We'll take it," he said, boldly. Somehow, once again, he found the money to purchase the land.

The "E." in his middle name must be "Enterprise." He once asked a graduating class, "If any of you has $3,000,000 to give to JMU, I'd be glad to name the new College of Business after you." That college was built as well.

His methods often were unorthodox, but the results were consistent. JMU's board members viewed him as outrageous and infuriating, but they gave into him regardless. "He can whittle and spit with the best of them," a JMU Board of Visitors rector said of Dr. Carrier's fund-raising Midas touch.

His operating mode was futuristic, always envisioning JMU ten to twenty years down the road. He's a risk-taker, his critics agreed, but they succumbed to his wily Southern charm.

Dr. Carrier could persuade bees to give up their honey, but it still required herculean effort. He was a man who rolled up his sleeves and got after whatever he wanted. He worked fourteen- to sixteen-hour days, often arising at 4 a.m. with a new mission in mind.

His energy was amazing. If he wasn't on the telephone, he'd be visiting with donors and legislators, meeting with faculty, mingling with students, speaking to parents and alumni, delegating to staff, picking up cans, attending games, knocking snow off shrubbery, or making notes for improvements. He also exercised, read voraciously, and was a family man.

He was a human hurricane. I asked him once how he was able to accomplish so many things. "You must take advantage of the moment," he replied. "You must have organization and structure, and you must have rules and control. But it can't be a detriment to innovation."

And who was more innovative than Dr. Carrier? "Through emotion, compassion, and force sometimes," he explained, "you pull people into your vision through your own drive and being in as many places as possible. Expansion and improvement should always go on. It should never stop."

He was as personal as he was powerful in presence, a broad-shouldered man with a prominent chin (he lost fifty-five pounds in retirement). People are drawn to him still, whether they are politicians, students, or families. He remembers birthdays, little children's names, and people's hardships.

It's very clear he cares deeply about others. He didn't just build a university; he built university families. He wanted to know about their lives.

"He doesn't ask good-manners questions," said a JMU vice-president who served under him. "He asks real questions."

JMU is his life even today, having moved from the university's president into the role of president emeritus. He maintains an office in the library named after him, and he shows up regularly in his early eighties, sharing office space with Jean Barnard, his trusted executive assistant of forty-plus years. Even now, in hindsight, he wonders how much more he could have done for JMU. There is no doubt that the most important and influential person in the history of James Madison University is Dr. Ronald E. Carrier.

Now that we've covered his hubris, we need to explore his humor, as they went hand-in-hand during his extensive development of JMU.

In a rush to get the new Madison Stadium (now Bridgeforth Stadium) built in time for the opening of the football season in 1975, the concrete still was wet with time running out. Dr. Carrier told the person in charge to hurry up the process. The man replied, "Dr. Carrier, you know Rome wasn't built in a day." Dr. Carrier replied, "I wasn't in charge."

On a separate occasion, he received a compliment from an alumna about JMU's improvement. "Dr. Carrier, the campus is beautiful," she said. "You and the Lord have done a magnificent job." Dr. Carrier said, "You should have seen the campus when the Lord had it by Himself."

Another alumna returned to campus after a long absence; she had attended the all-girls' college. Introduced to the JMU President, she inquired, "Tell me, Dr. Carrier, are the girls still required to wear hose for the evening meal?" His reply: "Not really. We're lucky to get them to wear shoes."

The governor of Virginia once summoned the state's college and university presidents to Richmond for a discussion on higher education. The governor wanted to have a "dialogue" with the presidents, but, after entering the room and berating them for ten minutes, he walked out. Dr. Carrier said to the others, "This was supposed to be a dialogue, but it seems like the governor was the only one doing any dialogue-ing."

Dr. Carrier, because of his glib manner, was in constant demand as a public speaker. Here are just a few of his funniest remarks:

"I was the tenth of eleven children. My parents weren't Catholic; they were just enthusiastic."

"I grew up in a large family in rural East Tennessee. I never slept alone until I was married."

"At the last speech I gave, I asked if everyone could hear me all right. A man in the back row said he couldn't hear. A man in the front row yelled, 'Come on up here. I can hear fine, and you can have my seat.'"

Dr. Carrier wasn't someone to mess around with. He didn't suffer fools easily. If he didn't receive the support he wanted for some JMU project, he was prepared to do it by himself. In fact, he preferred it that way.

Virginia's university presidents, it seemed, functioned by calling on influential alumni in the state's General Assembly to get bills passed. JMU had few alumni in such key political positions, which didn't faze Dr. Carrier.

"There's no reason why they wouldn't like me as their president," he reasoned. "They know I can't hurt them."

Protocol didn't stop him regardless. He merely bull-rushed his projects forward with remarkable success. He was a man on a proverbial roll.

"I knew we had to broaden the curriculum," he once said of his long-range plans for JMU. "What Virginia didn't have then were regional colleges, like you have in Berkeley with the University of California and all its campuses. Virginia had four women's colleges—Madison, Longwood, Radford, and Mary Washington—and three male institutions—Virginia Polytechnic Institute, Virginia Military Institute, and the University of Virginia.

"And then you had the Richmond Professional Institute, an art school that became Virginia Commonwealth University. So there were no regional colleges. We were the first of the four women's colleges to go co-educational. I realized that we had to increase the population. To do that, you have to have the resources, which meant building up our enrollment, which we did pretty fast.

"Then," he added, "we had to increase the majors. Remember, our school started in 1908 with only three majors: Home economics, physical education, and early childhood education. A lot of your female teachers chose early childhood. But, to get more majors, we needed more men."

Dr. Carrier tried to stump me. "How do you think, Lou, we started to get more male students?"

"Sports? Basketball?"

"You're half-right. But it was football, not basketball. Women don't play football. And there are more players on a football team than in basketball. So we started football to attract men."

I asked Dr. Carrier if there was resistance from the school's administration against his jumping into intercollegiate athletics right away.

"Not much," he said. "I didn't pay any attention to it anyway."

I inquired, long after the fact, why he picked me as the basketball coach.

"Well, Lou, you were young, you were an assistant at Rhode Island, so you already had college experience," he said. "You were enthusiastic, had a good personality, and so I knew you could recruit. "And," he added, "you were cheap."

I believe that last comment was Dr. Carrier's dry wit coming through once again. However, I did work cheaply.

"But *we* were cheap," he said. "We didn't have any money. When I hired Dean Ehlers as athletic director, I also made him the basketball coach. He said, 'I didn't know I was supposed to coach.' Like I said, we didn't have any money. He coached only one year until you came."

Dr. Carrier had a wide-ranging vision for enlarging enrollment. He started black fraternities and sororities on campus. He launched a transition program designed to bring in minority students who didn't quite qualify for regular admission. He got the state to pay their tuition, and then they took English, math, and history over the summer to qualify for the fall.

"One of those students, Pat Southall," he noted, proudly, "became the U.S. candidate for Miss Universe and finished runner-up in the world competition. She married the comedian Martin Lawrence. They had a child, then divorced, and she married Emmitt Smith, the football player.

"Preachers and other successful people came through that transitional program. We started a black gospel choir, (with) 180 members, who packed the hall on campus during homecoming weekend. They were so good that they played in black churches on Sundays around Virginia. Mamas would hear them sing and say, 'That's where I want my child to go to school.'"

As Dr. Carrier told that story, he shed tears. Here is a white man from the Deep South, from Bluff City, Tennessee, and he cared deeply about improving the lives of blacks. He truly was a man of the people.

"I believe this," he told me, "that there is a spark of genius in every student. You may not be the next heart surgeon, or the next Nobel Prize winner, or the next President of the United States. But it's our job as educators to ignite that spark, to allow that student to excel beyond his or her expectations.

"That's our first philosophy: Not to fail them but to encourage them. Our second philosophy: It's our job to build a campus where diversity is the chief characteristic and not try to mold students into a homogeneous environment but a heterogeneous environment, in order to develop their potential in their own special way."

To achieve those goals, Dr. Carrier relaxed what had been stringent campus rules at Madison. Sunbathing now was allowed. So was walking across the campus lawn. Suddenly, students appeared in bathing suits and walked barefoot across the green grass.

"The spring of my first semester here," Dr. Carrier recalled, "the dean of women came running into my office, screaming, 'They're out there on the quad, sunbathing. What are you going to do about that?' And I said, 'I'm going to go look at them.' And she said, 'But they might be having sex.' And I said, 'What's wrong with that?'"

Dr. Carrier was just getting started in modernizing the campus.

"I allowed beer-drinking in the dorms, because I preferred students drinking on campus rather than in town," he said. "But if they were in town, drinking, I didn't want them on the road. So I started the 'drunk bus,' where JMU students drove a school bus into town to pick up those who had too much to drink. That way, they wouldn't get into trouble with the local police. The 'drunk bus' still is in operation today."

With all the changes he instituted, what was his biggest challenge? "The psychological impact that we were a women's institution," he said. "I had to change that psychology. Remember, we had teachers who had taught in a single-sex institution. Athletics helped change that psychology after a year or two. So did our continuing to grow.

"Do you know that JMU now has 130 undergraduate majors—one of the largest in the nation in higher education? That's because I was doing my job. To do that, in the beginning, I let in men who were less qualified than women, in order to increase our male enrollment. Some of our million-dollar donors today were those very same men."

Nonetheless, he faced accusations of sexism. "I was sued by a young woman who didn't get into school because a less-qualified male had taken her spot," he said. "I had to travel to Philadelphia to meet with her lawyers. They told me that I had to change the way I was doing things. I told them, 'When I left Harrisonburg yesterday, I was school president. Unless somebody has taken my spot, I'm still president, and I'm going to keep doing the things the way I feel that are necessary.' Then I got up and walked out. I never heard back from those lawyers."

Just one more example of Dr. Carrier functioning as he darn well pleased. He's convinced that boards and committees stymie growth. Thus, he viewed them as hindrances. "They don't know what they're doing," he said, flatly. "You need them, primarily because they raise funds and help you with the General Assembly. So they cover you. But, sometimes, you have to do what you feel is best for the school, regardless of what others might think." Even if that meant confronting students.

One day, a bunch of male students gathered in front of Dr. Carrier's home on campus, hollering and carrying picket signs. Instantly annoyed, he went out to meet with the protestors.

After the Dukes nearly upset top-ranked and eventual national-champion North Carolina in an unforgettable NCAA second-round game, on March 14, a surprise post-season rally was planned in Godwin Hall. The team plane was late, but the fans weren't, packing the Electric Zoo, including President Carrier handling Duke Dog, the school's mascot, and his cheering wife, Edith. During this memorable event, Coach Lou's speech and the appearance of the now nationally ranked JMU team brought the crowd to its feet. Senior Linton Townes also gave a warm farewell to the JMU fans, as the UNC game was his last as a JMU Duke. Shortly thereafter, Townes was drafted by the Portland Trailblazers, with the 33rd overall pick in the second round of the 2003 NBA draft. Photograph courtesy of James Madison University Athletics.

"Lou, I can't remember what they were protesting," he said. "I do remember that the dean of students was standing there, and so was the chief of police, and they weren't doing anything. So I walked into the crowd and picked out the biggest ugly guy.

"I said, 'What are you doing in my yard?' He said, 'We're protesting.' And I said, 'Protesting, my ass.' I had come from Memphis, which had Dr. King, so I knew about riots. So I told this guy, 'You can come to my office any time you want to, and you can bring any issue, but you're not going to do it in my yard. Now if you're not gone by the time I count to fifteen, I'm going to whip your ass.' They all left. I never had another protest here in twenty-eight years."

Dr. Carrier was imposing, physically, so that protestor did the right thing. Dr. Carrier liked to refer to himself as "the last of the liberals," even though liberals weren't and still aren't all that popular in Virginia. He went to every dormitory at night, sat on the floor with the students, and listened to their issues. He and his wife, Edith, invited a group of students to their home every week for lunch. Dr. Carrier had a speaking rostrum built so that JMU students could voice their concerns and displeasures. He wanted an open-minded, fair-minded atmosphere on campus.

"My mother was open-minded," he pointed out. "She fed eleven children of her own, plus she fed black families. She baked cakes for them. We were poor, but we grew wheat, corn, and tomatoes. And we had a cow in the back.

"My mother thought I would be a preacher. I led the church service in Memphis from the time I was sixteen. I read the scripture, took up a collection. However, I was destined for education, especially after getting my Ph.D."

Dr. Carrier was like a preacher in visiting our locker room after home games. His presence was important to me and to my players, but it also was important to him. He told me later that the team needed his encouragement, to know that the president of the university was behind them and that the coach needed to know it as well. I, indeed, felt that way.

After JMU, I coached at the University of California, Berkeley, where protests were like a daily occurrence. But we experienced the same Free Speech Movement at Madison that originated on the Berkeley campus. Dr. Carrier let the Madison students protest anything they wanted—Vietnam, Cambodia, freedom, etc. He didn't care, as long as the protest didn't occur on his front lawn.

In the middle of all that protesting, in 1973, he launched a Reserved Officers Training Corps program at Madison, at a time when other campuses, nationally, were protesting against the ROTC, even violently. "I felt it was a good alternative for students, a career opportunity," he explained, "and it also attracted a lot of males. I had some faculty members who were opposed to it, but that was it. Our ROTC program has won the MacArthur Award, the highest national ROTC award, ten times or more.

"I started the school's marching band, even though the music department wouldn't accept it, saying it didn't want a stupid-ass band. So I put the budget for the band in the athletic department. You know what that budget is today? One million dollars. And our marching band now is the largest in the United States, with 497 members."

I asked Dr. Carrier about his proudest JMU achievement.

"The arboretum," he said of the 125-acre reserve named after his wife—the Edith J. Carrier Arboretum. "Where else are you going to find 125 acres, or a botanical garden, in the middle of a campus?

"It's a place to revitalize yourself. Our goal is to have all the native plants of Virginia and West Virginia growing there. There's a walking trail, and there are benches. If you've got too much stress, it's a place to restore your life. The students even have sex there."

As Dr. Carrier would add, as he had on another occasion, "What's wrong with that?"

James Madison University grew to 500 acres on his purposeful watch. His fingerprints are everywhere on this campus, but his pulse beat stayed calm, remarkably, through all of his extraordinary improvements.

"I never had any stress from all the changes," he said, "not one moment of stress in all those years. It never bothered me. I never got even with anybody, and I never held a grudge. I slept well at night—except, Lou, when you would lose."

I'm glad I won much more than I lost at JMU: 238–118, a .669 winning percentage. But Dr. Carrier was nothing less than completely supportive.

So, have I convinced you that he was a school president like no other? Until I'm presented someone else who is even remotely close, I rest my case.

The Edith J. Carrier Arboretum has become a natural sanctuary and oasis on the JMU campus not only for students, faculty, and staff, but also for parents and citizens from the burgeoning city of Harrisonburg. The late Dr. Norlyn L. Botkin, a revered professor of biology at JMU, proposed the arboretum in 1977 just when Dr. Carrier was moving full-speed-ahead with the campus's expansion. Dr. Botkin served as the arboretum's director from its official founding in 1985 until his retirement from teaching in 1999, and he is known for advocating the use of plants and trees indigenous to the region. Of the many contributions that both Dr. Carrier and Dr. Botkin made to JMU and the community, both have cited the arboretum as their respective proudest achievement at JMU. Photograph by Frank Doherty (original in color) courtesy of the Edith J. Carrier Arboretum at James Madison University.

Coach Campanelli and co-captains Pat Dosh and an injured Sherman Dillard share
the trophy after the Dukes won the JMU Invitational Tournament in 1976. Photograph
courtesy of James Madison University Athletics.

CHAPTER 8

Oh, No, Not Again

Here I was, starting my first season as a Division I head coach, 1976–1977. I had a new four-year contract and an upgraded schedule, including nine Division I opponents. And I was coaching, in essence, a new school. Madison College was a relic of the past. We now were James Madison University, playing on the same hardwood as college basketball's elite.

I was eager to prove that we belonged at that highest level, and I was confident that I had the talent to, at least, hold our own. Sherman Dillard was a proven scorer. Pat Dosh provided scoring and rebounding. Roger Hughett gave us productivity in the backcourt. That's a solid starting point.

We were young, with two seniors, backup players John Cadman and Van Snowdon. We added a promising newcomer in 6-foot-8 Steve Stielper, who, I felt, would contribute right away. That's an even better starting point.

Our opening game was against Virginia Military Institute, a Division I program. We would be tested from the very first tipoff. So we kept our practice intensity at a boiling point in priming for our November 26 debut. Then misfortune struck with the worst possible timing. Dillard, our go-to scorer, broke his foot in an exhibition game. He was lost for the season even before it began. Poof! As Yogi Berra once said, "It's déjà vu all over again." I knew exactly what ol' Yogi meant. Four years earlier, I lost my best player, Gary Butler, in the first half of my very first game as a college head coach. He, too, was lost for the season. Now it was happening all over again.

Why me? I paid my taxes on time. I made my players go to class. I drove the speed limit most of the time. I went to church regularly. Was I cursed? How would I make up Deadeye Dillard's twenty-two points a game? I mean, you don't replace Kobe Bryant overnight. Stielper could make up some of that scoring loss, but he was a true freshman, and I didn't want to put too much pressure on him. That would be grossly unfair.

And we were at a slight disadvantage even before losing Dillard, because we had no conference affiliation during our maiden voyage in Division I. We were a year away from joining the East Coast Athletic Conference. So we were a sea-going vessel that was leaving port without any ballast.

Without any conference games to pencil in, I scrambled about to find enough opponents to fill up a schedule. In the spring, I phoned every school I could think of in the East and South. I came up with eight Division I schools: VMI, Georgia State, South Alabama, East Tennessee State, Florida State, Austin Peay, Old Dominion, and The Citadel.

Those eight obviously felt they could beat us; otherwise, why schedule us? But I was in a bind. When you move from Division II to Division I, the NCAA considered it a "probationary year" if seventy-five percent of your schedule didn't include Division I teams. We were well under that percentage.

With Dillard down for the count, I feared we would be overmatched. Stielper was the X factor. He was young, but, like Sherman, he could score. I wasn't going to put the team squarely on his shoulders, even though he had some big shoulders. I just prayed he could contribute.

John Thurston, my assistant, first saw Stielper at the Five-Star Camp in Pennsylvania, the best basketball camp in the country. Anybody who was anybody, including Michael Jordan, went through the Five-Star Camp run by Howie Garfinkel, who assembled excellent competition and good coaching. I lectured there on four separate occasions.

Thurston saw Stielper play for a couple of days. Here was a great shooter with good hands but not very athletic—no quickness, no speed, no hops. He was a post-up guy who also had a sixteen- to eighteen-foot jump shot. Boston University and New Hampshire recruited him, but we really wanted him, which meant we had to out-recruit them. Thurston must have seen Stielper play twelve times, as Steve lived in a Baltimore suburb not that far from us.

We were successful in recruiting him, perhaps, because Stielper didn't have to beat out anyone at JMU. We immediately plugged him in as our big man, and he liked the fact that we would get him the ball. Why not? He could score against *anybody*. He put up thirty-six on Marc Iavaroni of Virginia one night in Charlottesville, and Iavaroni played ten years in the NBA.

But without Dillard, as expected, we got off to a rocky start. VMI beat us 85–77. We lost six of our first ten games, four of those defeats by three or fewer points. Florida State was our most formidable foe during that stretch, and we barely lost, 69–66, in Tallahassee. That was encouraging.

Stielper was a genuine find, and Dosh and Hughett picked up their games in Dillard's absence. What really hurt us was defense. We were slow, and, without quickness, we couldn't pressure anyone. We handed out points as if they were free candy samples.

We scored 100 points three times, ninety points six other times. That's great, but we couldn't stop anyone. We had eleven games where we gave up eighty to ninety-nine points. I'm a defensive coach, first, yet, during my first year of Division I, we held but one team below sixty points, Wilmington College, a Division II team.

Nonetheless, in the middle of the season, we got hot and won eight in a row and twelve of thirteen before The Citadel beat us, 79–72, in their rickety gym. Then, still on the road, I lost my fifth straight to Old Dominion, 97–77. We weren't yet at ODU's talent level, and I figured we might not be for a while.

Stielper was magnificent his first year, leading us in scoring and rebounding—20.9 points and 10.7 boards. Freshmen rarely put up such lavish numbers. Dosh, a junior, was equally impressive, averaging 20.3 points and 9.5 rebounds, an impressive rebounding average for someone 6-foot-3 1/2. Hughett, a 6-foot-2 sophomore, contributed 16.7 points a game. Those three stepped up, big time, in Dillard's absence.

We finished our first year as a Division I entry with a 17–9 record, seven of those losses coming against Division I schools. Some teams wind up 7–19 in their first year of Division I competition. You have to start somewhere, and we didn't embarrass ourselves, even while playing shorthanded.

I watched Stielper score with either hand, using clever pump fakes. Dosh was a junkman—spin moves, pump fakes, getting to the line, leading us in free throw attempts with 185. Hughett had an explosive first step and thus was tough to contain one-on-one.

We ran an offense called "three inside," based on some valuable time I spent with Bobby Knight at Indiana. We positioned our three top scorers—Stielper, Dosh, and Hughett—from the foul line to the base line. They would screen, pop out, and curl, working in perfect symmetry.

We put Jeff Cross, a 6-foot-3 freshman guard, and Jack Railey, a 6-foot-6 sophomore forward, on the outside. Though limited shooters at five points a game, they got the ball to the three scorers. Our free-throw shooting paid big dividends, as we shot 1,067 free throws to our opponents' 944.

We just couldn't extend our defense, although that liability actually paid lasting dividends one transformative evening. I had played man-to-man defense my first seventeen years of coaching. But when we played Austin Peay on January 3, 1977, we were down twelve points at halftime and with good reason. Their five guys were quicker than our five guys.

As I walked off the court at halftime, I said to myself, "You jerk, you can't guard these guys man-to-man. We're going to have to play zone."

I caught up to my assistants in front of the locker room. They said, "Coach, what are we going to do?" I said, "We're going to play zone." They said, "We don't have a zone." And I said, "We have one now."

Inside the locker room, I diagrammed a zone defense on the blackboard before asking, "How many of you guys played a 2–3 zone in high school?" They all raised their hands. I said, "That's how we're going to play Austin Peay in the second half."

Austin Peay had a strong offense against a man-to-man defense but not as strong, it turned out, against the zone. In the second half, they began taking bad shots. We sent five guys to the boards, outrebounded them, and, with thirty seconds to go, we had the ball down by two. But we turned it over, had to foul, and lost, 61–58.

The next morning, I announced, "We need to learn how to play zone defense." That's because, a week later, we played Florida State. They beat us by twenty the year before at our place. I called my buddy, Don Casey at Temple, to ask if he would send me some slides on how to play a 2–3 zone. He sounded shocked. "You want to play zone?" he asked.

I thought the zone was a lazy way to play, because there were no assignments. Rollie Massimino trained me on man-to-man defense. Then we traveled to Florida State, lost by three, and a light went on in my head. That unexpected defensive philosophy switch was a major turning point for me, so I asked myself, "Now that we're Division I, how are we going to be competitive night after night?" We needed the zone to neutralize Florida State, which had a very good team but didn't shoot well against us. Once again, we sent five guys to the boards and re-bounded their missed shots. Desperation, I discovered, can turn into revelation.

At that time, I had a pre-game and post-game radio show. I interviewed the opposing coach after the game, win or lose. A coach interviewing a coach is an unheard of concept today, but that's how we did it back then.

The coaching scene was totally different in those days. The night before a game, the two coaches went out for a sandwich and a beer. No trading secrets, just two guys enjoying each other's company. Coaches then didn't posture as much. Ten minutes before a game, the opposing coaches would shoot the bull. Then I'd interview the other coach afterwards. Civil-like.

But VCU's J. D. Barnett didn't want to visit at all. He strictly was game-face. If JMU hosted a tournament, we'd give a dinner beforehand, and all the teams showed up. Jim Calhoun, then at Northeastern, came down with his team. We wanted everyone to enjoy our hospitality—until it was jump ball.

I interviewed Hugh Durham of Florida State after our three-point defeat. He's got this squeaky voice, and he goes, "Lou, explain that 2–3 combo defense. I couldn't figure it out all night." I told him that we put it in at halftime against Austin Peay five days earlier. He couldn't believe it.

Before that interview, I stood in the hallway as Durham blew out his team in the locker room. He was pissed off that we played him so close. He calmed down on the radio, but he wouldn't play us again.

But Durham had taken his team to the Final Four, so this 2-3 zone must be effective. I now had the confidence to coach it, though, as a coach, you can't insert a new strategy if the players feel you don't believe in it. My players knew I was sold on man-to-man. As for the zone, Don Casey told me, "Lou, you have to sell it." That's what I did, and the players bought into it. Austin Peay became the evolution of the multiple defenses I taught at JMU, with great results.

Therefore, Dillard's injury was a blessing in disguise, because it made me change my philosophy. His absence also showed Stielper, Dosh, and Hughett that they could handle the scoring load. Stielper gained tremendous confidence right off the bat, telling himself, "Hey, I can play at this level."

Dosh was team captain as a junior and co-captain with Dillard the next year. Pat was my only two-year captain, for a specific reason: He was the voice of the team. He'd say, "Coach we have to leave on the bus trip at 6 o'clock. Maybe we could go to the dining hall first instead of eating food on the bus."

Team captains are made differently. George Toliver, my first captain at Madison, was the strong, silent type. He hardly said, "Boo." Dean Ehlers told me, "George is like the old pro. He puts his shoes on the same way, sits in the same spot. He won't be a cheerleader type." Pat was more of a character. He had a way with words, and guys listened to him. He had a great personality. He still has it, but I've always known that he is sincere.

Dillard, Stielper, Dosh, Hughett . . . I couldn't wait for the 1977–1978 season to arrive. Unbeknownst to me, the JMU students were just as excited.

Streams of toilet paper rain down on the Dukes after scoring the opening basket versus Old Dominion at home on February 8, 1978. The Dukes posted an impressive 74–65 win against their state rival. Photograph courtesy of James Madison University Athletics.

CHAPTER 9
Roll On, Dukes

To all of JMU's opponents, I plead not guilty. I had nothing to do with creating the Great Toilet Paper Toss at our basketball arena, Godwin Hall, a ritual that occurred after we scored our first basket at every home game. Regardless of what opposing coaches and even game officials might have suspected, it wasn't my idea. Honestly, people, it wasn't.

The Great Toilet Paper Toss was unveiled, or unrolled, at the beginning of the 1977–1978 season and continued the rest of my time at James Madison University. I'm ready, if necessary, to put my hand on *The Holy Bible* in order to prove my innocence regarding this tissue-d caper. However, if charged, judge, I didn't do anything to stop it either.

What a wild and crazy scene—hundreds of rolls of toilet paper cascading down to the floor from the student section, which took up one side of the always filled-to-capacity arena. Some grocery or drug store in Harrisonburg must have made a fortune off JMU's students, who continued buying toilet paper to demonstrate their zealous support of Dukes basketball.

Miraculously, we weren't ever assessed a delay-of-game technical. That's because our cheerleaders descended on the court in a hurry to clean up the scattered rolls. Don't ask me where all that tissue went, because I don't want to know. Nevertheless, we had created a clever home-court advantage.

The Great Toilet Paper Toss wasn't restricted to home games. When we played North Carolina in that memorable 1982 NCAA Tournament game in Charlotte, right after we scored our first basket, 1,000 JMU fans unleashed a stream of tissue. Before our cheerleaders could police the court, one of them was run over by a Tar Heel. She took a perfect charge but was unhurt.

This tissued bit of theater was an extension of the passion and interest in our basketball program. After moving up to Division I in no time at all, I sensed our fans becoming more rabid. They wanted to make Godwin Hall a tough home court, and they succeeded. Perhaps they watched Atlantic Coast Conference games on TV and saw the passion at Duke, North Carolina, and other ACC schools. Now that we were playing nineteen Division I schools in 1977–1978, up eleven from the previous year, maybe our fans wanted to jack crowd involvement up a notch.

I wasn't asked once to warn the crowd. Maybe the game officials were, subconsciously, impressed by the rabid enthusiasm at JMU and enjoyed working in such a fun environment. Opponents might have been ticked off, to the point where it affected their play, but that wasn't my worry.

The noise grew so loud inside Godwin Hall that the floor shook. And all because our students stood most of the game, 2,500 students on one side of the arena, shouting and stomping. It registered like a small earthquake. A game official stopped play one time after the visiting coach complained that it was hard for his team to shoot free throws because the floor was moving.

We had created a unique atmosphere by taking a program from puberty to manhood and establishing a tradition in the process. Perhaps our students felt that foot-stomping and tossing tissue would give their Dukes an edge. But I'm not aware of anyone confessing to being the instigator of the Great Toilet Paper Toss.

The stakes had been raised, regardless. We were eligible for the NCAA Division I Tournament. I was responsible for loading up the schedule, but, at the same time, I worried that we might be taking our share of lumps. The only way to find out was on the court.

We scheduled the Czechoslovakian National Team for an exhibition game. The Czechs had four 6-foot-10 players. People must have gotten excited seeing those tall trees walking around campus, for the game sold out. And it was a hard-fought game that was still tied after regulation. Then a funny thing occurred.

As I prepared my team for overtime, someone said, "Coach, they're leaving." I turned around and the Czech team was walking off the court. I ran up to their coach and said, "We still have an overtime period to play." He said, "We don't play overtime in exhibitions." And so the game ended.

Afterwards, I saw the Czech coach downtown. I was carrying a purple-and-gold JMU umbrella. He said, "Coach, why you carry the umbrella of a clown?" I asked him what he meant. "In my country," he explained, "all men have black umbrellas." Czechmate!

Preparing for the regular season, I put immediate pressure on my players by scheduling the University of Virginia as our opening opponent. And we played them in UVA's tournament in Charlottesville. I needed games, and I took them anywhere I could get them.

We weren't a pushover, because we had four guys who could put the ball in the basket. My only concern was that there was only one basketball for four players.

JMU students show their disinterest as opposing players are introduced prior to a home game. The students were known for innovating humorous antics such as this well before such displays became popular nationwide. Well before there were the "Cameron crazies" at Duke University, there were the "Electric Zoo crazies" supporting the JMU Dukes. Photograph courtesy of James Madison University Athletics.

President Ronald E. Carrier presents a trophy to Sherman Dillard in 1977 after he
reached the 2,000 point career mark, the first player to do so at JMU. Dillard ended
his career with 2,065 points and a 20.7 points-per-game scoring average. He was
also a three-time Academic All-American. Photograph courtesy of James Madison
University Athletics.

With Dillard, Stielper, and Dosh all proven point-makers, Hughett, willingly, gave himself up for the sake of the team by passing the ball more from the backcourt. Meanwhile, Stielper and Dosh respected Dillard's scoring ability. He became the school's first 2,000-point player. If there was a three-point shot when Dillard played, plus the bonus free throw, he'd have scored 2,500 points for JMU instead of 2,065.

Virginia coach Terry Holland didn't quite get me at first. He said, "Lou, you seem so out of place at James Madison with your Jersey accent and your rapid-fire manner of speaking. I need an interpreter to understand you."

Terry is a good guy. One time, while we were in the same gym evaluating talent, Terry told me how impressed he was by my personality. He watched me move from person to person in the gym, speaking to everybody from concessionaires to ushers, to the security folks. Well, I was trying to sell myself as well as the JMU program to everyone I could.

The Cavaliers really put it to us in the opener, 83–63. Though we played in the same state, I found out quickly that we weren't in their same league, talent-wise. Not yet, anyway. We won the third-place game the next night over Roanoke, 84–57. So the trip wasn't a total loss.

Once we got back home, the season warmed up. In fact, it turned red hot. We finished an astonishing 12–1 at Godwin Hall that season, and that one defeat was a squeaker—60–59 to Virginia Commonwealth in overtime. In my mind, it shouldn't have been a defeat. We had a one-point lead with six seconds to go in overtime, with VCU inbounding the ball under their basket. We put a man on the ball in case they wanted to throw a baseball pass. But the inbound pass was deflected, and it traveled sideways, away from the clockkeeper's vision.

The clockkeeper was a kind, decent man, but he didn't start the clock with the deflection, because he didn't see it. The clock didn't start until the ball was picked up near the corner. Instead of three seconds remaining, six seconds still showed on the clock. VCU's Edmund Sherrod dribbled down the court as we chased after him. He launched an eighteen-footer to beat us at the buzzer, by which time the game clock should have run out.

The clockkeeper felt terribly afterwards. He apologized. I didn't put the blame on him, because it was an innocent mistake. What are you going to say? VCU had a good team with Sherrod and Gerald Henderson, who went on the play for the Boston Celtics. But we would have beaten them, except for an unfortunate circumstance. We should have been 13–0 at home.

We played around the country that season in order to complete a Division I-dominated schedule. We made a swing through Tennessee to play Austin Peay and the University of Tennessee-Chattanooga (UTC) Moccasins. I had sent my assistant, Ernie Nestor, ahead to scout The Citadel against UTC. Afterwards, he called. I asked, "How did it go?" Ernie's reply was hilarious.

"Tennessee-Chattanooga is very good, a big, athletic team that presses full court," he said. "Their arena seats about 4,500. It's loud, and they play 'Rocky Top' Twenty times during the game. But the worst part is that they have an 'Intimidating Indian.'"

"What position does he play?"

"Coach, he's the Moc's mascot."

"Ernie, what are you talking about? Why should I worry about a mascot?"

"Coach, he dresses up in an Indian outfit—headdress, war paint, the whole deal—and he stomps around the visitor's side of the court during warm ups, carrying a six-foot pole. He scared the hell out of The Citadel players with his war cries."

"Where were the game officials?"

"They were nowhere to be found."

Sure enough, when we got to their place, the "Intimidating Indian" stomped and whooped on our half of the court. I forewarned our kids, so they just laughed at him. But, as Ernie said, there were no game officials on the court to, at least, monitor Geronimo, the mascot.

After our pre-game warm ups, we returned to the locker room, where I said, "We've seen enough of that clown." One of my players, Jeff Cross, said, "Don't worry, Coach, I'll take care of him."

I had no idea what Jeff had in mind, and I didn't ask. We went back onto the court, and the "Intimidating Indian" was dancing around at the top of the key, being a general nuisance as we practiced free throws.

Then it happened. Jeff grabbed a rebound and fired a two-handed overhead pass. The player on the foul line ducked, and the ball hit the mascot square in the face. He went whimpering off the court. Then the game started, and we didn't have to worry about the mascot the whole forty minutes. We kicked the "Intimidating Indian's" ass, and then we kicked Tennessee-Chattanooga's ass.

In fact, we won both our games in Tennessee—73–67 over Austin Peay and 76–67 over UTC. After the latter win, one of the local newspapers described us perfectly: "JMU: The best team you never heard of." It was quite a compliment and quite accurate.

We were gone twelve days on that trip. In between playing Austin Peay and UTC, we stayed in Nashville. With some time to kill, I got Grand Ole Opry tickets and took the team to the famous Ryman Auditorium. I wasn't a country music fan, but some of the guys were. The Opry had different acts, but we saw Porter Wagoner, a country music star and the man who discovered Dolly Parton.

An hour and a half into the show, Sherman Dillard found me and said, "Coach, we black guys don't dig country music. We'll wait for you in the lobby." The rest of us watched one more show before the entire team returned to the hotel. I told Sherman, "I'll make it up to you." A hotel bellman told me the best ribs in Nashville were at Mary's Shack, though it was strictly take-out. We ordered barbecue, brought it back to the hotel, found a room, and had a good time. On the road, you have to make your team happy.

We then lost to VCU, 64–54, in Richmond before heading next to the Rocky Mountains, where we played Utah State and the University of Denver—a short stopover that became a lasting memory.

At practice the night before the Utah State game, I felt we looked sluggish. So I called for a "cutthroat rebounding drill"—a three-man drill where you throw the ball off the backboard, and the man who gets the ball is on offense, while the other two are on defense. Then anything goes.

As luck would have it, Stielper jumped, lost his balance, and came down hard on his left elbow, which opened up like an artichoke. I felt awful. Besides, Utah State had a big front line, and Stielper stood 6-foot-8. Our trainer, Ron Stefancin, took Steve to the hospital, where he received thirty-six stitches. Ron told me at the motel, "Coach, Steve can't play. He's bandaged up. The elbow's stiff and sore."

I had a hard time sleeping. The next morning, Steve came to my room and said, "Coach, I'll play if you can find a football elbow pad to put over the bandages." We found one, and the doctor at the hospital cleared Steve for action, even though he could only straighten his left arm halfway. That didn't bother him, as he scored thirty-six points—one point per stitch. Talk about a courageous effort—thirty-six points with, basically, one good arm.

Stielper wasn't a gazelle, but he was so tough to stop in the post. We got clobbered that night, 102–66, our worst loss of the year. Stielper outscored his teammates that night, 36–30.

133

We couldn't leave Logan, Utah, fast enough. We had a flight from Salt Lake City to Denver, where the Mile High City was in a state of heightened anxiety. That's because the Denver Broncos were playing in the Super Bowl the next day.

Our situation grew comical after we boarded the plane. An announcement came that the aircraft was overweight. Passengers were asked to get off and in turn would receive a ticket for a future flight. Some did get off, but a second announcement came twenty minutes later, saying the aircraft still was overweight, and more passengers would have to deplane. I thought, "We have to fly over mountains, so we can't be overweight." Then, after another delay, came a third announcement: All luggage would be removed and would reach Denver on a later flight.

I had planned team practice that night. So I stood up and said, "You now have nineteen seats. We're out of here." We got off the plane and found ground personnel to retrieve our luggage. My players were right there with them on the tarmac, identifying our bags. That's how we got all of our bags.

Now we had to get another flight. We found Texas International, an airline I hadn't heard of, but it had plenty of seats. So we managed to get to Denver, but the insurance forms supposedly sent ahead in order for us to rent the vans that would transport us to the hotel weren't there. What next?

I found a limo service and arranged three town cars for our transportation. Getting in so late at night, we couldn't even practice. I chalked it up as a bad trip—my worst trip at JMU—and sent the team to bed. Denver beat us, 84–74, which made it even more miserable.

My players were resilient, and we won eleven of our next twelve games, eight of those victories coming at Godwin. After one of those home wins, I discovered that I still faced a language barrier in Virginia.

A fan approached me as I was leaving the court. He said, "Coach, I love the job you're doing, but I can't understand a word you're saying." To that fan, I was speaking a New Jersey version of Mountain Talk. But I said to him, "I have a hard time understanding what you're saying, too."

We finished the year 18–8, a respectable record considering those nineteen Division I opponents. We beat Old Dominion for the first time, 74–65—Hallelujah!—and you should have seen the floor shake at Godwin Hall. Dr. Carrier smiled broadly when he addressed the team afterward. And then we knocked off William & Mary, 68–65, in a thriller at Williamsburg.

The three-hour trip back from Williamsburg to Harrisonburg was the only time in my long coaching career that I broke a cardinal rule: No players drinking alcohol on the bus after a game. And, little surprise, the glib-tongued Pat Dosh was the instigator.

Following every road game, two cans of Coors Lite were waiting for me on the bus. And it sure tasted good after a win, such as the win in Williamsburg. We planned to stop on the way home, so the players could get some Popeye's fried chicken.

Somehow, Dosh found out there was a 7-11 en route. He sweet-talked me, saying some of the players were of drinking age, and could we stop off at the 7-11 to pick up some beer to drink with the fried chicken? "We'll drink the beer, Coach, then we'll go to sleep," Dosh promised. "You don't have to worry."

While on campus, I drank beer with JMU students in an effort to increase home attendance. Dr. Carrier drank beer with the students as well, not to mention his "Drunk Bus" policy. I couldn't be a hypocrite now.

So I told the driver to stop at the 7-11. The team manager went in and bought the beer, one per player. No one got crazy on the bus. The players had their chicken and beer, then they went to sleep, just as Dosh said they would. No harm, no foul. But, like I said, I never bent that cardinal rule again.

Twenty wins was a possibility before we lost our last two games, both on the road to The Citadel, 89–88, and Charleston Southern, 85–80. Had we won them, we still wouldn't have received an NCAA bid or even an NIT bid. Not after giving up eighty-nine and eighty-five points. Defense was our Achilles heel.

We weren't yet credible in the eyes of selection committes. Our name hadn't gotten out there yet and with justification. We couldn't expect too much too soon in terms of post-season tournament invitations.

I was proud of one thing: We made it through the season without any team rancor. There was just the one basketball, and we shared it without jealousy. Dillard led the Dukes with a 19.2 scoring average. I thought that was only fitting, since he was the school's greatest basketball player up to that point, and in the top five all-time right now.

JMU should feel honored that Sherman chose us in the first place. JMU hasn't ever had a finer student-athlete. And he was the school's first NBA draft pick—in the sixth round, 1978, to the Indiana Pacers.

Stielper's scoring average in 1977–1978 dropped four points to 16.8 points, but he led the team in rebounding with an 8.1 average. Dosh had a 13.2 scoring average as a senior, down seven points from his junior year, but he pulled down 6.5 rebounds a game. Solid numbers for a smaller-sized inside player who recorded a JMU-record 821 rebounds, still second on the all-time list. Hughett's scoring average was shaved in half at 8.4 points, but I came close to having four players in double figures. I can live with that.

That particular season touched my soul in a special way—special as in the Special Olympics. That's when I learned to coach in a different manner but, possibly, not so differently.

I received a call from the Special Olympics director in our area, wondering if I would like to coach the Virginia team in a springtime game against the Maryland team, which would be coached by Lefty Driesell from the University of Maryland. I agreed, though I told the director that I had no experience coaching Special Olympians, who deal with physical and mental issues that make everyday life challenging. The director said experience doesn't matter: "Coaching is coaching, and thanks for agreeing. It will be fun."

Our team was coed, with an age range from thirteen to fifty-four. I received a home-court advantage; the game would be played at Godwin Hall. I met the team and their two regular coaches, a man and a woman, one hour before the game. The players were focused as I spoke; their eyes were glued on me. One of their coaches advised me, "Just be yourself. They've seen you coach at Godwin before, and they don't want to be treated any differently."

I wasn't sure what instructions I should give them, because this was all so new to me. How much coaching did they even need? Their coaches said, "They're not real skilled, but they will do as you say." I emphasized to them the importance of staying with the person they're guarding. They shook their heads; they all seemed to understand.

Then the game started, and it was as if I had been talking to a wall. They were losing the players they were guarding right and left. It was like a fire drill. I was having the same defensive problems that I experienced with my Dukes during the season.

I felt lucky we were down by only six points at halftime. I didn't want to make them feel badly if they were doing the best they could. How could I know the difference? As I said, this was an entirely new approach for me.

While contemplating my halftime speech, I was surprised when one of their coaches said, "Let them know that you are unhappy with the way they are playing defense. Don't be afraid to raise your voice."

I had lectured my Dukes about sloppy defense, gotten even angry, but this wasn't the same thing. But just before I entered the locker room, I stopped and said, "Lord, forgive me. This is what they want me to do."

As I entered the room, you could heard a pin drop. Their eyes were fixed on me, waiting. Suddenly, I burst out, "What the hell is going on out there? Didn't I tell you to stay with your opponent? Stay with him! Got it!"

With that, I tore off my jacket and threw it on the floor. I wondered if Vince Lombardi ever did that? Then I wondered if they even knew who Vince Lombardi was. It didn't matter; I really had their attention now.

I used the blackboard, once again, to illustrate what we needed to do on defense and offense. They nodded their heads affirmatively, and then I said with firmness, "Let's go get 'em in the second half."

As we walked back on the court, one of their coaches said, "Good job. They needed to hear that."

Still unsure if I had taken the right approach, I just said, "We'll see."

The second half began, and, to my utter amazement, the players double-teamed Maryland's big scorer. We began getting steals and scoring baskets. Even though they weren't following my assignments exactly, something was working, so I kept my big mouth shut. We made a big comeback and won by six points, or a twelve-point reversal.

The players were so excited, they were jumping up and down. One of them, a thirteen-year-old girl, gave me a bear hug and said, "We did it all for you, Lou." It was a precious thing to say, and I couldn't hold back my tears. Such giving hearts these players had, and I had only met them two hours earlier.

I turned around and there was Lefty Driesell, a future JMU coach. He said, "How did you put that double team in at halftime?"

I replied: "Coach, they did it on their own. I had nothing to do with it."

What I learned that day is that every athlete, even Special Olympians, needs coaching. And every athlete, even Special Olympians, can be reached. I've very seldom left an arena with such fulfillment. "We did it all for you, Lou." How much better can a coach feel?

I coached Special Olympians the following year, against Lefty once more, and again at Godwin Hall. Lefty pulled a fast one this time. We were leading in the second half, when I noticed that he was using six players to my five. I said, "Lefty, what are you doing?" He said, "It's a Special Olympics rule; if you're down by five points, you can use a sixth player."

It didn't matter; as we prevailed again, winning by six or seven points. And we won it fair and square, my five players against Lefty's six.

My time with those Special Olympians was an experience I will always cherish. That indelible memory enriches my life to this day, right there with my JMU memories.

I'm so proud of what my Dukes accomplished on the court, and what they later accomplished in life. I prepared them for both worlds the best I could. One shining example would be Pat Dosh.

Less than a month after Pat graduated, I received a call from a headhunter at Johnson & Johnson, one of the nation's foremost pharmaceutical companies. He said one of my former players, Pat Dosh, had applied for a sales position job, and would I recommend him?

I didn't hesitate. "Hire him," I said. "He'll outwork anyone you can hire. He's a winner." Three months later, the same headhunter phoned me back and said, "Coach, we hired Pat, and you were exactly right. He has outworked everyone else, and he's already one of our top salesmen."

And Pat still reminds me about my reluctance to offer him a scholarship.

CHAPTER 10
Home Fires

Ralph Sampson was born in Harrisonburg and grew—man, did he ever grow—into the nation's No. 1 basketball recruit in 1979 at Harrisonburg High. As a teenager, he played in numerous pickup games on the James Madison University campus. Our gym became like his second hoops home.

Dell Curry, also born in Harrisonburg, played high school basketball seventeen miles away in Fort Defiance, graduating in 1982. He later developed into one of the NBA's deadliest three-point sharpshooters.

Moses Malone's hometown was Petersburg, Virginia, three hours from Harrisonburg. He visited our athletic director's office as a high-school senior in 1974. He then turned professional and became one of the most physically dominant centers ever.

Here were three players who could have made JMU a major contender in basketball. But I had to be realistic: Our chances of getting them to enroll at our school ranked between slim and none, with none dunking on slim.

And here we were, a remarkable story unto ourselves: A girls' school that became fully coed in 1971, added intercollegiate sports, and jumped from Division II to Division I in basketball in just four years. In fact, we were a *most* remarkable story.

Sampson, Curry, and possibly Malone were aware of our unique transformation, but, to those three prospects and to the nation in general, we still were perceived as a second-class institution *and* basketball program. But not for long; we would show them soon enough.

Sampson was so near to us that we shopped at the same supermarket. Harrisonburg High is a half-mile from our campus. Ralph came over in the spring and fall to play with our guys at Godwin. I'd poke my head in the gym and see this tall, skinny kid in the ninth grade. He already was 6-foot-7.

He wanted to play point guard in those pickup games, and he'd bring the ball up the court for his team. He didn't just want to stand in the low post; he told me that he wanted to develop his ball handling. He wanted to be a basketball *player.* Our kids liked playing with him, because it was a challenge.

Ralph had a nice personality, was rather soft-spoken. He was from a very nice family. You'd run into him at that supermarket, shopping with his mother. He was easy to spot above the shelves.

We did show interest in him, regardless of our remote chances. We had a meeting with Dr. Carrier in the conference room at Wilson Hall, the administrative building on the quad. We talked about what kind of summer job could we offer Ralph. We were a small town with no big industries, and we were up against basketball schools like North Carolina and Kentucky, with their prominent alumni.

There was a place in town called Lloyd's Steak House. We talked about getting Ralph a job there as a host. The one hangup: How much would that job pay? Well, the idea never got off the ground. Too bad, because Ralph would've been the world's tallest maître d'.

In the meantime, he kept growing. He was 7-foot-3 as a high school senior in 1979, when he averaged thirty points, nineteen rebounds, and seven blocks. Now the whole world wanted him.

Once the recruiting process began, he narrowed it down to seven schools, including JMU as a courtesy gesture. He extended our coaching staff a home visit. The Sampsons were courteous and congenial, as we were the local school in town. Sorry, Eastern Mennonite. Although sincere, the Sampsons wisely didn't show their hand.

James Madison hadn't yet arrived on the NCAA hoops scene. Deep in my heart, I knew we didn't have enough to offer Ralph. He and Sam Bowie of Lebanon, Pennsylvania, were the two top recruits in the country.

Ralph cut the list of seven down to three—North Carolina, Kentucky, and Virginia. He then picked Virginia, so he did stay home. Bowie selected Kentucky. Ralph topped out at 7-foot-4, became the College Player of the Year three times, and was drafted by the Houston Rockets as the NBA's top overall pick in 1983.

When Curry was in high school, he also played in our gym, though not as frequently as Ralph. Curry was a delightful young man, also soft-spoken, a country kid. Unlike Ralph, we thought we had a sleeper in Dell, because he hadn't gone to any basketball camps through his junior year. So he was somewhat undiscovered.

We thought we stood a strong chance of getting him. He could shoot the ball even then. But the summer before his senior year, he attended Virginia Tech's basketball camp. Once they saw his beautiful stroke, he was offered a scholarship on the spot. He then scored 2,389 points at Tech, which would have been the school record at James Madison. His son, Stephen Curry, is currently a standout NBA player with the Golden State Warriors and is, like his dad, a deadeye shot, who, in 2015, won the NBA's MVP award as well as the NBA championship against LeBron James and the Cleveland Cavaliers.

My first JMU assistant, Mike Fratello, also worked at the 5-Star Camp in Pennsylvania, the best basketball camp in the country. The camp's director, Howie Garfinkel, asked Mike if he would drive Moses Malone up to the camp. Mike got in touch with Moses and told him to catch a ride to JMU. The next thing any of us knew, there was Moses sitting in Dean Ehlers's office, asking Dean where he could find Mike.

This was before Moses's senior year. We weren't recruiting him; the big programs were after him. Dean worried that there might be an NCAA rules violation with Moses showing up like that at our place. As it turned out, nothing came of it. Moses turned pro right away, regardless.

I knew we weren't going to out-recruit North Carolina, Kentucky, Virginia, Maryland, or any other major program for a blue-chip player. We were considered a first-tier basketball program mainly because we were Division I, yet we were forced to win with players the major programs categorized as second-tier. We still had that fixed look of a mid-major.

But win we did once more in 1978–1979, posting a second straight eighteen-victory season, largely because of Steve Stielper. He had a career year—for himself and for JMU—averaging 25.7 points and shooting 59.8 percent. I'm sure that North Carolina, Kentucky, and others could have used him somehow.

Stielper was phenomenal: We *needed* him to be phenomenal, since Dillard and Dosh were now alumni. Our strategy was to get the ball to Stielper, then get the ball to him again. He wasn't the most athletic kid, as I've stated, but he stood out regardless. With such soft hands, he could latch onto bad passes. He shot with both hands, and he pump-faked players out of their jockstraps, which got him to the free-throw line, where he shot 76.1 percent.

He was first team All-ECAC South and second team All-State, a gross injustice, as he finished tenth nationally among Division I scorers. He was named honorable mention All-America by the Associated Press, only because JMU still lived under the radar. Stielper was unstoppable, pumping in fifty-one points against Robert Morris University, hitting twenty-two of twenty-five field goals.

We had only one other player in double figures that season: Linton Townes, who averaged 11.5 points as a freshman, even though he still looked like he could use another meal. So you can see how much we relied on Stielper. Our next three scorers were Hughett, now a senior, at 8.8 points, and two sophomores—Steve Blackmon at 7.4 and Tyrone Shoulders at 6.7. Our team captain, senior Jack Railey, averaged 5.2 points.

We finished 18–8, while facing eighteen Division I opponents. We improved on defense, cutting our per-game yield from 70.8 to 64.9 points. That was a positive jump, but we were a year away from showing significant improvement. It's easier to find good shooters than good defenders for a specific reason: Kids would rather shoot the ball. To our credit, we shot 52.3 percent that season, a fabulous team average. Even better, we took mostly good shots.

It's also easier to find good rebounders than good defenders. I don't know why that is, but we always seemed to out-rebound our foes. The margin in 1978–1979 was 1,003 to 871, a sizable difference. We made up for our lack of quickness with toughness. Stielper pulled down nine rebounds a game, while Townes, Blackmon, Shoulders, and Railey were each good for five more. Those guys liked to crash the boards, and it all added up for us.

We lost to Virginia again in the season opener in their tournament by a 71–58 score. We came back the next night with a big win over George Washington, 82–62, in the third-place game. We had three 100-point games that season, but Old Dominion got us again at its place, 75–65.

We were stuck at that 17-, 18-win level. As a coach, I wanted more, to climb into the twenties, where the NCAA Selection Committee might actually see us, even with a telescope.

Fortunately, we had Stielper coming back for another year. After his lights-out junior season, an ECAC all-star team was assembled to travel to Europe for a series of summertime exhibitions. Naturally, I nominated Steve. The coaches were Don Casey of Temple and Bob Weinhauer of the University of Pennsylvania. I sent them a film of Steve's fifty-one-point game. Then Don—we'd played freshman ball together in college—called to say that he was passing over Steve because he was too slow. I couldn't believe my ears. Too slow, yet he averaged 25.7 points?

A week later, Don called me back. He had to let a player go in training camp. He asked: "Is that Stielper kid still available?" Steve just happened to be working for JMU buildings and grounds that summer, and he gladly accepted the invite.

Guess what happened? He led that all-star team in scoring *and* rebounding. Needless to say, I really let Casey and Weinhauer have it after they returned home.

They told me how much the whole team enjoyed Steve, on and off the court. He has an engaging personality and a sharp mind. He made the trip zip by, for he's almost impossible to beat on sports trivia questions. He's also good at impersonations. He can do a one-man skit of *The Wizard of Oz*, playing all of the characters, from the Wicked Witch down to the Munchkins. Toto, too. He drew crowds wherever he performed on that ECAC trip. There are many things in life that catch your eye but only a few that capture your heart. Well, Steve captured both the eye and the heart.

I took a journey myself that same offseason, an inspiring trip to Taiwan. Here's how it all came about: I attended the NCAA's Final Four in 1979—as a spectator, while dreaming of being a participant—when I bumped into Bill Wall, the executive director of ABAUSA, the Amateur Basketball Association of the United States of America. Included in Bill's responsibilities were arranging for foreign national teams to play exhibition games in the States and also finding coaches in the States to help teach basketball overseas.

Bill needed a coach to help train the Republic of China (Taiwan) National Team for a big international tournament, the Jones Cup in Taipei. The trip lasted thirty-two days, and the ABAUSA would cover my air travel, lodging, and meals, plus a stipend of $600. That's not a lot of money, but I thought the experience might be beneficial.

I got the green light from Dean Ehlers, but I wasn't sure what Dawn would say, with three young children at home. Dawn, always the real trooper, said she could handle it alone for the month that I would be gone. "If this is something that is good for you professionally, go for it," she said. For the umpteenth time, I realized I had married the right woman.

I wouldn't be the head coach in Taiwan but an assistant to a twenty-seven-year-old coach who had won the National Club Championship the past season. My job would be to teach man-to-man defense, even though I now was teaching the zone in the States. But I could do both, and I was provided a translator.

Upon arriving in Taipei, I was greeted by a delegation headed by my host, Rich Lee, the editor of the *China Post*, an English-language newspaper. On the ride from the airport to the hotel, suddenly the car's front windshield shattered, and glass was flying every which way.

"Everybody down!" a voice called out.

One thought immediately crossed my mind: "Terrorists!" My next reaction: "Will I ever see my family again?" My heart was racing. Too frightened to move, I stayed down until the driver made it to the hotel safely. No one ever explained to me what had just taken place, but what a greeting!

I began teaching man-to-man techniques, and the Taiwanese players, though small in size, were responsive. The biggest player was 6-foot-4, but he was quick and had a good shooting touch. I gave each player a nickname, which made communication much easier.

Daily practice lasted two hours. With the extra free time, I worked with the national women's team as a volunteer. Additionally, I gave clinics to coaches and kids. My efforts were most appreciated.

"Lou," Rich Lee said after I had been there a week, "you're working hard. To show our gratitude, we're giving you a $200 raise and a nicer hotel room with a view of the mountains."

Working hard hasn't ever been an obstacle for me, once I learned proper study habits in school. We were scheduled to play ten tournament games in a 15,000-seat arena in Taipei. The size of that building told me that the Chinese take their basketball very seriously. The big game, I was told, would be the opener against South Korea, whom the Taiwanese hadn't beaten in ten years.

The crowd atmosphere for that opener was electric, with shrill, piercing whistles that cut right through me. Dead fish were hurled onto the floor along with heads of lettuce and cabbage. I nicknamed that arena the Cabbage Patch.

Well, the Taiwanese won that game by a point; the streak had been broken. Their fans stormed the court and tossed the head coach up in the air and caught him, too, as he wasn't more than 140 pounds. I stayed, protectively, in the background. Sometimes, it's good to be the assistant.

The celebration was just getting started. A Chinese Basketball Federation official spoke to the team, telling the players how proud he was of their valiant effort and how they had brought much honor and glory to their country. He did everything but pin medals on their game uniforms.

The players and coaches were taken to a local nightclub, where we received a standing ovation. The beer started flowing, and a number of toasts were given. The team captain, whom I nicknamed "Baby," was called up to sing a tune. The head coach did likewise. Then I heard, "Coachee." My turn.

I begged off but was told that I would be insulting the country if I refused to sing. Fortunately, the bandleader had an American songbook. I spotted "You Light Up My Life," a tune made famous by Debby Boone, the daughter of singer Pat Boone, who was famous when I was a teenager.

I'm not Frank Sinatra, except that we're both from New Jersey. But I got through the song, the team cheered, and we celebrated until 5 a.m. We had to play again in twelve hours. I was worried that the team wouldn't get enough rest. I was told, "Coach, enjoy the moment. This is a special night."

After that sensational start, we finished the tournament with a 5–5 record. Everyone seemed happy with the outcome, and I couldn't have been happier with my time in Taiwan. On my last day, the head coach and team captain took me to an art gallery and let me pick out two oil paintings for Dawn.

It was a long time to be away from my family, and I missed them terribly. Dawn enjoyed being a mother, and that's why she was a great mom. And she was a great coach's wife; she allowed me to do the things professionally to enhance my career. When I left for Taiwan for thirty-two days, I thought I was pushing the envelope, but she understood. She always did. And that time in Taiwan made me, Coachee, love coaching even more.

Coach Lou doing a little "chalk talk" during a timeout at a home game in the Convocation Center.
Photograph courtesy of James Madison University Athletics.

CHAPTER 11
Staying Strong

I read this parable once, which I accepted as a prophecy of success:

A Cherokee elder was teaching his grandchildren about life. He said to them, "A fight is going on inside me . . . a terrible fight between two wolves.

"One wolf is Evil. It represents fear, anger, envy, sorrow, regret, greed, arrogance, self-pity, guilt, resentment, inferiority, lies, false pride, and superiority.

"The other wolf is God. It stands for joy, peace, love, hope, sharing, serenity, humility, kindness, benevolence, friendship, empathy, generosity, truth, compassion, and faith.

"The same fight is going on inside you and inside every other person, too."

The grandchildren thought about what was said for a minute, and then one child asked his grandfather, "Which wolf would win?"

The old man simply replied: "The one you feed."

I applied this good vs. evil parable to coaching. The wolf I wanted to win, of course, was the wolf closely allied with God. Because evil, ultimately, cannot win, while good can only lead to further goodness, kindness, self-fulfillment, and victory in the end.

Also, good intentions are the best way to achieve brotherhood and the necessary bonding that I instilled in all my James Madison teams. We didn't have the prized recruits that the top-10 programs had, but we did have a special closeness. I preached to them the benefits of staying together, believing in one another, sharing the basketball, and committing to defense in order for us to triumph through, basically, overachievement. Those were the only ways my teams—my wolf—would win the fight.

I entered another season, 1979–1980, with that same principle of needing to play over our heads to succeed. My players bought into this principle, but, realistically, only a certain amount of success was attainable for JMU.

We were strong enough, mentally and physically, to win at home, which we proved once again with a 14–2 record, even though that second defeat was a killer. We weren't nearly as consistent away from Godwin Hall, especially against the one school we'd been trying to catch up to in ability. That was, of course,

Old Dominion. But we had other travel issues. We weren't king of the road. King? We hadn't even worked our way up to prince.

Opponents figured out that the best way to beat us was to throw a human curtain around Steve Stielper. After his record-setting junior year, he was surrounded as if he were a head of state. Suffocating defenses restricted our main threat, and Stielper's scoring average dropped from 25.7 to 18.4, and his shooting percentage fell from 59.8 to 48.4.

We simply didn't have the manpower to pick up Stielper, especially after Linton Townes, our second leading scorer at 14.6, played in only ten of twenty-six games because of academic issues. We then became a one-horse team, and that horse was corralled most of the time. Defenses made Stielper work so much harder, and it was equally hard for us to get him the ball.

Twenty-one of our twenty-six games were played against Division I teams, up from nineteen Division I games the previous winter. We really needed Townes, who had emerged as a sophomore, but we lost him on a technicality. He was eligible by NCAA standards yet ineligible, by one unit, by super-strict JMU standards.

Our athletic director, Dean Ehlers, was a stickler for adherence to rules. JMU's rules were tougher, actually, than the NCAA's rules when it came to eligibility. That same technicality later was amended at JMU, but not before the 1979–1980 season played out.

As it turned out, it was a blessing for Linton, who became a better student over the next two years. I told Linton that I had been down that same road in college, and you can't cut it that close. The wolf will be at your throat.

Stielper, to his credit, stepped up despite the hounding pressure. He set JMU career records for scoring, 2,126 points, and rebounds, 917. I have great admiration for Steve, who carried us even when the load was overbearing. JMU's never had a better big man than Steve Stielper.

We had problems that season with consistency. We won our first four games, all at home, then lost our next three games, on the road, to East Carolina, UNC-Wilmington and Virginia Commonwealth. Then we won our next six. We played this same topsy-turvy basketball the rest of the season.

In the process, we established a heated rivalry with Virginia Commonwealth (VCU). Every game between the Dukes and Rams was a battle. Literally. Tempers flew and fisticuffs nearly occurred several times.

On one such occasion, while fighting for a loose ball in front of our bench, Steve Blackmon and a Ram had to be separated. Blackmon was a tough kid from Washington, DC. You didn't want to mess with him. J. D. Barnett, the VCU coach, tried to restore peace. I told J. D., "Be glad there was no fight, or your kid would have slept tonight in a hospital."

VCU won the first game, 80–59, at its place, and we beat the Rams in the return match at Godwin Hall, 53–51, in overtime. The crowd at the Richmond Coliseum—VCU's home court at that time—was brutal. I received a security escort to and from the locker room, plus a security guard was positioned behind our bench, which made me feel protected but only for a short while. Then I turned around and the guard was facing the court instead of the crowd.

"Excuse me, sir," I said, "Aren't you facing the wrong way? All you'll be able to do is get the knife out of my back. Please turn around." He complied, and I got out of Richmond with my life.

Besides beating VCU, we knocked off William & Mary twice, 63–58 and 57–49, which were positive signs. But we lost to Old Dominion—twice—by scores of 52–44 and 83–63. I now was 1–8 against ODU. Forgive me, Dr. Carrier. We also got clobbered at Virginia Tech, 66–40. We did reverse the losses to East Carolina, 63–52, and UNC Wilmington, 68–60, at our place.

We ended the year 18–8, meaning that we were stuck on eighteen wins for the third straight season. I felt pressured, because I was eager to take the next step. But we were spinning our wheels.

I could feel the wolf's glare and asked myself, "How are we going to get better? Will we ever dance at the Big Dance?"

We had only been a Division I program four years, but I was growing impatient. My father told Dr. Carrier that I would win for him, but I wasn't winning enough even to please myself. I was staying on myself harder than I stayed on my players in practice, and I'm a hard-nosed coach.

Not that there weren't positives that season. David Dupont, Dan Ruland, and Charles Fisher had promising freshman debuts. Dupont averaged 6.8 points, Ruland 5.9 and Fisher 5.2, all three shooting slightly above fifty percent. Although they played in every game, you couldn't expect them to light up the scoreboard as Stielper did when he was a freshman.

Blackmon, a 6-foot-4 junior, was second on the team in scoring, 9.3, and rebounding, 6.1, behind Stielper's 8.1 boards. Tyrone Shoulders, a 6-foot-6 junior, was third in scoring, 7.6, and rebounding, 5.7. Despite Shoulders shooting only 43.3 per cent, we shot 49.1 as a team. I could live with that.

We made significant improvement on defense, yielding only 62.6 points a game, a fourteen-point drop from the year before. Unfortunately, our scoring average was 68.2, down eleven points from the previous season because of the tightening-up job on Stielper.

We still had an opportunity to make it a happy ending. We knocked off visiting St. Francis University of Loretto, Pennsylvania, 84–69, at Godwin Hall to end the regular season, which earned us a spot in the first East Coast Athletic Conference post-season tournament. As luck would have it, our quarterfinal opponent would be that same St. Francis team we had just beaten by fifteen points. Three days after that win, we met again at our place, and we hit the court with the highest expectations.

Then our stratospheric high turned into a cataclysmic low and all because we couldn't shoot straight. We clanked shots all night long. They played a zone, jammed up Stielper, and made us shoot from the outside. If we had Townes, a great perimeter scorer and zone buster, it might have been different. But their kids were loose and confident, figuring they had nothing to lose, and they beat us, 58–54. That second home defeat was a real killer.

I was so devastated that I felt the wolf gnawing at my suit coat as I walked back to the locker room. Dean Ehlers and Dr. Carrier were there as always, fully supportive, or so I hoped. They had every reason to be upset, anticipating that the Dukes would be moving on to the semifinals.

Dr. Carrier addressed the team, congratulating them on their effort and on their winning season. What other college president is so consistent in that regard? Dr. Carrier was a class act once again, and the players, though downcast, appreciated his sincerity as always.

Then he said, "Coach, I want to see you outside." I didn't know what for, because you never knew what Dr. Carrier was thinking. I wasn't expecting a new contract. I was more worried about whether I still had a job.

"Coach," he said, "I want you to get away from basketball for a while. Take your family skiing at my lodge up at Massanutten Mountain, which is thirty minutes away. Call my secretary, pick up the keys, and she will give you directions." He recognized my distress; he's always been that perceptive.

Dawn and I took our three kids out of school for a few days, and we went skiing. I had skied before, but I was a novice who made my way down the hill with a snowplow style, while trying to avoid fast breaks or moguls.

Coach Lou with Brooke, Racelle, Kyle, and Dawn in their backyard in 1980. Harrisonburg was a great place to raise a family. Photograph courtesy of Lou Campanelli.

Driving up, I thought about putting too much pressure on myself. With coaching, it's like this: The losses always stay with you longer than the wins. Thus, it's easy to burn out. You grind, and you grind. Then the gears stop.

Arriving at Dr. Carrier's lodge, we built a fire and played games. I was able to devote full attention to my family. The season was over, and I couldn't bring it back. Dr. Carrier forced me to step back and take a deep breath. And it worked: I felt refreshed, restored, and renewed.

After returning, I gathered my staff and said, "Let's get ready for recruiting." When I told other head coaches what Dr. Carrier had done for me, they seemed stunned. "Really?" they said. "You work for a good boss."

I can't ever thank Dr. Carrier enough for believing in me, because other presidents or athletic directors with Type-A personalities might have padlocked my office and bid me goodbye after such a disappointing ending. Coaches, as a rule, are given a short leash, which they aren't holding.

Dr. Carrier showed great compassion and unwavering confidence in helping me become the coach I wanted to be. With his amazing insight, he felt my pain. Now I needed to reward his confidence in me.

What's sad is that we were a better team than St. Francis. If we played them ten games, we'd have won nine. Even Dr. Carrier believed that. He played freshman basketball at East Tennessee State, so he knew the game. He was intuitive about almost anything, even hoops.

The loss to St. Francis was Stielper's final game for JMU. How were we going to replace his productivity? I worried about slippage, perhaps a .500 record. Coaches worry year-round. It's in our blood type.

Tom Dulaney was the Dukes' radio play-by-play announcer at that time. His nickname was "Crash," because he owned a single-engine airplane. He inquired about my future plans.

"Lou, how long do you think you'll stay at JMU?" he asked. "And do you think you'll ever get to the NCAA (Division I) Tournament here?"

A double-barreled question, but I didn't hesitate. "Crash, I told Dawn that we're not leaving JMU until we *do* get to the NCAA Tournament."

I had no thoughts of leaving JMU at that time. I was more worried about what might happen the following season. The wolf was crouched outside my office door.

CHAPTER 12
Breakthrough

There was no way of anticipating that the 1980–1981 season would change James Madison University basketball forever. The school's most productive player, Steve Stielper, now was property of the NBA's Indiana Pacers, an eighth-round draft pick in 1980. I wasn't sure if we could replace his scoring output even with a group effort or if we had the sufficient firepower to win.

I enlarged our Division I competition from twenty-one to twenty-three schools, which brought us our greatest challenge yet. And, before that season played out, we would face four schools ranked in the Top 20, including a No. 6 (Notre Dame) and a No. 3 (Virginia).

This was another monumental step to respectability, a step I hoped we could take without falling flat on our backsides. With so much uncertainty, how could I harbor any high hopes for my Dukes?

Our first game was against No. 17 St. John's in its own tournament. I was flattered that St. John's legendary coach, Lou Carnesecca, invited us. At the pre-tournament coaches luncheon at the famous 21 Club in New York City, I walked in as Zsa Zsa Gabor walked out. Big deal. She wasn't nearly as pretty as Dawn.

Our kids had a chance to play Big Apple basketball, of sorts, at St. John's campus in Jamaica, Queens. I threw my players to the wolves from the get-go, and they played well in a 67–58 defeat. That energized my hopes. We edged a good Weber State team, 49–47, in overtime in the consolation game, yet another confidence booster.

We left New York with a split and the knowledge that we could play winning defense. The kids rolled up their sleeves at that point and went to work. I worried about making the schedule too tough, but the players responded by implementing my multiple defenses to near perfection. We would finish sixth nationally in scoring defense that season with a 57.2-point average. Our shifting defenses confused teams; we picked their pockets.

After the St. John's tournament, we won four of our next five games, losing only to West Virginia Tech, 80–78, when Sedale Threatt, a complete unknown, went off against us with thirty-eight points. How did I know that he would play twelve years in the NBA?

We next traveled to Virginia Tech's tournament and drew twelfth-ranked Texas A&M in the opener. The Aggies' coach, Shelby Metcalf, was known as "The Sage of the Brazos." At a cocktail party the night before the tournament, I asked Shelby, "How are my little Dukes going to do against your team, with all that size? You've got a seven-footer, Rudy Woods, and your front line is known as 'The Wall.' Besides, you're 'The Sage of the Brazos.' How are we going to play against all *that?*"

Shelby had that Texas accent. He said, "Coach, you got to understand that, in Texas, at the back of every basketball press release is a football release." He wasn't kidding. The University of Texas's sports information director, Jones Ramsey, said, "The No. 1 sport at Texas is football. The No. 2 sport at Texas is spring football." Texans do take their football seriously.

Texas A&M did have a solid basketball team, and they beat us close, 51–47. The next night, we beat Pittsburgh, 77–69. That was a huge win, our first against a Big East team. Pitt had Sam Clancy, a talented player who went on to the NBA. He looked like a house, with thighs like fire hydrants. We jumped on them early, got them off-balance, and never looked back. Linton Townes played strong in that game, and our young guys hung really tough. We had gotten over a big hump. We were making some noise.

I now had the confidence that we could give anybody a game. We were developing into a solid program. The basketball world was about to discover the Dukes of James Madison University.

What turned us around were the three sophomores—Charles Fisher, Dan Ruland, and David Dupont—who came of age as starters. Junior forward Linton Townes, back for a full season, became our dominant scorer. A surprise happening was Steve Blackmon, who really stepped up as a senior. Another senior, Tyrone Shoulders, dropped from starter to substitute and accepted it willingly, which made him a great team captain.

Our eighth opponent was No. 3 Virginia at JMU. I thought Godwin Hall would explode that evening with 7-foot-4 Ralph Sampson returning to Harrisonburg, his home town where he once played pickup games with my guys in our gym. Cavaliers coach Terry Holland graciously agreed to play us at our campus.

Dan Ruland (6-foot-8) scores inside against 7-foot-4 All-American Ralph Sampson, of UVA, at home on December 30, 1980. The Cavaliers eked out a 53–52 win in a boisterous Godwin Hall. Sampson was from Harrisonburg. Two years later, Ruland was a third-round pick (#70 overall) of the Phildelphia 76ers in the 1983 NBA draft. Photograph courtesy of James Madison University Athletics.

What a night that was, and it's Leo Zindler's fault that he wasn't there. In the fall of my first season at Madison, 1972–1973, Dean Ehlers and I went downtown to sell season tickets. We stopped in the Alfred Neys Clothing Store, owned by Zindler, who said, "Why do I need a season ticket? I'll be able to just walk up and get a ticket anytime."

Well, eight years later, we're playing Virginia. Zindler, a UVA alum, phoned. "Lou," he said. "I need a ticket for the game." I said, "Sorry, Leo, we're all sold out." He couldn't see the smile on my face.

That Virginia game was JMU's biggest-ever regular-season basketball contest and the biggest game ever on the JMU campus, regardless of the sport. How much bigger does it get than Ralph Sampson, literally and figuratively? Virginia had three other solid players in Jeff Lamp, Lee Raker, and Othell Wilson. Rick Carlisle, the current coach of the Dallas Mavericks, played off the bench on that team.

What was my game plan? What else?—jam up Sampson! Ruland couldn't be left naked in the post, playing Sampson one-on-one, not with an eight-inch height disadvantage. So we fronted Sampson and gave Ruland weak-side help. A frustrated Sampson wound up with eleven points and fouteen rebounds. We weren't a team of giants, but we had giant-sized hearts.

By executing on defense, playing smart, and taking good shots, we actually led for thirty-nine minutes. Then Raker hit an outside shot with fifty-two seconds left that put them up by one point. We missed two shots in the last ten seconds, and they sneaked out with a 53–52 victory.

Walking off the court, it was a pathetic scene. Virginia's players weren't smiling, even though they had won. They seemed in shock. Our players were in tears. Terry Holland told me afterwards, "You have a tough team, and your guys played really well tonight." He might have been in shock, too.

The headline in the next day's newspaper read: "Sampson Chained (11 Points)." Don't forget, Virginia would be the Atlantic Coast Conference regular-season champion that season and finish third in the NCAA Tournament. James Madison? We definitely were on our way.

We split with Old Dominion, losing close at our place, 65–63, then beating them in Norfolk for the first time, 73–65. The gap had narrowed. We defeated Richmond not once, not twice, but three times. We wound up with a 21–9 record, a high-water mark at JMU. We could have been 27–3, because we lost

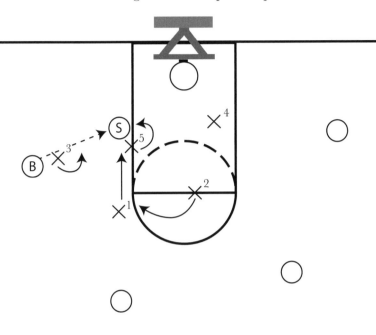

JMU's Defense in Its December 30, 1980 Game versus Virginia and Ralph Sampson

Designed by Morgan Pfaelzer for Coach Lou Campanelli. © George F. Thompson Publishing.

This is how Coach Lou drew up JMU's defense:

- Double team from the ballside elbow (X^1 and X^5).

- Dig from the passer (X^3) and elbow (X^2) on the pass into the post.

- X^4 is the rebounder on the weak side.

Note: Ralph Sampson (S), UVA's All-American 7-foot-4 center, was held to 11 points in a tough one-point win for the third-ranked Cavaliers on JMU's home court.

B = basketball   O = UVA's offensive player   X = JMU's defensive player

JMU's Defense in Its December 30, 1980 Game versus Virginia and Ralph Sampson

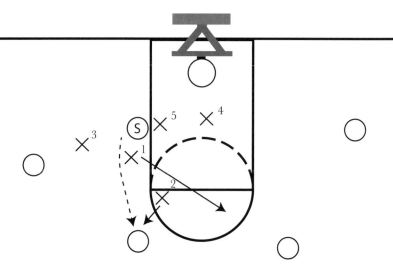

Designed by Morgan Pfaelzer for Coach Lou Campanelli. © George F. Thompson Publishing.

This is how Coach Lou drew up JMU's defense:

- X^1 and X^2 do the "X move" out of a double team, and X^1 runs across the high post.
- Sampson (S) passes the ball.
- X^3 continues to guard the perimeter shooter; X^5 continues to guard Sampson; and X^4 protects the inside and readies for a rebound.

Note: Ralph Sampson (S), UVA's All-American 7-foot-4 center, was held to 11 points in a tough one-point win for the third-ranked Cavaliers on JMU's home court.

B = basketball   O = UVA's offensive player   X = JMU's defensive player six games by two or fewer points, including William & Mary once and Virginia Commonwealth twice. Our biggest loss was nine points, against both St. John's and No. 6 Notre Dame. But we were in every game, something new.

Winning is vital, because, when building a program, you're not going to grow by accepting moral victories. Becoming a winner is a gradual process. Getting together is the beginning, then sticking together translates into unity. But it's how hard you work that makes you successful. Fortunately, I had a team with a strong work mentality. We didn't back off from anybody, even in practice. JMU's trademark was that we wouldn't be intimidated.

Our starters were marksmen: All five shot 51.0 percent or better that season. The scoring was balanced, with Townes our leader at 15.3 points per game. Opponents shot 43.4 percent; our defensive play was magnificent. And we had timing, playing our best basketball at the end of the season, building toward an even stronger finish at the ECAC Tournament in Hampton, Virginia, that might impress the NCAA Selection Committee.

We were at a rarified high, right before we hit a bottomless low. Wilbert "Buddy" Mills, a former player and team captain in 1975–1976, passed away, unexpectedly, on March 5, 1981, the night before we opened against William & Mary in the tournament.

The tragic news came out of the blue. I got a call from Ernie Nestor, my one-time assistant who was coaching at Wake Forest. I thought he might be phoning to wish me luck in the postseason.

"Lou, are you sitting down?"

"Yes," I said, getting nervous.

"I have sad news," he said. "Buddy Mills had a brain aneurysm, and we lost him this morning."

I couldn't believe it. I hadn't ever lost a player. Buddy, twenty-nine, was getting married, having just announced his engagement. I was shocked and saddened at the same time. The Lord called him away far too soon.

Buddy's loss was bigger than just losing a player. He led us to the NCAA Division II Tournament as a senior. Beyond that, he was a special individual. After getting his degree, I invited him to be a graduate assistant, giving him the opportunity to earn a master's degree in physical education. His desire was to be a teacher and coach, and he wound up doing both at Fieldale-Carver High School outside of Roanoke.

Everyone who knew Buddy loved him. He was the happiest guy, the nicest young man I ever coached. He didn't have an enemy in the world. He remained loyal to Madison, where he averaged 7.8 points over four years as a decent jump shooter and consummate role player. Each summer, he brought his high-school players to participate in our team camp.

His death broke my heart. On the 3.5-hour bus ride over to Hampton, I kept thinking about him and his wonderful family. I hadn't told the team yet, then brought them together when we got there. I informed them about Buddy and asked that they keep him in their prayers. They knew him from summer camp, and everyone enjoyed him, which was easy to do. He was a peach.

I told the team, "Let's dedicate this weekend in Buddy's honor." I said it mat-ter-of-factly—no "Win one for the Gipper" speech—unaware that the weekend was about to get crazy. "Let's win *two* for Buddy" would take some doing.

In the semis, William & Mary's ball-control offense slowed the game down, almost to a crawl. Without a shot clock, plus our confounding defense, I figured on a low-scoring contest that would stay tight until the final buzzer. And that's exactly what transpired.

We grabbed the lead, 44–42, with a few seconds left. But we missed a free throw, and the ball went to Billy Barnes, their star player. He dribbled to half-court and launched a Hail Mary shot, unbelievably swishing it at the buzzer. This portended to overtime, because the NCAA hadn't yet adopted the three-point shot.

But, hold on! Did the official call a charge? No overtime? We just won?

Charles Fisher somehow had positioned himself directly in front of Barnes and drew the charge as Barnes flattened him like a Mack truck. Fisher was as still as a statue when contact was made, and Barnes initiated the contact. But how does someone call a charge at such a critical moment?

My heart was in my throat, but game official Austin McArthur did rule it a charge and disallowed the basket. That took a ton of guts, but it was the correct call. We won in the most unusual way imaginable. And Fisher wound up as the ECAC Tournament's most valuable player. Who else?

I'm sure Buddy was smiling down on us.

We were one game away from the Big Dance, and our opponent would be Richmond, which had just upset Old Dominion. We had beaten Richmond twice, 92–73 at Godwin and 69–63 at their place to end the regular season. An old axiom in sports declares that it's hard to three-peat against one team in the

Coach Lou celebrates with his son, Kyle, after the Dukes defeated Richmond 69–60 in Hampton on March 7, 1981, to win the 1981 ECAC Conference Championship. Photograph courtesy of James Madison University Athletics.

Charles Fisher after the Dukes won the 1981 ECAC Championship. For Fisher, it was a shining moment not only to cut down and wear the nets, but also to receive the MVP award. Photograph courtesy of James Madison University Athletics.

same season. Surely, we knew Richmond's strengths and weaknesses, but the Spiders knew ours just as well.

Well, we did three-peat at the Hampton Coliseum, winning 69–60 to earn the ECAC's automatic NCAA bid. Our scoring was spread out. Blackmon had a career-high twenty-one points, while Townes added eighteen points and twelve rebounds. But our entire team came to play that day.

I was so excited about this breakthrough performance. We were one of the nation's tournament-level teams at last. It was such a numbing experience. I said to myself, "Is this really happening? Where do we dance?"

After watching so many teams cut down the nets after winning a championship, I always wondered what that feeling would be like. As the new ECAC champion, I climbed the ladder and cut it down. The feeling was awesome. Holding the net high, I looked at the smiling players down below and felt like we had climbed Kilimanjaro. After I climbed down, one of the players said, "Coach, did we really do this?" What I was feeling at that moment was better than all of the Christmases in my life combined.

Leaving the court, I said, "Buddy, this one's for you."

We arrived back at JMU on Sunday afternoon, greeted by a crowd of 2,000 ready to celebrate. There was an impromptu pep rally outside Godwin Hall. JMU had gotten its first taste of championship life in a major men's sport. But it wouldn't be the school's last such taste in basketball.

March Madness, here come the Dukes! But with whom do we dance?

Selection Sunday is when the NCAA announces its tournament pairings. Coaches and players usually gather inside a gym or another campus facility together with students and season-ticket holders, eager to hear where they will be playing. It's a most-anxious, annual happening.

Only that particular Sunday, I was with my assistant, John Thurston, driving directly from Hampton to Buddy Mills's memorial service. I missed being with my team at such a momentous time, but my first duty was to Buddy. Heading back to Harrisonburg, we heard on the radio that we would play Georgetown in the East Regional. John and I impulsively started cheering. Rich Murray, our sports information director, and my other assistant, Bill Leatherman, had gotten the team together for the announcement.

We didn't know much about Georgetown, but we didn't care who we played: We were *in* the tournament. On Monday, we began gathering film and tape on Georgetown. We were in a hurry to prepare, because we played the Hoyas on Thursday in Providence, which meant we bused to Washington, DC, on Wednesday to catch a flight to Rhode Island.

We already had beaten a Big East team, Pitt, but Georgetown didn't know that much about us because we weren't on TV. So they weren't familiar with our style, and they didn't know how motivated we were. We felt an advantage, even if we were a No. 11 seed to the Hoyas' No. 7.

Taking the court at Providence Civic Center for the pre-game warm ups, one sign caught my eye: "JM Who?" That was the first time I had seen or heard that expression, but it wouldn't be the last. I thought: "I hope, by the end of the night, they'll know who we are."

I wasn't worried about my team. They had a quiet sense of confidence. Nothing bothered them, not even Georgetown, which wasn't quite yet "The Beast of the East." But the Hoyas still had some snarl to them.

Their best player was All-America guard Eric "Sleepy" Floyd. What a shooter! I remember later on, in the NBA, his scoring fifty-one for the Golden State Warriors in a playoff game against the Los Angeles Lakers—twenty-nine in the fourth quarter to seal the upset.

The Hoyas had another good player, a forward named Larry Spriggs. But Sleepy was the man. Coach John Thompson's style was a full-court press, and the Hoyas pressed us all the way. But Dupont and Fisher got the ball up the court by keeping their composure, thereby defying the hounding Hoyas.

Offensively, Fisher banked in a jump shot, and I heard Al McGuire, the great Marquette coach who became a TV analyst, shout into his microphone, "Off the window!" We trailed 39–36 in the second half but kept our poise, controlling the tempo as always. Then—wham! bam!—we ran off nine straight points to seize the lead and put the Hoyas away, 61–55.

Sleepy Floyd scored twenty-three points, but no other Hoya hurt us. Townes led us with nineteen, while Fisher scored fourteen and Blackmon twelve. We shot fifty-three percent from the field and eighty-five percent from the line, including clutch free throws down the stretch. One of the Three Amigos, Joe Hepworth, ran out of the stands to give me a bear hug with seconds remaining. He was so excited for me. That particular memory is special.

JMU had its first NCAA Tournament victory—we were 0–3 in the Division II tournament—and it felt so sweet. JM Who? Figure it out.

Charles Fisher breaks away for a layup versus Georgetown in the Dukes' 61–55 win in
the first round of the 1981 NCAA East Regionals in Providence, Rhode Island. Fisher had
great ball awareness as he and his teammates broke down court against the favored Hoyas,
coached by Hall of Fame Coach John Thompson. Photograph courtesy of James Madison
University Athletics.

Once you win a tournament game, you feel like you really belong. If you're one and done, you don't even know that you were in the tournament, because you're home before you know what hit you. But win one, and you're there for the weekend. You are one of the guys.

Our locker room was joyous, but the joy was temporary, because we next faced a team of giant redwoods. Notre Dame was big—the biggest team we had ever faced. They had an NBA front line of 6-foot-11 Tim Andree, 6-foot-9 Orlando Woolridge, and 6-foot-7 Kelly Tripucka. Their backcourt of 6-foot-5 John Paxson and 6-foot-3 Tracy Jackson also would play in the NBA. Paxson became a great shooter on those championship Chicago Bulls teams with Michael Jordan and Scotty Pippen.

Notre Dame's firepower came from Tripucka with an 18.2-point average, then Woolridge at 14.4, Jackson at 12.9, and Paxson at 9.9. Andree got what was left, 2.2 points, but he rebounded, and he was huge, something we weren't.

Our tallest guy was Ruland at 6-foot-8. When we went out for the opening tip, we looked like a high-school team, while they looked like an NBA team. I told our team before the game: "We've played Virginia and St. John's, teams as good as Notre Dame, guys." But they weren't as tall, and we didn't beat Virginia and St. John's, though I didn't mention that.

We were a resilient bunch, and, though we couldn't see over Notre Dame as a whole, we battled them hard, trailing, 40–37, with 7:30 left to play. The Irish scored the next five points. Then it was hard for us to catch up, because, uncharacteristically, we shot fifty percent on free throws, while Notre Dame was seventy percent from the line. Three days from St. Patrick's Day, the Irish triumphed, 54–45.

Though inside shots were hard to come by that game, Blackmon and Townes each scored twelve points. Defensively, we held the Irish down in points, but we couldn't hold them off. But I was immensely proud of the way we fought. And there was no doubt that we gained some new respect, having been seen on national TV. After the game, Notre Dame coach Richard "Digger" Phelps offered the following wrap-up: "James Madison is one of the most difficult teams to play any time. That's a credit to Lou Campanelli. They never quit. We were never in a position to blow open this game."

The future looked bright for JMU with four starters returning—Townes, Fisher, Dupont, and Ruland. These four, once seen as below the radar as big-time

Coach Lou's teams were known for their swarming, aggressive, and creative defenses. Here, Charles Fisher and Dan Ruland trap Notre Dame guard Tracy Jackson in the second round of the 1981 NCAA East Regional. The Irish were a second seed in the tournament, and, once again, the Dukes proved they could play with any team in the nation. Photograph courtesy of James Madison University Athletics.

After hearing chants of "Who the hell is JMU?" in the Dukes' 1981 NCAA first-round win versus Georgetown, students responded with a sign of their own versus Notre Dame, in second-round action in the NCAA East Regional in Providence, Rhode Island. Photograph courtesy of James Madison University Athletics.

college recruits, now played above that same radar. We were gaining recognition as the "Rocky" of college basketball.

That season was a confluence of an extraordinary high, a tournament bid, and a dismal low, the death of Buddy Mills. But his legacy would live on at JMU. I've since lost two other players, Troy Keyes and Randy Michie, who helped bring respectability to JMU basketball. I'm grateful to all three.

In January 2000, when Sherman Dillard was the Dukes basketball coach, a beautiful team room was constructed inside the Convocation Center, a 7,400-seat facility that replaced Godwin Hall before the 1981–1982 season. The team room was named for Buddy Mills. His family was there for the dedication. So was I, traveling from the West Coast. Van Snowdon, one of Buddy's teammates, donated the money for the room, specifying that it be named after Buddy.

It was the perfect tribute for an unforgettable person.

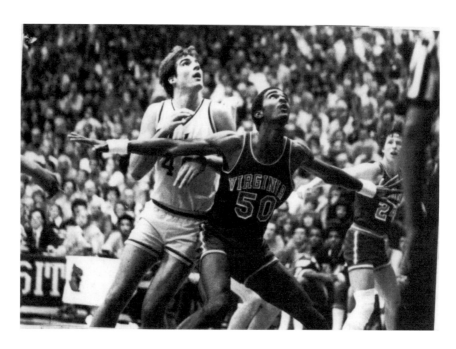

JMU Center Dan Ruland, in the white uniform, battles National Player of the Year Ralph Sampson, of UVA, in the December 30, 1981, game played in a jam-packed Richmond Colliseum. Photograph courtesy of James Madison University Athletics.

CHAPTER 13
Golden Hoops

The timing was fortuitous or ill-fated, depending on one's outlook. But James Madison University reached its basketball zenith during the golden age of college hoops in the early 1980s. There hasn't been another decade to rival that momentous era in the NCAA's dribble-and-dunk world—five glorious years of superb individual talent coupled with the two most unbelievable championship game upsets. Between 1980 and 1985, my Dukes just happened to hit their pinnacle and JMU's overall apex in basketball, at this same marvelous juncture. How marvelous?

When the National Basketball Association, in 1997, picked its fifty best players over its first fifty years, twelve were college kids during the first half of the 1980s—Charles Barkley (Auburn), Clyde Drexler and Hakeem Olajuwon (Houston), Karl Malone (Louisiana Tech), Scottie Pippen (Central Arkansas), David Robinson (Navy), John Stockton (Gonzaga), Isiah Thomas (Indiana), Kevin McHale (Minnesota), Patrick Ewing (Georgetown), and Michael Jordan and James Worthy (North Carolina).

That is a remarkable assemblage of talent. Also noteworthy, two other Top 50 members, Larry Bird of Indiana State and Earvin "Magic" Johnson of Michigan State, who completed their college careers against each other in the 1979 NCAA title game, are given credit for transforming the NBA into a marquee, money-making enterprise. Before Bird and Magic, the NBA lacked a full-season national television package, let alone national appeal.

Those first five years of the 1980s produced other big-time college stars: Ralph Sampson (Virginia), Chris Mullin (St. John's), Mark Aguirre and Terry Cummings (DePaul), Darrell "Dr. Dunkenstein" Griffith (Louisville), Sam Perkins (North Carolina), Danny Ainge (Brigham Young), Dale Ellis (Tennessee), John Paxson (Notre Dame), Eric "Sleepy" Floyd (Georgetown), Waymon Tisdale (Oklahoma), Paul Pressey (Tulsa), Len Bias (Maryland), Mark Price (Georgia Tech), Buck Johnson (Alabama), Sam Bowie and Kenny "Sky" Walker (Kentucky), and Xavier McDaniel (Wichita State).

Some of the players in this last group will be included among the NBA's top seventy-five players when its seventy-fifth anniversary takes place in 2021. And there haven't been two more stunning NCAA title games surprises than North Carolina State shocking Houston in 1983 and Villanova, coached by my buddy Rollie Massimino, toppling Georgetown in 1985.

Reflecting on those five years, one simply goes "Wow!" What great players and what an unparalleled time in undergraduate basketball. College hoops took off right then. The NCAA tournament grew in importance, with expanded TV coverage. So, if you made it to the tournament, you received tremendous exposure for your university.

Besides those great players, there were great college coaches in the 1980s: Dean Smith, John Thompson, Jim Valvano, Rollie Massimino, Lou Carnesecca, Bobby Knight, Mike Krzyzewski, Guy Lewis, Pete Carril, Wimp Sanderson, Dale Brown, and so on. That was a fun time, a historic period. Even the basketball rim looked golden in the eighties.

During that run, my Dukes reached their peak success with twenty-four victories in 1981–1982, still the high-water mark at JMU. And we achieved it after increasing our Division I foes to 28, including tournament teams. Twenty-four wins, and JMU had only played NCAA men's basketball for nine years.

Even with that ambitious scheduling, we won our first eight games—twice against Virginia Commonwealth, the first time at VCU, 47–45, and then 54–46 in the *Richmond Times-Dispatch* Tournament ten days later. As fate would have it, we next played Virginia twice in a row, in the *Times-Dispatch* Tournament championship game and then at UVA. Our valiant effort against the Cavaliers the previous season got their attention, and they had our number this time, 57–44 and 73–65. Yet they didn't succeed in pummeling us. We were nobody's punching bag.

Those were four brutal games against two schools in the span of two weeks, but Dean Ehlers felt the Richmond tournament would help our power rating. I had to agree, though guarding Ralph Sampson twice in four days, let alone twice in one season, was asking quite a bit. He was unchained this time, with twenty-two points and fourteen rebounds against us the first game, and fifteen points and fourteen rebounds in the encore. At least, he never scored thirty against us, as he did other teams. And I'm sure the NCAA Selection Committee took notice of our playing an Atlantic Coast Conference team, one of the best

Guard David Dupont looks for an opening against UVA's guard Jeff Jones in the January 2, 1982, game in Charlottesville. Photograph courtesy of James Madison University Athletics.

A happy Coach Lou congratulates team captain Linton Townes with the game ball after he scored his 1,000th point in 1981. For his career, Townes scored 1,380 points and had 507 rebounds and 191 assists. Photograph courtesy of James Madison University Athletics.

teams in the country. With our beating VCU twice and toughening up our Division I schedule, the selection committee was keeping a closer eye on us.

After those four games, we began to roll. We posted a 13–2 record the rest of the regular season, with winning streaks of seven and six games. We knocked off Old Dominion twice, 60–48 and 43–41, for our first-ever regular season sweep of the Monarchs. The NCAA selection folks likely subscribed to our campus newspaper, *The Breeze*, after that impressive double. And I thought, "It took some time, Dr. Carrier, but we finally had mastered ODU."

I felt assured that we could compete against the better programs, and my players certainly wanted that opportunity. This was something they needed and JMU also needed: The challenge. My Dukes were maturing as players, physically and confidently. Townes was a senior. Ruland, Fisher, and Dupont were juniors. They didn't play scared; quite the opposite.

Those four really bonded. They believed in one another, and they grew in confidence together. Watching them play, you sensed that this fearless team, even if knocked to the floor, would get up and deliver a knockout.

They really took pride in their defense. Our multiple schemes took hold that season. We kept teams off-kilter as defense became a huge weapon for us. We finished fifth nationally in scoring defense, yielding fifty-two points a game. Those Dukes played tough, they played smart, they played with discipline, and they played as a unit. They played the game *the right way*.

In my thirteen years at JMU, and I can't stress it enough, this was my best team. Not so much for the 24–6 record but in how we functioned, always as a *team*. Like coaches on the court, they implemented exactly what my staff asked them to do, largely by controlling the game on the defensive end.

I normally played eight men: Townes, Ruland, Fisher, Dupont, and Darrell Jackson as starters and Derek Steele, Keith Bradley and Woody Boler off the bench. They all knew their roles. They weren't always going to get their shots, because our emphasis was to get the ball inside, where contact led to free throws.

Our only ECAC South regular-season defeats were to Richmond, 56–51 at their place, and 68–66 in overtime to VCU at our place. But, in beating VCU and ODU twice each, it gave us a favorable power rating. Richmond had talented kids, and we always had to play our best to beat them. We just didn't execute that night. And ODU had Mark West, a talented 6-foot-10 player who would enjoy some good years in the NBA.

I've always maintained that you must get your team playing its best basketball heading into February. And we were 9–3 from that point forward, including the postseason. One of those wins was positively "horrifying."

On February 10, we played the University of New Orleans in the Big Easy. UNO had a gym known as "The Chamber of Horrors," because UNO had won thirty-nine consecutive games there. During the game-day shoot-around, I told the team. "If we win, there's no curfew. Just be on the bus at 9 a.m. to go to the airport. But if we lose, it's back to the hotel for the night."

There's nothing like natural motivation to inspire a team, especially in a fun place like New Orleans. And, I added, "If you do the town, please stay together and don't do anything to embarrass yourselves or our program." My pre-game talk couldn't miss or so I thought.

The game started and—Boom!—we were down quick, 7–0. I called a time-out, and all I said was, "What's it going to be, fellas, Bourbon Street or back to the hotel?" My Dukes erased that lead and won, 59–55.

As I walked off the court, feeling good about snapping that streak, I bumped into the New Orleans baseball coach, Ron Maestri, who had a concession stand in the gym. He handed me a cold beer and said, "Coach, you deserve it. Teams don't usually win here." It was the first post-game beer I'd ever had before reaching the locker room. Tasted good, though.

My Dukes were on the bus at 9 a.m. the next morning, with no incidents reported from the previous evening. Did they fill up on booze to celebrate? Daddy wasn't going to ask them. It's all about enjoying college life and making it fun, even if on the sly. I doubt Dr. Carrier, especially Dr. Carrier, would have interrogated them either. Not the "Drunk Bus" president.

I use the term "Daddy" only because I tried to be a father figure to the team. A caring coach should be a father figure; we teach the players, and we guide them into adulthood. Some of my players needed more guidance than others, but most of them came from good families, with mothers and fathers. I tried to supplement away from home what the parents would want.

That's why, every year that I was at Madison, we invited the whole team, including student managers, over to our house for Thanksgiving dinner. There wasn't time for them to go home, because the season started right after Thanksgiving. We roasted two turkeys, which Dawn enjoyed doing. Most Italian women love to cook for their families, and Dawn is such a good cook. My teams loved the home-cooked hospitality; it was so much better than having Thanksgiving dinner in some restaurant.

We beat William & Mary at JMU, 54–44, prior to the New Orleans trip. We beat them again, 56–55, on the road after the bayou visit. Playing William & Mary was like having a root canal; they played slower than you preferred. Their goal was to hold teams between forty-five and fifty-five points, while our goal was to score between fifty-five and sixty-five. They controlled the ball, and they had good shooters, so it was hard to pull away from them. Getting up ten points on that bunch felt like a twenty-point lead against other teams.

So which team did we draw in the ECAC South Tournament semifinals in Norfolk? Yep, William & Mary. We were the No. 1 seed in the tournament with a 10–1 conference record, and we beat William & Mary, 64–49, for the third time. Any trifecta is worth celebrating, but we needed another trifecta against Old Dominion in the championship game the next night to earn an automatic NCAA bid.

The third time against ODU was like watching paint dry. We lost, 43–41, scoring our fewest points all season, while giving up our fewest points. ODU was now our master again, by a basket. Both teams shot poorly, though both played solid defense. The problem is, in a low-possession game, you don't have a big margin of error. Afterwards, I was left with an immediate sense of panic: There might be no NCAA Tournament bid for my Dukes.

Even though we were 23–5, the NCAA Selection Committee hadn't ever picked an at-large team from our conference. ODU got the automatic bid as the ECAC champion. I felt that we would, at least, get an NIT offer. Dean Ehlers was non-committal; he didn't know what the committee would do.

"Stay by the phone on Sunday, Coach, and I'll give you a call," he said.

Would prayer help? I prayed that beating VCU and ODU twice each would impress the committee. I prayed that having two All-ECAC South first-team selections, team captain Townes and Ruland, would make the committee sit up and take notice. I did everything but resort to a novena for special intentions. You can only ask the Man Above for so many favors.

We had a four-hour bus ride Sunday back to Harrisonburg from the ECAC tournament. Dawn and the kids knew I would be waiting by the phone at the house for the important phone call. So they watched a home movie—I don't remember which one—as I pondered our fate.

Finally, the phone rang about 4 p.m. Dean Ehlers said, "Coach, we're going to Charlotte."

"We got an NIT bid?" I asked.

"No, Coach," said Dean, a man given to brevity. "We got an NCAA bid."

"What?" I reacted.

With that, I took the phone, which had a long cord, and threw it against the ceiling. Dawn and the kids came running in, and we had a group hug. Just then, I looked out the window, and here came Dr. Carrier and his wife, Edith, walking up the path with a bottle of champagne and four glasses.

We had a quick toast, and I then I joined the team to watch the selection show. I walked in with a deadpan look, because I didn't want to tip my hand. We heard our name called early, because they did the East first. Then it was pandemonium. These are such joyous occasions, the fruits of your labor.

"Fellas," I said, "we have to make a good showing, to represent our conference well and to prove that we belong in the tournament, because our selection this time is going to be controversial."

Sure enough, in the next day's newspapers, the University of Nevada at Las Vegas and Bradley University screamed bloody murder, saying, "How could you pick James Madison over us?" Well, we had played a strong schedule, and we did well against it. We *did* belong.

I also told the team, "We're playing a Big Ten team in Ohio State, and they're as excited to be in the tournament as we are. This is an opportunity to show the country that we're deserving of this bid." And, following our impressive performances, the win against Ohio State and the two-point loss against NCAA champion North Carolina, JMU's critics were eating their words. JM Who? Get lost.

As a fitting conclusion to the 1981–1982 season, at least in the Campanelli household, I was named Virginia College Coach of the Year. This meant I had to give a speech at the Virginia Hall of Fame banquet in Norfolk.

The principal speaker was George Steinbrenner, the owner of the New York Yankees. To my utter delight, I was seated between two Yankee greats, Bill "Moose" Skowron and the legendary Mickey Mantle, both now retired. I was beside myself, because I was a huge Yankees fan as a youngster. Joe DiMaggio was my hero, and then Mantle became my hero after Joltin' Joe retired. At the banquet, I found the Mick to be quite candid.

"Coach," he said, "I came along too soon."

"What do you mean, Mick?"

"The biggest contract I got from the Yankees was $100,000, my last year as a player," he said. "I practically had to beg them for it. Nowadays, you have guys batting .240 earning more than a million a year."

That's so unjust, I agreed, for there was only one Mick.

I wasn't a big George Steinbrenner fan. He fired Yankee managers right and left, and he was in the news as much as his players, and I didn't like that approach. But he gave an eloquent and motivating speech that night with a strong patriotic message. I gained a new appreciation for the man.

As I sat there listening to him, I counted my blessings. Here I was, sitting with my boyhood heroes, and I had just hit my peak as a coach. My life had come together in the best possible way. I felt like a million bucks.

JMU's new 6,426-seat Convocation Center, opened in 1982, was a necessary addition to accommodate JMU's expanding sports and entertainment programs. It was also the first building to be built east of Interstate 81. The "Convo" replaced Godwin Hall (not pictured but to the right of the parking lot) as the home of the JMU basketball team. The woods (top) beyond the Convocation Center became part of the Edith J. Carrier Arboretum in 1985. Photograph courtesy of James Madison University Libraries: Special Collections.

CHAPTER 14
An Electric Jolt

After two straight NCAA tournament appearances, James Madison University forfeited its image as college basketball's biggest secret. Before the 1982–1983 season, *Sports Illustrated* sealed our fate by rating us No. 17 in the country, the first time JMU had ever climbed into the Top 20. Although flattered, I knew we didn't deserve that rating.

We had lost our scoring power when Linton Townes left for the NBA. We had no marksman to replace him. JMU was ranked seventeenth strictly off what we did the previous year. We would need every ounce of that same unity, smartness, confidence, and grit to carve out a third straight twenty-win season.

We'd also need a little extra boost from our zealous fans in order to achieve that end result. We already had the Great Toilet Paper Toss going for us. Perhaps something new, and equally innovative could turn the Convocation Center into the Convocrazy Center—a madhouse for visiting teams to venture into at their own peril. But what would that innovation be?

Then, on cue, an electric guitar rang out, reverberating throughout the arena. Perhaps it happened by accident, but that electric guitar, coming from the student band, suddenly took center stage. The guitar's relentless twang filled the building with its zany sound, and it also filled our opponents' ears. Conveniently, the guitar was positioned right above the visitors' bench.

Our students were passionate about basketball, and that passion kept firing up, higher and higher, like some emotional wattage getting charged. And so JMU's Convocation Center became christened as the "Electric Zoo."

College basketball should be enjoyable for everyone involved. This isn't the NBA, where you aren't a graduate of the New York Knickerbockers or an alumnus of the Boston Celtics. This is your school, which makes the pride you feel for it so *personal* and thus more meaningful.

The Convocation Center was the perfect size, with the perfect acoustics, for a winning environment. That said, there still was an adjustment period for my Dukes. We had a phenomenal 119–22 record (.844 winning percentage) during ten seasons at Godwin Hall, with its 5,000 fans. The Convocation Center's seating capacity was 7,400—by design. Dr. Carrier's handiwork was present once again.

Before it was constructed, he asked me: "How big should it be?"

"I don't know, Dr. Carrier," I said. "I'm a coach, not an architect."

"Coach," said the ever-wise Dr. Carrier, "it's always better to build it a little smaller than too big. You don't want to have empty seats."

He was correct, as usual. A zoo can't be as large as a game preserve. The Electric Zoo was a perfect fit and a perfect nightmare for visiting teams.

We opened at home by stifling VMI, 58–33. The Keydets were outplayed and drowned out. The "Zoo" was positively rocking. Virginia, aware that we were the No. 17 team in the nation, played us next at our place. That was one day when the music died. The No. 1-ranked Cavaliers smoked us, 51–34—the fewest points scored by JMU during my thirteen years there.

That was an absolute crusher; we had no perimeter game minus Townes. That defect became readily apparent to our opponents. We weren't No. 17 for very long; we had to find a whole new way to win.

We recovered to win at Maine, 58–53, and then returned home for a convincing 66–57 victory over VCU. Strike up the band! Then it all fell apart. In ten previous seasons at Madison, I hadn't lost four games in a row. Then it happened within ten days—and by the combined margin of ten points.

We were invited to the Cardinal Classic, a tournament on the Ball State campus in Muncie, Indiana. Our first opponent was Louisiana Tech, which had an unfamiliar player named Karl Malone. Who knew, right? Well, "The Mailman" would deliver 20.9 points and 10.3 rebounds as a sophomore. And Tech nipped us, 62–61. Dan Ruland said Malone was the strongest player he had ever faced. We played Fairleigh Dickinson the next night in the consolation game, and lost again, 65–62. And I was used to winning consolations.

Next up was the Kodak Classic in Rochester, New York. We drew No. 9 Iowa, coached by Lute Olson, in the opener. We lost, 47–45, and then fell to St. Bonaventure, 58–54, in yet another consolation disappointment.

There was no consoling me when we returned from Rochester. I needed to make a change. The team was in a funk, and so was David Dupont. His poor shooting was affecting the team. He was a senior, but I had to do something, because junior Derek Steele was playing well off the bench.

So I took David out to lunch to break the news: I was starting Derek. David broke down and cried. I really felt badly, because he was such a wonderful kid.

But I needed to relieve David, our captain, of whatever pressure he was feeling. Making him the sixth man, I hoped, would restore his shooting eye. I did that for four, five games, and David didn't mope. He contributed, and his shooting touch came back.

A coach can't know, for sure, how such changes will work out. You can push the right button or the wrong button. David had been prominent in our success, so naturally he was upset. But the *team* is my responsibility. And I had to think of myself, too. My job was to win, not play favorites.

I then promoted David and moved Derek back into a reserve role, which he accepted with poise. I now had three productive guards for the rest of the season. Derek brought us a different dimension: He was strong, quick, and a good passer, he could penetrate, and he was great against the press. But then, as a bonus, he became a difference-maker as a shooter.

Still, I scrambled to find the right lineup. Townes left such a big void. The previous season, I had six players with nine or more starts. This time around, I had nine players with nine starts.

Each of my Dukes had a different quality. Greg Mosten was a good rebounder. Darrell Jackson was a great athlete. Bob Donohue was a spot-up jump shooter. Keith Bradley was a fierce competitor. I hoped that, collectively, they could replace Townes. Alas, I discovered, they couldn't.

They played tight, so we weren't as good offensively. It was like an emotional claw had grabbed them, and they couldn't free themselves. Fortunately, our multiple defenses got us over the hump. After upgrading to twenty-nine Division I teams, we had to bear down harder, players and coaches alike, in order to reach the twenty-win plateau and to keep the NCAA Selection Committee interested in us.

The NCAA is all about "power wins," so I continued to challenge my Dukes with demanding schedules. But I was concerned that their confidence had slipped after two tournament failures, and with that early No. 17 ranking, everyone was gunning for us. We weren't the hunter anymore; we were the hunted. I had to find a way to bring out the hunter in us again.

After winning three of the next four games, evening our record at 6–6, here came Old Dominion. This was a make-or-break game, something we needed as a springboard. Otherwise, it might capsize our season.

Desperate, I needed a motivating brainstorm. And *The Daily News-Record*, our Harrisonburg newspaper, provided that motivation the day of the game. "Hapless Dukes Host ODU."

I took one look at that headline and said, "Thank you, *Daily News-Record*, you just gave me my pre-game speech." And I would give it my best Al Pacino delivery. Hey, we Italians stick together. I cut out the article, because I needed to make a dramatic showing. The game would be televised on ESPN, which added urgency to my speech.

I called our team manager, Patti Przybocki, and asked her to meet me in the team room and to bring a screwdriver. We had a small bulletin board in that room, and I tacked the article to it. Then we loosened the screws to the board, just the right amount. Now the scene was set.

I walked into the team room after the players had gathered. Without saying a word, I paced back and forth, and they could see that I was fuming. They all wondered, "What's wrong with Coach?" They didn't have to wonder much longer.

"Hapless?" I shouted, pointing at the bulletin board. "Now we are hapless?"

I had everyone's attention. "Hapless! That's the worst thing anyone can call you."

I paced and fumed some more; I sensed the tension building. Al Pacino, I'm sure, would have approved of my thespian flair.

Suddenly, I whirled and ripped the article off the bulletin board. Then I tore down the bulletin board, thanks to those loosened screws. Everybody was stunned. "What's with Coach? Has he gone nuts?"

I proceeded to rip the article to shreds, then I threw the shreds down on the floor and stomped on them. The players' expressions were priceless, but I had reached them, just as I planned. Then I stormed out of the room.

I made it onto the arena floor just in time for the National Anthem. After the players completed their pre-game drills, they returned to the bench. I saw the fire in their eyes. "Hapless Dukes?" Now we'll see who's hapless.

We jumped on Old Dominion like a bunch of bullies, and they didn't know what hit them. We had them down, 22–4. They were breathing hard and were already beaten. We rolled to a 63–52 win as the Electric Zoo went bonkers. The guitarist's twang sounded like Jimi Hendrix that night.

Paul Webb, the Monarchs' coach, caught up to me afterward. "When I read that headline this morning," he said, "I knew we were in trouble."

We now had beaten ODU four out of the last five meetings, a turnaround that pleased Dr. Carrier—no end. We needed a win over a good team, and that headline did the trick. We became a much looser team after that; we had gotten our mojo back. We were Hapless Dukes no longer.

Starting with that ODU game, we were 8–1 at home and 11–4 overall the rest of the regular season. Twenty wins now was a more realistic objective. But it's tough to win twenty games at JMU after losing a key player like Linton Townes. Hey, we're not talent-stacked like the ACC or Big East. We recruited guys that we unearthed here and there, and we managed to come up with a few gems. But after we started winning, the gems became much harder to find, because we weren't the only school panning for gold.

Look, college basketball is competitive. Coaches are working hard to keep their jobs, and if they're lazy, they're not going to last long in this business. So they're beating the bushes, just as we did. And kids do want to play. After our NCAA Tournament success, kids started thinking, "James Madison is too good. I'll go to Richmond or George Mason."

Down the stretch in 1982–1983, we took our lumps. We lost back-to-back road games, 72–65 at William & Mary and 58–43 at Old Dominion. Hey, we didn't own ODU. VCU also got us on the road, 59–53, and William & Mary caught us at home, 59–55, with the Tribe's grinding, ball-control attack.

We had beaten New Orleans in their "Chamber of Horrors" the year before, and now we played them at our place. We won the rematch, 56–44, and their coach, Don Smith, wasn't pleased with the officiating. He took a handkerchief out of his pocket and put it over his mouth and nose. He, in effect, was calling the officials "bandits." Walking onto the court looking like a bank robber, he received a second technical and was ejected. He passed by our bench en route to the locker room. I said, "Coach, what the hell are you doing?" He replied, "I'm going to get me a beer."

We finished the regular season at 17–10, an impressive record considering our inconsistent offense. Ruland was our top scorer with a 15.1 average, along with 6.7 rebounds a game. Danny had a strong senior season and was named ECAC South Player of the Year. But we didn't have a No. 2 scorer like we did the year before. Twenty wins wouldn't be easy.

We qualified for the ECAC South tournament at the University of Richmond's Robins Center. Navy was our semifinal foe, and we took care of the

Middies, 72–58. Ruland led us with eighteen points. Charles Fisher added twelve, and Steele had twelve off the bench. Diminutive Derek had become a force.

Now 18–10, our title-game opponent was William & Mary, which already had thumped us twice. Continuing our frustrations against the Tribe's slow-it-down tactics, we trailed by ten points with ten minutes left. An NCAA Tournament bid was slipping away from my Dukes, not to mention twenty wins. I called a time-out.

"We've got to get after these guys full-court," I said. "We can't let them run the clock." The NCAA had no shot clock yet, so it was up to our defense to turn things around. We weren't a pressing team, normally, but time was getting short. We pressured the Tribe and forced some steals. We kept chipping away, making them take bad shots, until we tied the game with the clock about to expire. Then our mighty mite took over.

With four seconds left, Steele hit a pressure shot from the top of the key, a two-pointer at that time. Fouled in the act of shooting, he made the free throw, and his three-point play gave us a season-saving 41–38 victory. Derek had eighteen of our forty-one points and was named tournament MVP, all 5-foot-7 of him. One tough, pocket-sized Duke.

Hello, again, March Madness, for the third consecutive year. Or as the great Count Basie phrased it, "One more once."

My Dukes, at 19–10, had overcome their offensive deficiencies with defensive tenacity, which wasn't ever more tenacious than during those last ten minutes against William & Mary, which, by the way, later changed its mascot from an American Indian to a Griffin, a mythical figure that is the body of a lion and the head of an eagle.

My Dukes had become the hunter once again, recovering from that early four-game losing streak. They also overcame that thirty-four-point clunker against Virginia. And they took care of that regular-season sweep by William & Mary when it counted the most. They had done everything, in my mind, but end the Cold War and invent the microchip. How could I not love a team with so much heart? They wanted that March Madness three-peat so badly, and they made it happen.

Our reward was to play in the NCAA's East Regional in our new "home" away from home, the state of North Carolina, this time in Greensboro. Our first-round opponent would be the West Virginia Mountaineers.

Senior center Dan Ruland shoots over a West Virginia defender in the first-round game of the 1983 NCAA East Regional in Greensboro, North Carolina. The Dukes won 57–50, extending JMU's reputation as a "giant killer" during the NCAA tournament. Ruland, who finished his career at JMU with 1,255 points and 640 rebounds, was co-CAA Player of the Year. Photograph courtesy of James Madison University Athletics.

The Dukes' bench reacts after a score against West Virginia in their first-round game in the 1983 NCAA East Regional. Bob Donohue, a 6-foot-3 senior forward, had a stellar game coming off the bench and scoring 12 points against the seventh-seeded Mountaineers. Photograph courtesy of James Madison University Athletics.

Bad blood now existed between West Virginia and JMU. Normally, coaches are respectful before the NCAA Tournament, praising one another's programs but also realizing how difficult it is to qualify for the tournament. West Virginia coach Gale Catlett took the opposite approach. He said, "James Madison is only successful, because they hold the ball."

What a cheap shot! During our three-year tournament run, we averaged fifty-seven points and held opponents to fifty-one points per game during the regular season. We weren't run-and-gun, but we weren't hold-the-ball-until-midnight either.

Catlett had thrown down the gauntlet. I picked it up and threw it right back in his face. "Gale Catlett is only famous," I responded, "for getting the University of Cincinnati on probation, from which they've had a hard time recovering." Mull on that, mouthy Mountaineer.

Needless to say, there wasn't the obligatory pre-game handshake between coaches. There wouldn't be the obligatory post-game handshake either. So what? I didn't need to interact with Catlett.

We kicked West Virginia's butt, 57–50. They had a 5-foot-10 guard, Greg Jones, who was a catalyst for the Mountaineers. Our 1-3-1 half-trap defense (page 29) bothered him, because he had a tough time seeing over our taller defenders. Fisher led us with thirteen points, sinking five free throws in the final 2:30. Ruland added eleven points and twelve rebounds, and we got a huge game from reserve Bob Donohoe, with twelve points. It was such a sweet victory, our twentieth. The "Hapless Dukes" had reached twenty wins for the third straight year.

JMU also had three consecutive NCAA Tournament first-round victories. But, as fate would have it, our second-round opponent would be North Carolina for the second straight year. And North Carolina was laying for us.

The NCAA could have placed us in another regional, but, for three years running, we got stuck in the East. The Tar Heels must have caught considerable heat back home after little ol' JMU played them tough the year before. They wouldn't be surprised this time around.

They jumped on us early, got us back on our heels, and we couldn't make up much ground. They had lost James Worthy, but they still had Michael Jordan and Sam Perkins. And their new big man, 6-foot-11 Brad Daugherty, was a future NBA No. 1 overall pick. That's the North Carolina way.

The opening tip off in the Dukes' second-round game versus second-seeded North Carolina in the 1983 NCAA East Regional. Photograph courtesy of James Madison University Athletics.

The Tar Heels had us down, 28–17, at the half and never looked back, thumping us, 68–49. Perkins had eighteen points and Jordan seventeen. Fisher led the Dukes with sixteen points, while Ruland added fifteen.

Sadly, it was time to say good-bye to three instrumental factors in JMU's meteoric rise to respectability: Fisher, Ruland, and Dupont. Ruland would become a third-round pick of the Philadelphia 76ers and Fisher a ninth-round pick by those same 76ers. Without those three and Townes before them, I wouldn't have had the same success at JMU. I owed them so much.

An era was ending, and I knew it. We couldn't have predicted what we were getting in talent when those four came to college; how can you really project potential? But JMU won't ever forget them. They brought with them the essential intangibles—young men of character with a solid work ethic on the court and in the classroom, plus natural enthusiasm, leadership, and the ability to bond.

There couldn't have been that three-year NCAA Tournament run without them, not to mention the unprecedented glory that they brought to JMU. Those three years still feel like a fairy tale. Right afterwards, the Electric Zoo experienced a power short.

Coach Lou and the Dukes celebrate after senior team captain Dereck Steele hit the winning shot to beat Old Dominion 69–67 at home in the Electric Zoo on February 1, 1984. Photograph courtesy of James Madison University Athletics.

CHAPTER 15
Afterglow

Success is the incubator of opportunity, even for a mid-major basketball program such as James Madison University. After JMU's first appearance in the NCAA Division I Tournament in 1981, I received a call from a major college program, which was seeking a basketball coach. Similar calls followed our next two March Madness appearances in 1982 and 1983.

What was I to do? I wasn't looking for a new job. In fact, I rejected each offer. I was happy at JMU, but that didn't stop the telephone from ringing.

The first call came from Georgia Tech, which was moving into the competitive Atlantic Coast Conference and wanted me to fly down for an interview. Only two coaches were being interviewed, Bobby Cremins and myself. My interview went well, and it was a wonderful opportunity. Georgia Tech had the smallest arena in the ACC, but it was upgrading. Atlanta is a major city, and the school had a solid academic rating.

But it would have meant a move into the Deep South, and here I was a Northerner already dealing with conservative Southerners. Don't misunderstand. I enjoyed Harrisonburg. But I wasn't a good ol' boy, and, additionally, I didn't want to abandon JMU. So I turned down Georgia Tech, and Cremins took the job.

When you have success, people inquire about you, and I felt I owed it to my family to investigate any new opportunity. I didn't want to be one of those nomadic coaches who keeps jumping ship every few years, taking four or five jobs. But I didn't want my ship to sink either. Businessmen change jobs if there is a better offer. I was a businessman, too, just with a whistle.

Hubie Brown phoned after the '82 season. Hubie and I went way back to our high-school coaching days in New Jersey during the early 1960s. He now coached the New York Knicks, he needed an assistant, and would I be interested? It was another great opportunity, and I gave it serious consideration. But I turned Hubie down, because I didn't feel the NBA lifestyle was right for me. My son, Kyle, then thirteen, was disappointed with my decision. He looked forward to seeing his idol, Julius Erving, the incomparable "Dr. J," performing at Madison Square Garden.

Meanwhile, I was soul-searching, asking myself if I could take the JMU program further, past the second round of the NCAA Tournament. Would we even make it back to March Madness? Staying or leaving, it wasn't about the money. If it were only that, I would have taken the Ole Miss job. They wanted to triple my salary.

After the '83 season, the University of Mississippi contacted me. Ole Miss plays in the tough Southeastern Conference, and it offered to come up to Virginia and fly Dawn and me down to Oxford. I gave it serious thought before explaining to them that I knew the confederate flag was flown at Ole Miss, and I would have a hard time being in the home of a black student-athlete and having to deal with that issue. So I politely declined the interview. They said they understood, and I know that racial attitudes have changed in the Deep South in the ensuing forty years.

I still loved my job at JMU, an idyllic situation. We now lived in our second home in Harrisonburg, a beautiful area called Forest Hills. I could walk to my office in the Convocation Center in five minutes. Or I'd hop on my trusty moped, cut through the woods, and be at my office in two minutes. I left the moped unlocked outside the Convo Center, and it wasn't ever touched. Riding it to the bank in town, the moped was just as safe. My family and I felt protected in Harrisonburg. I couldn't have asked for a better coaching environment.

The only question mark for me was the basketball program. After building it up to Division I tournament level and maintaining it there for three years, it would be difficult to keep it there. We lost some key players, and where—and how soon—would we find the players to replace them? Therefore, I wasn't anticipating an NCAA four-peat. I was wondering, instead, if a winning record was even conceivable the following season.

JMU and its fans continued to have high expectations, but my next Dukes team would be inexperienced. We had some promising youngsters whom we felt would be good down the road. But we had too many role players and not enough tilt-the-court guys.

I continually reminded myself that the game is called "basketball." Even with all its intangibles, you still have to fill up the basket to win. A mid-major is blessed to have freshmen help it out right away. We got lucky with Dillard, Stielper, and Townes, but now our tank was running low on luck.

During JMU's 1983–1984 season, we lost seven games by no more than four points. Why? Inexperience. Those Dukes played, count 'em, six overtime games, which is unheard of. Until that season, we had no more than three overtimes in a season, and that happened only once. Fortunately, we were 4–2 in those six OTs, yet it was a struggle hanging tough in close games.

We finished a disappointing 15–14, though we weren't too far off from another twenty-win season. It's a slim margin between winning and losing, but that margin also defines exactly who you are. You either have the players to get it done or you don't. No alibis. It was a big falloff for the Dukes any way you look at it, a major letdown.

We knew beforehand that teams in our conference would challenge us. The ECAC South was a tough conference, mid-major or no mid-major, with great coaches and great men, in Dick Tarrant at Richmond, Paul Webb at Old Dominion, and the Parkhill brothers, Bruce and Barry, at William & Mary. I had such respect for those coaches, who made the conference tough because of their ultra-competitiveness. Most of the games were hard-fought, nip-and-tuck. If you won by nine points, that was a rout. Dean Ehlers was one of the administrators who put that conference together. Thanks, Dean.

We competed hard, regardless of our record, that winter. Our go-to guy was our smallest weapon, Derek Steele. Now a senior and team captain, Derek led us in three categories—twelve points a game, plus assists and steals. Freshman guard Eric Brent averaged nine points, while sophomore forward Eric Esch added seven points a game. We just lacked a big-time scorer.

Before that season, I thought if we could reach seventeen wins with our youth and inexperience, it would be a successful year. We almost got there. Our fifteen victories did represent our twelfth consecutive winning season at Madison. Conversely, those fifteen wins also represented a steep drop. You're down to the discouraging level of average, instead of a cut above the norm.

Searching for positives, we achieved some glory. As green as we were, we split with Old Dominion, Richmond, and George Mason. And we narrowly lost to Virginia, 53–50, in Charlottesville. The kids showed plenty of heart and some moxie, too. They coulda been a contender if . . . oh, well.

Hope still remained for us, as every school gets into the East Coast Athletic Conference tournament. Only, this time, we didn't get an automatic bye into the semifinals. We played George Mason in a first-round game and pounded the Patriots, 63–56. Our youngsters came through. We were then eliminated by Richmond, 65–57, in the semis. Johnny Newman, a deadeye shooter for the Spiders, kept pumping in jumpers from another planet. He was otherworldly. Richmond went on to win the ECAC tournament.

Our mission, as always, was to keep opponents' scoring in the fifties. That became imperative in '83–84. Only we held teams to sixty or fewer points eighteen times, compared to twenty-four times the season before. Offensively, we scored sixty or more points fourteen times, compared to sixteen the previous year. As a result, winning came down to minute margins.

Of course, winning depends on talent. And, so, why wasn't I able to find those same diamonds in the rough that I was so successful in digging out previously? I asked myself: Had I had lost my recruiting knack?

I'm hard on myself, just as I'm hard on my players. But, in truth, I hadn't stopped recruiting; I still worked at it diligently. We ended up with some able talent in Brent, Esch, and John Newman. But our John Newman wasn't the Johnny Newman of Richmond. We just didn't have enough offensive punch to lift us up to twenty wins.

I prayed a lot that season, holding onto my rosary beads. I prayed that our new guys would develop into the guys we had lost. In retrospect, I was too optimistic. A mid-major must be lucky, because recruiting requires more guesswork, more projection, and less certainty. Dean Smith, Bobby Knight, and their big-time ilk had far less guesswork.

But, in retrospect, what if we didn't land Stielper? What if Dillard went to Richmond? What if North Carolina took Dupont as a walk-on? What if Townes went to Liberty Baptist? What if, what if? I felt fortunate that it worked out for us—three NCAA Tournament berths in a row. Did luck or fate have anything to do with our success? Absolutely. Those players fell into my lap. If they hadn't, I might have been coaching in Chattahoochee!

After the 1983–1984 season, I wondered once more if I needed a new challenge to re-charge my battery. That thought stayed with me much longer this time around, though I still kept my foot on the recruiting accelerator. I wanted so bad to bring March Madness back to JMU. I certainly didn't want our devoted fans tossing toilet paper at *me*.

Things didn't improve the following season. There was a zoo break at the Electric Zoo, and all the animals ran amok. The electric guitar popped

JMU's Offense in Its January 12, 1985 Game versus Navy and "The Admiral"

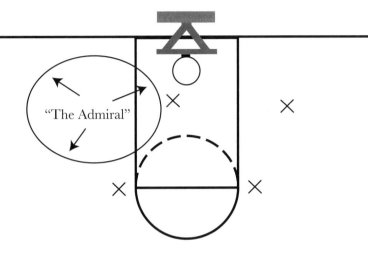

"The Admiral"

Designed by Morgan Pfaelzer for Coach Lou Campanelli. © George F. Thompson Publishing.

In JMU's first game versus Navy in Annapolis, JMU's shots were affected in the circled area against Navy's 2–3 zone defense. David Robinson ("The Admiral") blocked 10 shots, and Navy won the game, 79–65.

Note: "The Admiral" was 7-foot center David Robinson, an All-American at the Naval Academy and NBA Hall of Famer.

X = Navy's defensive player

JMU's Offense in Its February 9, 1985 Game versus Navy and "The Admiral"

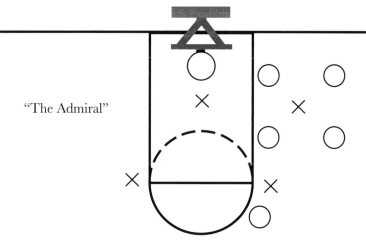

"The Admiral"

Designed by Morgan Pfaelzer for Coach Lou Campanelli. © George F. Thompson Publishing.

In the second game versus Navy in Harrisonburg, JMU reversed the ball to the side of the court opposite David Robinson ("The Admiral"). The Dukes took all shots from that side of the court, and, in doing so, JMU won the game, 65–62. Robinson still ended up grabbing 20 rebounds, but he had few blocked shots.

B = basketball   O = JMU's offensive player   X = Navy's defensive player its strings. Life had changed, and the Dukes stumbled home 14–14, not to mention 7–7 in the ECAC South, a second straight .500 conference record. Our hot-air balloon had deflated, and we floated back down to Earth.

But without making this a coaching copout, we were about as good as we could be, considering that we had only seven games where we held teams under sixty points and just once over our last eighteen games. My multiple defenses scheme clogged like the carburetor in an Edsel. I no longer had the players to make that motor hum.

One of my more recent recruits, sophomore forward Newman, led the Dukes in scoring with a 12.6 average. Senior forward and team captain Darrell Jackson, the last integral link from our NCAA Tournament run, added ten points a game, while Brent contributed nine per outing.

The season wasn't a total loss. We did have some feel-good wins, beating Old Dominion, 80–68, and rallying from a thirteen-point deficit with 11:40 left to beat Virginia Commonwealth, 66–65, at a time when VCU was nationally ranked. The "Zoo" felt really electric during those two home wins.

After Navy drilled us, 79–65, a game in which David Robinson blocked ten shots, we got the Middies on our court, looking for revenge. How could I nullify Robinson? Well, he blocked those ten shots on one side of the basket. So I swung our offense over to the other side of the court, away from "The Admiral," in order to anchor his presence. And it worked as we won, 65–62. Navy went on to win the ECAC championship after we lost to William & Mary, 68–61, in the first round of the tournament in Richmond.

I hadn't a clue at that moment that my coaching career at James Madison University was about to end following thirteen non-losing seasons. But what kept playing in my mind was this recurring thought: "Maybe I need to fall in love again." With the game of basketball, I meant.

I realized that I needed to make a move. It was time. Dean Ehlers and Dr. Carrier sensed my restlessness, and I didn't want to cause them any unnecessary angst. They had given me an opportunity to make a name for myself; I owed them so much. The last thing I wanted was to lessen their confidence in me, or to disappoint them, or to lose our close friendship.

I had a few more years left on my JMU contract, and I never felt threatened by either man. Regardless of when I left, it would be painful and all because of the deep respect I felt for those two men. The bottom line, however, was that I coveted a new challenge.

Coaches don't always get that choice; athletic directors often make that choice for them, by firing them. Coaches are better off in making that choice for themselves, by leaving on their own terms. Though it sounds hokey, if you stay too long at the fair, you'll eat too much cotton candy, and you'll get a tummy ache. You get the point.

I didn't want to be a mediocre coach. We'd fallen to 14–14, and I was staring mediocrity in the face. It's only natural that Dean and Dr. Carrier wanted to get back to the NCAA Tournament. They had added money and scholarships into the program, and I wanted to see them reap the rewards.

I felt frustrated, a feeling I disliked intensely. Gone was that buzz we had on campus when everybody was excited about March Madness. Two years had passed without that same buzz. Even Dawn said, "Maybe it is time for you to leave." She added that a change of scenery might be good for me.

Something else was working against me. I was hearing through the grapevine that opposing coaches were telling recruits, "You don't want to go to James Madison. Their coach isn't going to be there much longer."

Recruiting is nasty; lies are spread like feed. Coaches will resort to *anything* to win over a kid. But I also had to be honest about my situation.

A mother of a kid we were recruiting in North Carolina asked me point blank: "Is it true that you won't be at JMU much longer?" I didn't know. "Coaches come and go," I told her. "You have to pick a university based on its own merit. I've been here thirteen years; I could be here another thirteen years."

Or not. I didn't know myself if I would be leaving. At the time she asked me, I had no other promising opportunities. That same kid decided on James Madison, but, after I did resign, he transferred to UNC-Charlotte.

If I were to leave JMU, it had to be with no regrets. I had stayed there thirteen years, an uncommonly long time for one coach in one place. Some coaches keep the Bekins moving company's phone number in their back pocket. I had given JMU everything I had for those thirteen years—the best thirteen-year run the Dukes may ever have in basketball. My teams played in five NCAA Tournaments, twice in Division II. Since I left some thirty years ago, JMU has made only two men's NCAA Division I Tournament appearances, the last time in 2013.

A coach's competiveness is like that wolf in the parable—a wolf that keeps stalking you, insisting that you need another challenge. It's really all about soul-searching. Do you go, or do you stay? And, if you stay or if you go, is either decision the right decision? The wolf keeps after you.

Look at my good buddy, Rollie Massimino. He left Villanova for UNLV. I asked him why he would leave a small Catholic school, where he won a national championship, and go to a sprawling place where he'd be dealing with a totally different kind of player and environment? Maybe Rollie needed another challenge, too. The same wolf might have been stalking him. So he took the UNLV job. Did it work out? He told me he loved the weather. But he only stayed two years. Perhaps that wolf was a werewolf.

All the coaches attend the Final Four, which was in Lexington, Kentucky, in 1985. And wouldn't you know it? There was Rollie with his Villanova Wildcats, joining Memphis State, St. John's, and Georgetown—three Big East schools and Memphis State. I had to be there for my good buddy.

That same weekend, I met Dave Maggard, the athletic director at the University of California's Berkeley campus. He interviewed me, then asked if I'd be interested in coming out for a visit. I accepted his invite. I didn't know much about Cal, other than it had planted the seeds of campus unrest nationally during the 1960s and that the renowned Pete Newell had coached basketball there. His book was one of the first two books I read on basketball techniques, along with Ed Jucker's of Cincinnati.

Villanova then beat "The Beast of the East," Georgetown, in that historic upset. Unbeknownst to me, three hours before that title game, Rollie was on the phone with Dave Maggard, recommending me for the Cal job. The biggest moment of Rollie's coaching life, and he was looking out for me. What a friend!

Dawn thought California sounded great, with its beautiful scenery and the warm weather. We wouldn't have to bring our snow shovel, that's for sure. Maggard told me he was looking for a "tough, hard-nosed coach from the East who could teach defense." Cal won the NCAA championship in 1959, lost to Ohio State in the 1960 title game, and hadn't made a postseason appearance since, even in the NIT, in twenty-five years. Maggard sounded desperate.

The Pacific-10 was a prestigious conference. UCLA was the most dominant team in NCAA basketball history, then with ten national championships. This was the very challenge I needed, to take on UCLA.

I've held onto this relevant quote over the years:

"Challenge! Every man has within him the ability to do great things. His touchstone is challenge. No matter what his field of endeavor, a man must measure himself against the demands of his world, to rise to the challenge . . . ultimately. This is the reason men build bridges, climb mountains, and do a thousand other things that manifest personal achievement and satisfaction."

After visiting the Berkeley campus, I returned to Harrisonburg, newly inspired. I weighed my decision for a week, then accepted Cal's offer. The hard part was saying good-bye to Dean Ehlers and Dr. Carrier. I knew I would break their hearts. But, at the same time, I wanted this new opportunity, so that balanced things out. I had given them my very best; I never do anything half-assed. So I couldn't feel guilty about leaving.

I went up to Dr. Carrier's office with my heart in my hand. I told him I needed a new coaching challenge and that Cal hadn't won in a very long time. But, first, I visited with Dean to inform him of my decision. Dean then told Dave Maggard, "Lou will win for you." The same words that my father said to Dr. Carrier thirteen years before.

I know Dean and Dr. Carrier understood that it's difficult for a mid-major to stay up there with the regal likes of North Carolina, Duke, Kentucky, and Kansas. After meeting with these two great men, I gathered my JMU players and told them why I had to go. There were mixed emotions, obviously.

There wasn't anything left to hold me in the East. My parents had passed away while I was at Madison. My kids were excited by the move. They pictured swimming pools and the Pacific Ocean. A Cal alumnus already had offered us his place at Lake Tahoe. Dr. Tom Davis, the Stanford coach and a nice man, offered Kyle a scholarship to Stanford's summer basketball camp.

Flying out west, I told Kyle: "No skateboarding in California—you're a basketball player. And no eating sprouts—you're Italian." I don't know why I said that but Kyle remembers. And he's never eaten sprouts in front of me.

Dr. Carrier, Dean Ehlers, and I have a bond that will be eternal, whether I live on the East Coast or West Coast. That's why cutting ties at James Madison University proved difficult for them and for me.

Just how strong were those ties? Dr. Carrier attempted to re-hire me after I got to Cal. John Thurston, my assistant, replaced me as JMU's coach. He was 5–23 his first year and left after a few years. That's when Dr. Carrier tried to lure me back. Taking a chance that I was unhappy at Cal, he phoned. I assured him that I was happy and couldn't leave, because I was building a program to get to the NCAA Tournament, just like we did at JMU.

Later on, Dean called to see if I would bring my Cal team to JMU for a game. I told him I couldn't do that; it would be too tough on my emotions. I told him that I would come back to campus, perhaps for a summertime visit.

I have come back many times, for Homecoming and for the dedication of the Buddy Mills Team Room at the Convocation Center. I returned, also, for my induction into the James Madison University Athletic Hall of Fame in 1999, being honored for my 238–118 (.669) record and those five appearance in the NCAA tournament.

Someone once said: "No one can cheat you out of ultimate success but yourself." I didn't cheat myself at JMU, and I didn't cheat JMU.

I won't ever forget my Dukes. I pushed them, and they responded. I made them successful, and they made me successful. We owed one another a great deal. They all graduated, and most of them led successful lives. I wanted them to be something more than a team—more like a family that depended on one another and enjoyed one another.

Patti Przybocki Martin was our team manager. She's now married with three children and living in Georgia. She e-mailed me recently with memories of her time with JMU basketball.

"There are a few sayings that I remember from Coach," she wrote, "that I even use with my own children every now and then. I remember Coach saying that a person is really lucky if he or she could call five people their true friends. That is so true. I would be hard-pressed to find five true friends like that in my life today.

"Coach was all about respect, treating yourself and others around you with respect. If the team was eating breakfast at a hotel and some of the players looked like they had just rolled out of bed, Coach would say, 'At the least, you can wash your face and comb your hair before you come down to join the team.' I took this to heart . . . honestly, everybody can wash their face and comb their hair before they start the day.

"I remember one time at practice, none of the players was getting the drill right. Coach looked up and said, mostly to himself but loud enough for everyone to hear, 'Why did I ever choose a career that depends on teenagers?' He pulled both hands to his head and sort of fell to the floor. That was funny, but maybe you had to be there.

"When Coach interviewed me to become manager, he said there would be no dating the players. I was thinking, 'Of course!' I became the head manager. My responsibilities were to have all the supplies ready for practice. I was allowed to register early with the players to make sure my classes weren't scheduled during our practice hours.

"One of Coach's game-day habits was that he would nervously scrape the skin off the side tips of his fingers. That must have hurt. For Coach, I always had several sticks of chewing gum at the ready. I took unofficial stats during the first half and had them ready for use during Coach's halftime talk.

"Coach became like a father figure to me. He always asked about my parents and how they were doing, even before he met them. Coach has always been a very thoughtful and sincere person.

"And Mrs. Campanelli was/is the most supportive, friendly, and gentle person I've ever known. She was always busy with something for the family and always ready with a laugh or smile. Kyle, Brooke, and Racelle were wonderful kids, and I baby-sat them on a couple of occasions. Now they're grown up, and we still exchange Christmas cards."

Patti also recalled that my assistant, Bill Leatherman, had this tradition: He had to make a hook shot from half-court at each facility in which we played, and he was always successful. Before one game, he predicted to Patti that the Dukes would win by eleven points, and we won by that exact margin.

I'm sorry that Bill had run out of eligibility. I could have used his hook shot at JMU my last two seasons there.

CHAPTER 16
Making New Believers

After moving to Cal in the spring of 1985, officially as the Golden Bears' new basketball coach, I took a more serious look around. I noticed that the landmark bell-tower on campus, the Campanile, had a familiar ring. I told Dave Maggard, "We haven't won any games yet, and you've named the tower after me. What's going on?"

Dave was confused, but he got a chuckle when I explained that campanile, in Italian, is campanello. The "bell." Campanello. Campanelli. Close enough.

Now would that bell ring for Cal and for me? I needed to make that happen and quickly. Cal's basketball program had the bell sound of a thud.

When I looked at Cal's campus, it was very attractive—woodsy and set back against the rolling hills of Strawberry Canyon. But, when I checked out Harmon Gym, where the Bears played, it was an eyesore.

Dave had been reluctant to show me Harmon on my previous trip, fearing, I guess, that I might turn down the job right then. Who built that gymnasium, anyway, Julius Caesar?

"It needs a lot of work," Dave said before I stepped inside.

"How much?" I asked, now worried.

"It's very outdated," he replied.

He wasn't kidding. I walked onto the court for the first time as Dave stood, nervously, off to the side. But I loved the gym's coziness; the seats came right out to the court. I turned to Dave and said, "I can make this place a pit, a place that teams won't like to come into."

And he said, somewhat relieved, "I'm glad you feel like that."

Painted lines were all over the court, serving various Cal sports. Sandbags, of all things, raised and lowered the basketball hoops; it had been that way since the gym opened in 1933. I told Dave the sandbags and those extra lines had to go, and he agreed to eliminate them. He then proceeded to improve the gymnasium's lighting along with the basketball offices.

Harmon was the Pac-10's most outdated gym. Only the success of Cal basketball, I figured, would turn Harmon into a recruiting advantage. I couldn't show recruits a sandbag or a "gym." So I renamed it Harmon Arena.

205

Dave Maggard reminded me so much of Dean Ehlers: Good men who kept their word and were supportive of me as a coach. But Cal's president when I got there, Ira Michael Heyman, was nothing like Dr. Carrier. Heyman didn't attend many games, let alone visit the locker room after games. Maybe, though, that was a good thing.

"I don't care if Heyman doesn't help us," I told Dave, "as long as he doesn't hurt us."

I was unaware of "The Streak"—Cal hadn't beaten UCLA in twenty-six years or fifty-two consecutive games—until I held my first Berkeley press conference at the Faculty Club on campus. I told the press I expected to win, that I was used to winning. We had been to the NCAA tournament five times at James Madison, and that's where I wanted to take the Cal program. And we needed to fill up Harmon Arena every game, like at JMU, to give us an advantage.

Then someone in the back of the room asked about The Streak.

After Maggard explained it to me, I announced, "We'll beat their ass the first time we play them." The place erupted, and the press must have loved my bravado. Later, Dave said, "Gee, Lou, you really went out on a limb there." I said, "What the hell did you hire me for? Of course, I expect to beat them. You have to have expectations." Then Dave felt good about it.

College basketball analyst Billy Packer told me that the fifty-two-game losing streak was, at that time, the longest losing streak in college basketball history between two rivals. And since Cal and UCLA belonged to the same University of California system, I naturally expected my statement to wind up on the locker room wall at the University of California, Los Angeles. What did I care? I said what was in my heart, and I believed it. Now I had to convince my players that they were good enough to beat UCLA.

I called a team meeting and said, "We expect to win. Mediocrity is excellent in the eyes of mediocre people, and we don't want to be mediocre. You've had enough of mediocrity. We're striving for excellence."

I wasn't exactly short on talent. I inherited two solid big men in Dave Butler and Leonard Taylor, both of whom would play professionally overseas—Butler as a Rhodes Scholar. And I had two exciting point guards in Kevin Johnson and Chris Washington, though there was friction between them. I removed that friction by making Kevin my point guard and Chris my shooting guard, though Chris felt I had switched the wrong man.

As my assistants, I brought along two JMU connections—Sherman Dillard from the Maryland staff and Ernie Nestor from Wake Forest. Ernie had coached Sherman in high school, so it was like reuniting a family. I kept Derek Allister from the previous Cal staff.

I didn't know how soon I would need to lean on Derek, but it happened the first day of fall conditioning, when the basketball team started a six-days-a-week training program of lifting weights and running. At the time, Ernie and I were on a recruiting trip in Boise, Idaho. I called back to see how training was going, and Derek said everyone's there but Kevin Johnson. I asked, "Where's Kevin?" Derek said he could see him through the window at Harmon, on the baseball diamond, playing shortstop.

I was furious. I told myself, "He's going to test me. He's strong-willed, but so am I." I told Derek, "Put down the phone, run down the Harmon steps, run over to the bleachers, leap over the dugout wall, go out to shortstop, and get him up in the office—right now. I'm going to hold."

Five minutes later, K. J.'s on the phone. "Hey, Coach," he said, casually. "How's recruiting?" I said, "What are you doing?" K. J. said, "Coach (Bob) Milano said I could play baseball." And I said, "Oh, really. Your teammates are up in the gym starting a conditioning program, learning what it takes to win. You're on a basketball scholarship, and you're playing baseball? That's not going to fly. Meet me in the office tomorrow at 3 p.m. In the meantime, decide whether you want to play basketball or baseball. Maybe coach Milano will put you on a baseball scholarship."

At 3 p.m. the next day, K. J. entered the office. I asked him point blank, "What's your decision?" He said, "I want to play basketball." I said, "Well, you don't miss pre-season conditioning." Then I went to the baseball office and confronted the coach. I told him, "You can't pull that kind of crap, letting a kid do whatever he wants, when he's on a basketball scholarship. Maybe that's why Cal's been losing all these years."

I had no problems with K. J. after I laid down the law; he never missed another pre-season workout. But we all needed to be on the same page if we expected to win. I wanted everyone to be in top shape when we started practice October 15. I expected them to achieve in the classroom, too. And K. J. would graduate from Cal, just like he promised his grandmother.

K. J. was a special player; I saw that on tape. I didn't have anyone like him at JMU. You couldn't miss his tremendous athletic ability. He'd take an outlet pass and be down at the end of the court in no time. I told K. J., "You can be an NBA point guard, but you've got to give up the ball to an open teammate." That had been a sore point on the team, I was informed.

"And K. J.," I added, "the three-point shot is coming into effect next year. So develop your three-point shot. Sherman can help you; he's a 2,000-point scorer. If you shoot the three, pass the ball, and learn to play defense, your potential is unlimited."

He bought into what I was saying. A year later, K. J. and Reggie Miller of UCLA were the two best three-point shooters in the conference. K. J. was the seventh player taken in the 1987 NBA draft. He became a three-time all-star, had his number (11) retired at Cal, and he's now a two-term mayor of Sacramento, in the state capital. Before that, he started St. HOPE, an after-school program in the Sacramento area. As mayor, he saved the NBA franchise for Sacramento when it appeared the Kings were skipping town. And, when the NBA punished Los Angeles Clippers owner Donald Sterling for making racist remarks in 2014, there was K. J. acting as a spokesman for the NBA Players Association, calling for the severest penalties on Sterling, which then were enacted by new NBA Commissioner Adam Silver.

K. J. is a natural leader, and he always was articulate. Here's something I learned recently from Jon Wheeler, K. J.'s teammate at Cal. Wheeler and David Butler watched K. J. mixing easily with some Cal students back in 1987. David said to Jon, "K. J.'s going to be Governor of California someday." When Wheeler told me that story, I said, "I wouldn't doubt it."

K. J. thanked me later for developing him as a basketball player, but he said that I was "too hard" on him. I told him, "If I hadn't been hard, K. J., you wouldn't be where you're at. You had to be challenged and pushed."

Before that first season at Cal, Sherman, Ernie, and I checked out the six power conferences in the country, and we couldn't find one school from any of those conferences that hadn't, at least, made the NIT—except for Cal—in twenty-five years. That's what I was dealing with in 1985.

From the very start, Dawn noticed that I was coaching with more "urgency" than at James Madison. Well, Cal was a tougher job than at JMU. The difference? JMU was my baby; I raised it, made into what I wanted. But Cal had forgotten how to win. Its fans, unlike at JMU, didn't even know how to cheer. Early in my first season at Harmon, I stood up and yelled at the fans, "Cheer or go home. This isn't an opera." I needed to light a fire. After that, they started getting involved.

So here comes UCLA, after I had predicted that we would end The Streak. I saw UCLA on film and told my team, "We're better." They had Miller and Pooh Richardson, but I truly believed we were the stronger team.

Sports Illustrated phoned before the game, and the reporter said, "Coach, if you knock them off, we'll give you a two-page spread." My old friends, the Three Amigos, flew out for the game. Dawn decided that I should wear my black velour sport coat; she considered it lucky, because I wore it at JMU when we beat Old Dominion, right after we were called the "Hapless Dukes." ABC-TV wanted to mic my pre-game speech at Harmon, which I agreed to do, because we needed all the publicity we could get.

We set up a trapping defense that worked that day, but we couldn't stop Reggie Miller. He hit some deep shots from twenty-eight feet. UCLA was up six points with nine minutes left. I called a time-out and said, "I'm not interested in moral victories. You guys have done that before. Play to win."

Harmon was electric that day; the Electric Zoo without the guitar. Cal's Straw Hat Band—a college band unlike any other—had the crowd going, like it was the Final Four. This was our moment, now we had to seize it.

Right after the time-out, Chris Washington stole the ball and scored, and that's when we broke their momentum. We pulled ahead and won, 75–67. Washington had twenty-two points. We had ended The Streak, just as I predicted.

After the post-game interviews, I called Ernie and Sherman into my office, just the three of us. We toasted the win with champagne. I told them the day before that we would win the game; I believed it more than they did. We drank out of our glasses, and I poured the rest of the champagne over our heads. I told them that I couldn't have done this without them, and let's remember this moment for the rest of our lives. We were all in tears.

Making it even more memorable, I heard the Straw Hat Band playing. I looked inside Harmon and 2,000 people still were there, singing and danc-ing—two and a half hours after the game. Moved beyond words, I drove to Dave Maggard's house before heading home, where the Three Amigos waited for me, wanting to re-live every play in the game. It was just a special day.

Not only did I have to change Cal's basketball outlook, I had to change Cal's image. On a trip south to play UCLA and USC, we stayed at a Marriott in Marina

Del Rey. As the bus pulled into the hotel lot, I saw the marquee: "The Marriott Welcomes the Cal State Berkeley Basketball Team."

I was irate. "Stop the bus," I ordered the driver, who then hit the brakes. I told the team manager, Ron Tiongco, "You go inside and tell them to put the 'University of California Basketball Team' on that marquee in five minutes or we're going to check into someplace else." I could hear the players giggling on the bus. Ron went into the hotel, and people came running out in less than five minutes with a ladder, and they put the correct lettering on the marquee, as the players cheered and clapped.

I wasn't an alumnus of the University of California, just as I wasn't an alumnus of James Madison University, but I wasn't going to stand for either school to be referred to incorrectly. At Oregon State, the public address announcer said, "And now the starting lineups for California Berkeley . . ." I let him know about that, too, telling him, "In the Pac-10, we are the University of California or Cal, and I won't accept anything less than that." He got the point. The University of California is among the world's greatest academic institutions, and it should be recognized properly.

JM Who? Cal State Berkeley Who? It's the same thing—disrespect.

My first Cal team finished 19–10 and made it to the NIT, losing our first-round game to Loyola Marymount, 80–75, after playing poorly. The next year, with Kevin Johnson and Chris Washington as seniors, we finished 20–15 and were invited back to the NIT. We beat Cal State-Fullerton, 72–68, and Oregon State, 65–62, to advance to the third round.

I hoped the next NIT game would be at Cal. But an American Indian festival had been scheduled inside Harmon that same week. I was furious. How could Cal have scheduled away that arena time? Didn't Cal think we would, at least, make the NIT? That's the losing attitude I faced in Berkeley, the very same attitude I was still trying to change.

So we had to fly to Little Rock, then take a bus to Pine Bluff, where we lost to Arkansas-Little Rock, 80–73. I know we would have won that game had it been played at Harmon, which would have put us into the NIT semifinals at Madison Square Garden in New York City.

After losing seven seniors, we fell to 9–20 my third year. But that wasn't my first letdown at Cal, because Jack Snead had re-entered my life.

I had forgotten about Snead, the kid in the orange tennis shoes whom I kicked off the Madison team bus after he dressed improperly for an away game, the same Snead who quit the team and then dropped out of school. Well, here I am in Berkeley, and so, it turned out, was Jack Snead.

When I first got to Cal, Sherman came back from lunch with a look of disbelief. "Coach, you're not going to believe who I just saw on the plaza: Jack Snead." I said, "Stop pulling my leg." "No, Coach, his hair is long and straggly," said Sherman, "and he's bent over a little bit, but it's him."

I had bumped into Snead at a Harrisonburg mall eight years after he left JMU. He said, "You didn't tell me that Buddy Mills passed away. I would have gone to his service." I said, "Jack, I didn't know where you were." He yelled at me, and I told him, "Get the hell out of here." I had no further contact with him until one day he came into my Cal office, when I wasn't there, and left me a note—a weird note.

He signed it, "Skull and crossbones." I called Dave Maggard, who said that skull and crossbones possibly meant "death." Dave called in the campus police, plus a handwriting expert, who read the note. I was told, "Protect yourself." I asked, "How?" I was advised, "Get a bulletproof vest."

A what? But, feeling unsafe, I did find a bulletproof vest to wear under my jacket around campus. Snead was instructed to stay 100 feet away from Harmon, a restriction he then violated. So I kept looking over my shoulder. Only the bulletproof vest proved cumbersome. After a while, I got tired of it, buried it in the trunk of my car, and forgot about it.

While I was away on a basketball trip, Dawn had a flat tire on the car. The guy who fixed it opened the trunk to get the spare tire and found the vest. He said to Dawn, "Hey, lady, does your husband rob banks?" I hadn't told her about the vest. I didn't want to frighten her. Well, I frightened her.

She's thinking, "Does my husband have a second life?" After I got home, I explained everything to her, and then it passed. I never heard from Jack Snead again. The whole thing had been so bizarre.

I had no idea what then happened to Snead until I received a newspaper obituary from Virginia, which said he passed away, at fifty-two, in Oakland on September 5, 2006. I don't know from what, but he died "peacefully" and was buried in Lovingston, Virginia.

The obit said further that Snead, son of an Army brigadier general, showed early talent as a short-story writer and caricaturist. After leaving Madison, he transferred to the University of Arizona, then moved to Berkeley in 1983, two years before I arrived. I was worried that he followed me there. He was active with the Berkeley Lutheran Church, including a Bible group, and he worked with the needy. He coached basketball (I'm not sure in what capacity), and he was a serious student of World War II, including D-Day details. Health and injury issues restricted his mobility.

The obit told me more about him than I ever knew. Jack Snead represented a weird episode in my life, divided into two phases. Oh, yes, I gave the bulletproof vest back to the authorities.

After experiencing that losing record my third year at Cal—my first non-winning season as a college coach in sixteen years—we recovered with a 20–13 record in 1988–1989. Leonard Taylor, our dominant big man, returned that season after missing a year with spinal stenosis. He kept us in games. We received a third NIT invitation and rolled over Hawaii, 73–57, before losing a tight one to Connecticut, 73–72, after leading most of the way.

I had promised Dave Maggard, the Cal alumni, and the media that I would lead the Bears to the NCAA Tournament, and that's what happened my fifth year. We were 22–10, my best season in Berkeley. I deadpanned it again on Selection Sunday, knowing in advance that we had made the Big Dance.

I joined my team for the announcement at the school's football facility, Memorial Stadium. It was pandemonium and a milestone—Cal's first NCAA tournament showing in thirty years or since Pete Newell's Bears lost to Ohio State, 80–60, in the 1960 title game after edging West Virginia, 72–71, for the national championship the year before.

The players were thrilled and deservedly so. We had a 7–2 road record in conference play. We came from sixteen down to beat Stanford and its star center, Adam Keefe. Our center, Brian Hendrick, hit the shot to win the game. Those Bears were a fun bunch to coach.

So which team did we draw in the first round but Bobby Knight and his Indiana Hoosiers, which meant we had to play smart and take care of the ball. We didn't have enough depth to play man-to-man that season. So we played more zone, which was our strategy against Indiana.

I told our kids beforehand, just like I told my kids at JMU, that you don't want to be one and done. It's important to win your first-round game. And we beat the Hoosiers, 65–63, in Hartford, Connecticut, nearly 3,000 miles away from home. We had few fans there, but my kids were strong-willed. Keith Smith, our best player that season, hit two free throws with three seconds left, enabling us to advance. Roy Fisher and Hendricks also played standout ball that game and, really, throughout the season.

Our second-round opponent was Connecticut. For the third time as a coach, I played a second-round NCAA Tournament game against a team in its own state, after twice facing North Carolina in North Carolina. UConn, which played ten games at the Hartford Civic Center that season, beat us handily, 74–54. It was like a home game for them. The NCAA got away with that crap in those days. UConn was a good team, but still . . .

Two losing seasons ensued at Cal, 13–15 and 10–18. But I was dealing with something far more crucial—nearly losing my wife.

In 1988, my son, Kyle, came up from Santa Rosa Junior College, where he was playing basketball, to watch our Midnight Madness on October 15, the official start of fall practice. That was the night I actually suited up. My idea was to take the first charge of the season. And so, after I participated in pre-game layups, Keith Smith ran—smack!—over me after the opening tip. I fell back on my butt, and then I came out of the game.

After the game, Kyle drove Dawn home. I was two minutes behind. Then catastrophe struck. A drunk in a truck ran a red light and plowed broadside into them on the passenger's side, where Dawn was sitting. The door caved in, so Dawn was pinned in. A Cal alumnus got there immediately and phoned for help. I arrived, spoke to the drunk, and ordered him not to step out of that truck until the fire department came. I might have threatened to strangle him.

Kyle wasn't injured, luckily, but the firemen needed the "Jaws of Life" to pry open Dawn's door and free her. It was a nightmare. They took her to Highland Hospital in Oakland. They did all these x-rays, and her pelvis was shattered into thirty pieces. I stayed there all night, distraught.

She was transferred to Alta Bates Hospital in Berkeley and put into traction. Dr. John Debenham, Cal's team orthopedist, couldn't find a local surgeon who would take Dawn's case; it was that critical. He recommended Dr. Michael Chapman at the University of California in Davis. "He's the best," Dr. Debenham told me.

The surgery lasted six hours. I found a church and prayed: "Dear God, let her live, let her walk, let her have a normal life. She has three kids." Dr. Chapman came out of the recovery room, looking exhausted. "I think we nailed it," he said. "Thirty screws and four L brackets are holding the pelvis together; Dawn is bone on bone. A year from now, after the pelvis has stabilized, she's going to need a hip replacement."

I told the doctor, "God bless you."

Dawn was in various hospitals for nine and a half weeks. She couldn't eat, and her weight went down to nothing. It was horrible. I don't know how she got through it. I don't know how I got through coaching. I told my staff to take over; I told the players I'll be back when I'm able to function. I'd visit Dawn in the hospital, and I'd cry in the parking lot. I didn't want to cry in front of her.

The drunk driver, who was uninsured, went to jail for six months.

I had befriended Tommy Lasorda, the manager of the Los Angeles Dodgers, after I came west. It's an Italian thing. He called Dawn in the hospital and told her, "I'm going to take you dancing when you feel better." What a sweet man. We played Villanova at our place that season, and we won a close game. Rollie took the time to go see Dawn.

She's lucky she wasn't paralyzed. She is so tough that I nicknamed her "Nails." Christmas is very important to Dawn. From her hospital bed, she arranged for gifts to be there for her family on Christmas Day. She has improved physically through exercise classes, but, reluctantly, she had to give up tennis, which she loved playing. But what a comeback!

Kyle was devastated about the accident, but he made first team all-conference at Santa Rosa JC and then transferred to an NAIA school, Southern California College. After that didn't work out, he wanted to play for me at Cal. I tried to talk him out of it, but he came, I played him off the bench, and he did a good job. Let's be honest, what coaching father wouldn't like to coach his son?

Some fans saw that as nepotism. My brother, the Bear, came out to a game, and this one Cal alum really was on me the first half. The Bear said nothing, but when that alum got on Kyle in the second half, that did it. The Bear went up a few rows, grabbed the alum by the tie, and told him, "You can criticize the coach, but not my sister-in-law or nephew." Or else. The alum, scared out of his wits, didn't say another word. The Bear is some man.

My situation had changed by then at Cal. Dave Maggard left to become the athletic director at the University of Miami in Florida. I was fired seventeen games into the 1992–1993 season with a 10–7 record. A lot of speculation

Coach Lou, his son, Kyle, and Michael Jordan reunite in 1987 at a Nike Coaches Trip in Newport Beach, California. Photograph (signed by Michael Jordan) courtesy of Lou Campanelli.

followed about why I was let go, but Maggard wanted a tough, hard-nosed defensive coach, and that's what Cal got when it hired me.

I wasn't any different a coach at Cal than I had been at James Madison. But there was a big shift in the Cal administration. A new athletic director, Bob Bockrath, and a new chancellor, Chang-Lin Tien, came in with different agendas, and they decided to make a coaching change . . . abruptly.

Two weeks before I was fired, I was congratulated by those men and also by two of college basketball's coaching legends, John Wooden and Pete Newell. We had just beaten UCLA, 102–81, at UCLA. Wooden and Newell were at the game, seated side by side. I saw them afterwards, and Wooden said, "You know, Coach, this is the worst loss for the Bruins in the history of Pauley Pavilion." He would know that as "The Wizard of Westwood." Newell, the former Cal coach, naturally was pleased.

That victory was emotional for our team for another reason. Three nights before, we lost a one-point game at USC when Jerod Haase, our freshman guard, unfairly was called for an off-the-ball foul with one second left, enabling a Trojan to hit both ends of a bonus free-throw situation for the win.

After the game, at the hotel, we got a call that Jerod's father had died. I had to tell Jerod the bad news. I advised him to go home and be with his family in South Lake Tahoe. We would take him to the airport in the morning so he could fly home. I felt terrible for Jerod, a young man of strong character.

Both his parents were Cal grads, but, after he spoke with his mother, she told him that his father wouldn't have wanted him to miss his first UCLA game. So Jerod told me that he wanted to play this game for his dad. I had my assistant, Jeff Wulbrun, take him to dinner and to Venice Beach to try and lift his spirits. And Jerod—what heart!—contributed sixteen points to the victory. That game became therapeutic for him.

When I got back to Cal from that trip, Bockrath wrote me the following note: "Congratulations on a great win over UCLA, and you're doing a great job with a young team." Then Tien phoned to say, "Coach Campanelli, I saw the win over UCLA on television, and you're doing a great job with a young team." Two weeks later, they obviously felt differently, and I was let go. And, to think, the year before, I was offered the St. John's coaching job, to replace the great Lou Carnesecca. I turned it down. I didn't want to uproot my family and move across the country again.

Did I fail Cal? I graduated twenty-four of my twenty-eight players. I lifted its basketball program back to prominence. I ran a clean program. I accepted the challenge of taking the Cal job with three goals in mind.

The first goal was to beat UCLA the first time we played them and end the twenty-six-year, fifty-two-game losing streak, which we did, 75–67, in January 1986.

The second goal was to lift Cal out of basketball anonymity, which we did with three NIT appearances in my first four years.

The third goal was to return Cal to the NCAA Tournament after a thirty-year absence, which we did my fifth year, beating Indiana in a first-round game.

I delivered on all three goals, but I guess I stayed too long at the fair.

After I was dismissed, the only time in my life that I had been fired, I felt empty and also unappreciated for all I had done for Cal. At the same time, I felt for my family. I think this hit Dawn harder than anyone. She was angry for a long time. And, with my firing, Kyle left Cal and transferred.

I needed some place to grieve, and I decided to get as far away from Cal as possible. I thought of Hawaii. Then Ken Rawlings called. He's a Cal booster and owner of Otis Spunkmeyer cookies. Ken offered me his home in Carmel, to stay as long as I needed. So I went down there for two weeks. Dawn and the family came down for a day. Otherwise, I'd walk the beach in the morning, read a book, and take another walk later in the day.

One morning, I'm walking the beach, wearing a hooded sweatshirt, baseball cap, and glasses. Because I hadn't shaved since I got there, I was almost in disguise. I saw this couple coming toward me, walking their dog. As they passed by, the man said, "Coach, you got screwed."

How did he even recognize me? The couple kept right on walking, and so did I. But, even when you're grieving, there are surprise moments. On my last night in Carmel, I went over to the Mission Ranch, which Clint Eastwood owns, to have a drink. I met this nice couple from Ohio, who remembered James Madison beating Ohio State in the 1982 NCAA Tournament.

There's a piano bar at the Mission Ranch, and, at the end of the night, I was asked to sing. I started to beg off, but the next thing I know, I'm standing on the piano lady's bench, singing, "When Irish Eyes Are Smiling." And I'm Italian! As I'm singing, I'm laughing and crying, and having a good time for the first time in two weeks.

How do I explain those tears? Sometimes you cry when you're sad, sometimes you cry when you're happy. Maybe I washed the pain away, but I went to bed that night feeling better. Getting away those two weeks worked out well. I drove home, rolled up my sleeves, and said, "It's time to get back to work."

I did some advance scouting for the Portland Trail Blazers. Then I coached a year of pro ball in Japan through the recommendation of Pete Newell. I was offered $75,000, but I said I needed $100,000. And I got it, plus a $10,000 bonus later on for winning the championship. I coached in Japan eight months, with four days off to come home for Christmas. Dawn didn't accompany me overseas. On my off days in Tokyo, I volunteered to help coach boys and girls basketball at St. Mour's High School. Every job I've ever had, I put my heart into it, but that school kept me going mentally.

Then I did advance scouting for the Cleveland Cavaliers for three years. The first season, I had half the country, then the next two seasons I had the whole country as my territory. I once had nineteen games to scout in twenty days in twenty different cities. Advance scouting is the toughest job in the NBA because of the travel, which is why I gave it up.

After that, I was coordinator of basketball officiating for the Pacific-10 Conference for six years. If Pac-10 game officials were frightened to see me, a former coach, at various campus arenas, grading their performances, they needn't have been scared. I'm not revenge-minded.

This book, in fact, is the first time in twenty-two years that I've talked publicly about my firing at Cal. I could say a whole lot more, but for what purpose? I know who I am, and I like who I am. And what I've accomplished in coaching, and in life, is enough to make me sleep well at night.

I now volunteer at a Bay Area high school, working with young players, teaching them the game I love and the way I love it best—play hard, play together, play defense. Those three tenets I've used my entire coaching life. Do them consistently, and you have a chance to be successful.

Reflecting on my career, my mind often wanders back to Virginia and life in the Shenandoah Valley framed by the beauteous Alleghany and Blue Ridge mountains. That bucolic landscape reminds me of an American folk song written in 1882, a lovely piece that is so pertinent to my own life:

"Oh, Shenandoah,
I long to see you,
Away, you rolling river.
Oh, Shenandoah,
I long to see you,
Away, I'm bound away
'Cross the wide Missouri."

I've crossed that wide Missouri often, by flying over it or mentally picturing its scenic banks. The West Coast now is my permanent home, but the beautiful Shenandoah Valley always will have a meaningful place in my heart.

Mike Schikman (left), David Dupont, Coach Lou, Dan Ruland, Dean Ehlers, Linton Townes, Joe Pfahler, and Pat Dosh, were reunited in Carrier Library during Coach Lou's visit to JMU on January 25, 2014. The portrait of James Madison, the university's namesake and the fourth President of the United States, beckons above. Photograph courtesy of Lou Campanelli.

CONCLUSION:
Looking Back

Dave Newhouse

The roots of James Madison University basketball—the men who seeded it, tended to it, and watched it flower—gathered in a conference room at the Carrier Library, seated below two portraits of relevance: President James Madison, "The Father of the Constitution," and Dr. Ronald E. Carrier, the father of what became James Madison University.

Dean Ehlers, the athletic director during JMU's basketball emergence, was joined by Lou Campanelli, the coach who made it happen, and five of his players—Joe Pfahler, Pat Dosh, Linton Townes, David Dupont, and Dan Ruland—plus Mike Schikman, legendary "Voice of the Dukes" who called their games on local radio.

"Dr. Carrier was my Sunday school teacher in Memphis," noted Ehlers. "I coached at Memphis State, then retired to go with the Memphis city schools as a first-time athletic director. Our job was to integrate the schools, during the time that Dr. King was shot, in our community. We operated during this difficult period, sometimes by the seat of our pants.

"Then Gene Bartow, who replaced me as Memphis State's coach, said I needed to get back into college work. I told him that I was done when I left Memphis. But, as fate would have it, I had a note back at my office to call Dr. Ron Carrier, who then offered me the athletic directorship here at Madison. He talked about what he hoped Madison would become. He also told me that I would have a problem winning over the women, who had a strong sports program."

Ehlers smiled in reliving those distant memories.

"Our first football season," he said, "we recruited players out of the registration line. They not only didn't win a game, they didn't score. The scholarships for basketball came a year or two before I anticipated, but that's Dr. Carrier.

"I like to believe that we became competitive pretty quickly. Then we brought in you guys, five of the best basketball players we've ever had here. But, with all respect to Lou, I tried to hire four other guys first."

Group laughter ended the library-like mood in the room.

"I'm not going to take that personally," said a grinning Campanelli.

"This guy," said Ehlers, looking at Campanelli, "is one of the best coaches I've ever known. He played a style where I always felt that we were in the game and had a chance to win. He was always positive about what he believed in, that defense wins games. That's why we upset Georgetown and Ohio State in the NCAA Tournament. He was a plus for this university."

Pfahler recalled his recruiting trip to Madison College, believing the school was located in West Virginia. He made it to Harrisonburg on a balmy spring day and, on a whim, became Campanelli's first scholarship player.

"I didn't feel like a pioneer," Pfahler said. "I did think we would play a different style of ball than those 54–51 games. But they got us wins."

"Joe was the most basic fundamental point guard you ever saw play," noted Dosh. "He rarely went behind his back or through his legs. He never turned the ball over, and he was an unselfish assist man."

Dosh, a productive scorer, was a primary target of Pfahler's passes.

"I played at St. John's (High School) in Washington, DC, in as good a Catholic league as you will find," said Dosh. "I had a good senior year, with twenty-three points and ten rebounds a game. JMU saw me play eleven games before offering me a scholarship. Eleven games! I guess, at one point, the light went on with Coach. But the approach that appealed to me was doing something different, taking a program in its infancy and building it into something."

"I heard, when I came to the Valley," interjected Schikman, "that Pat Dosh was the single dirtiest player you've ever seen, grabbing shirts and shorts."

"I remember trying harder than everyone else," countered Dosh.

"And I remember Pat getting twenty-two rebounds against Austin Peay, a pretty athletic team," said Campanelli. "Typical of Pat, he always knew where the ball was going. He had that knack. Grabbing people? Incidental contact."

Pat Dosh is a JMU Sports Hall of Fame inductee. Not so incidental.

Townes's parents were high-school teachers. After his father turned to preaching, it was "ordained" that Linton would attend college. Campanelli gave him a scholarship, though he wasn't considered the best player at his high school.

"I was just happy to be here," said Townes. "(JMU) was advancing forward, which was great for me."

Ruland, in high school, was "undisciplined, a follower instead of a leader," he said. He attended Fork Union Academy—"the year that changed my life around"—before enrolling at James Madison, the one college that believed in him even while he was struggling.

"Every day of my life," he said, "I can't tell you how much it means to me to have been a part of this program, of this group of guys. We had the right chemistry. We had the right leaders. My four years at James Madison University were the best four years of my life."

There were affirming nods from others seated around him.

"I was a role player in high school, even though we won the state championship," said Dupont. "But I was the only one on the team who got a scholarship."

Ruland believes those JMU Dukes were "a team of role players, with the one exception, Linton, who was a skilled player."

"I always could depend on them," said Townes. "I could close my eyes and pass the ball, and I knew David would be there."

"There were no egos on the team," Campanelli said. "You all came to college with modest expectations, which made you work hard and made you successful. And your intelligence is why we could play these different defenses."

Schikman, JMU's iconic play-by-man from 1981 until his retirement in 2014, paid Townes the ultimate compliment. "There's no better shooter in this school's history than that man there," Schikman said. "He had the purest shot."

Schikman, who didn't see Sherman Dillard or Steve Stielper play, wasn't through complimenting. "These guys," he said of Townes, Ruland, and Dupont, "played beautiful basketball. Every possession was important. Their switching defenses stunned people. I knew they were going to beat Ohio State in the NCAAs when I saw Eldon Miller, the Buckeyes' coach, trying to teach his team the 2–3 zone the day before they played JMU."

"We had a commitment to play team defense," said Ruland. "There was no way alone I could have stopped Ralph Sampson. I'm not athletically capable of doing that. But we were committed to helping each other on defense. I know teams hated playing us for that reason alone."

"And they were a great cast of characters," added Schikman. "David Dupont had more ads in *The Breeze* campus newspaper about his legs. Guys, remember: 'Nothing hotter than David Dupont's legs?' Charles Fisher was a 6-foot-2 center in high school. Coach made him into a point guard."

The five players in the room were more relaxed in discussing their head coach in front of him years later, when he no longer could discipline them by making them run extra laps after practice.

"He was a dictator but a good one," Pfahler said.

"When he imposed discipline," Schikman, who also announced JMU football, recalled, "you kids could handle it. Today, unfortunately, kids don't get that. The game has changed. I knew all of your parents. Today, we have more single families, more single moms. You can't do the same things in basketball and football that you did even ten years ago. That's because we have a softer culture. All our dads taught us to get up in the morning, go to work, don't complain. We don't have that today. Coach Camp learned from Rollie Massimino."

"It wasn't always hunky-dory," said Townes. "We have a good feeling now, but Coach was tough. Every day, we were tired. But we were working hard for a purpose, so you'd have to say he was fair."

"Here's what he was like," Dosh pointed out. "He made you give him everything you've got and then some. If you've done that, you have nothing to be concerned about. If you don't, it's not going to be a good relationship."

"He made the players closer," added Townes, "because we all knew what we were going through together. I played seventeen years of pro ball. I would feel sorry for young guys coming through who didn't have the discipline and fundamentals that Coach taught me."

Those fundamentals and that discipline pulled JMU through against favored Ohio State and Georgetown in the NCAAs. All those defensive schemes made JMU more than a token opponent against two of North Carolina's most-gifted teams ever.

"We never felt that, because we were down, we couldn't catch up," said Dupont. "With the way we played—we just kept working—we were in games. We were better defensively than offensively, except for Linton."

"It was bend but never break," said Campanelli. "The players were so close that it was hard to get them apart. I can still visualize it."

"You guys were relentless," added Schikman. "I can't recall too many possessions you took off, whether it was against Luther Rice or Ohio State."

"We weren't intimidated," Townes said.

Campanelli then took the time to explain himself and his coaching philosophy in a language that, possibly, his players hadn't heard before. "I had an edge,"

Linton Townes and Coach Lou pose during Townes's visit to JMU's 1983 summer basketball camp after Townes's rookie season with the Portland Trailblazers. Photograph courtesy of Lou Campanelli.

Junior guard Derek Steele (5-foot-7) works his way around a West Virginia defender in the JMU win against the Mountaineers in their first-round game in the 1983 NCAA East Regional in Greensboro. Photograph courtesy of James Madison University Athletics.

he said. "Hopefully, that edge rubbed off on the players. If a coach doesn't demand, you're not going to get far. If you're not pushed or challenged, you're never going to reach your potential. If I didn't help you reach that potential, I would be cheating you."

Campanelli was challenged as well by Ehlers, who scheduled tough non-conference competition. The Dukes rose to that challenge, building a reputation as fearless underdogs.

"Looking back on my career, that's the one thing I was able to do here," said Ehlers, "by getting people to play us, knowing we had a good program that played by the rules and we were worthy. Hugh Durham, the Florida State coach at the time, said, 'We're not going to play you anymore.'"

Ehlers, Madison's athletic director for twenty-two years, built a program based on fairness. He didn't browbeat his coaches or hold them on a short leash.

"There's a winner and a loser, and you can't win every game," he said. "When you play good competition, you're not always going to win. And I knew that Lou coached as well when he won as when he lost."

The Electric Zoo came up.

"They talk about the 'Cameron Crazies,'" Schikman said of Duke University's rabid basketball fans. "We had the 'crazies' before they did. This place would get *insane*."

The two-point loss to North Carolina in the 1982 NCAA Tournament came up. "Dean Smith was God!" Ehlers exclaimed.

And, for one shining moment, Campanelli made Smith a pre-game prophet in what remains JMU's most famous basketball game, albeit a two-point loss to the evenutal national champion.

"I would say so," Schikman agreed. "The only thing that would compare in JMU sports was beating Virginia Tech in football in 2012. But basketball was much bigger than football on campus."

The broadcaster addressed the five players at the table.

"The one thing you guys did," he said, "was to put JMU on the map."

Sometimes, then, there is history couched in a 52–50 defeat.

"Even though we lost to North Carolina, we felt very, very proud," said Ruland.

"We represented the school probably as well as we could have," Dupont stressed.

"That's it," Ruland concurred.

Madison College's NCAA Division II Tournament Results

Year	Round	Opponent	Result
1976	Regional Semifinals	Old Dominion	L 77–86
	Regional 3rd Place Game	Morgan State	L 81–86

The Dukes have appeared in the NCAA Division II Tournament one time, under Coach Lou. Compiled by Mikki Soroczak for Coach Campanelli.

JMU's NCAA Division I Tournament Results

Year	Round	Opponent	Result
1981	First Round	Georgetown	W 61–55
	Second Round	Notre Dame	L 45–54
1982	First Round	Ohio State	W 55–48
	Second Round	North Carolina*	L 50–52
1983	First Round	West Virginia	W 57–50
	Second Round	North Carolina	L 49–68
1994	First Round	Florida	L 62–64
2013	First Round	Long Island	W 68–55
	Second Round	Indiana	L 62–83

*1982 National Champion

The Dukes have appeared in the NCAA Division I Tournament five times, three times (1981–1983) under Coach Lou. Compiled by Mikki Soroczak for Coach Campanelli.

"I want the school to have that same feeling now," Townes said, "to be just as successful as we were, because it was such a good feeling for us."

The wise sage at the far end of the table was heard from again.

"I think I read once," said Ehlers, "where John Wooden asked his players after practice, 'Can you go inside, look yourselves in the mirror, and say, I did the best that I could?' I think you people, after that North Carolina game, could go inside and say, 'Hey, we did the best that we could.' But I want you all to know that what you did here at JMU is appreciated by this old man, who's about to turn eighty-four. We came a long way, baby."

Campanelli, a pasta lover from New Jersey, had a confession to make: "I like grits. I still eat grits to this day. I make them myself."

His players weren't shocked. His coaching demeanor, after all, was gritty.

Dosh had a closing thought on this Sunday morning get-together of January 26, 2014—a roundtable only in spirit as the gabfest occurred at a rectangular table.

"I'm sitting back and thinking that what happened here at JMU is pretty unique," he said. "How did it happen? What is the road map for somebody else to take with this book? A lot of people will read it for different reasons. A lot of coaches across America may want to understand how you take a college program from nothing to this. How do you do it?

"What took place here starts at the top. You've got to have a president like Dr. Carrier, whose vision wasn't to see the school as it was but what it will be. And then you need people to get in line under that vision, like an athletic director with high integrity, who heeds the rules, who doesn't have any issues, and who steers the athletic program in the right direction."

The eloquent Dosh was just warming up. "Then you have to hire the right coaches," he said, "who are trying to make this vision real, coaches who can't get the four-star and five-star athletes. They've got to find these precious jewels that others have no interest in and see what they can become, to get everything you can get out of them, which Coach was able to do. And then you need the final piece—a community fan base that rallies around you. So you have this whole team, from the top down to the fan, all of these pieces falling together into place to make this whole thing happen. That's what happened here."

The final word, as it should have been, belonged to Coach Lou, without whom JMU's historic ascendance wouldn't have been remotely possible.

"I want to thank you guys for coming this weekend," said Campanelli, choking back tears. "I have such respect for Dean Ehlers, who was a great mentor. He's a superstar. I feel blessed that the Lord put me here. I came together with Dean and Dr. Carrier, and we delivered this program. Together with you players, we surpassed our wildest dreams. I love you guys."

"And Lou," said Ehlers, "I love you, man."

Then there were handshakes and hugs, for it was time to hit the road or catch a plane, as families were waiting elsewhere. But these men who are linked forever by their singular story are a family separate unto themselves.

JM Who? Lou Campanelli's Dukes knew exactly who they were.

AFTERWORD:
Coaching in America's Birthplace

I **never envisioned that I**, Louis Paul Campanelli, a pipefitter's son from Elizabeth, New Jersey, would become a part of United States history. A small part, granted, though U.S. history wasn't even my best subject in school. And here I was, working at a university named after a U.S. President who just happened to be the Father of the Constitution.

No other basketball coach at that time could make that claim. I was also coaching in, perhaps, the most historic of all fifty states. In basketball parlance, I was certainly flying high above the rim. My life had turned out perfect, landing a dream job in the very state that laid the groundwork for the good ol' USA. Yes, Virginia, you are the impetus behind the United States of America.

Usually asleep in history class, I wasn't aware until I came to JMU that Virginia actually planted the seeds that grew this nation, both politically and geographically, and that it is the Mother of U.S. Presidents. Four of the first five Presidents were Virginians: George Washington, Thomas Jefferson, James Madison, and James Monroe. Only John Adams (Massachusetts) interrupted that run. Virginia can claim four other natives who became President: William Henry Harrison, John Tyler, Zachary Taylor, and Woodrow Wilson. That's eight U.S. Presidents in your U.S. presidential scorebook.

I soon learned that the first permanent English settlement in America occurred in Virginia at Jamestown in 1607, and that, twelve years later, the folks in Jamestown established America's first representative legislature, the House of Burgesses. Virginia was just warming up in terms of historic happenings.

I soon learned a great deal about the French and Indian Wars fought in greater Virginia and that some of the fiercest fighting during the Revolutionary War and Civil War took place in Virginia. Those last two wars *ended* in Virginia, when Lord Cornwall surrendered to General George Washington on October 19, 1781, after the Battle of Yorktown, and Commanding General Robert E. Lee of the Confederacy surrendered to Commanding General Ulysses S. Grant of the Union in the McLean House in the village of Appomattox Court House on April 9, 1865. My history knowledge was improving.

If not for Virginia, there would be no West Virginia or Kentucky, as pieces of the original Commonwealth were broken off to form those two states. And Virginians, in hindsight, showed early on that it is possible for the old and new among us to coexist when tobacco-growing colonist John Rolfe married Indian maiden Pocahontas in 1614, bringing temporary peace to an unsettled situation between the native Indians and the newly arrived foreign colonists.

How did Virginia get its name? From Queen Elizabeth I of England, the *virgin* queen. Who suggested the name? Supposedly, Sir Walter Raleigh in 1584, the same year Queen Elizabeth gave him her permission to colonize the Virginia region. See how it all came together?

Virginia also is known as Old Dominion. No wonder that name haunted me, and it's been around since Shakespeare was writing sonnets. Speaking of literature and higher learning, William & Mary College, founded in Williamsburg in 1693, is our nation's second oldest college—after Harvard in 1636—in addition to being a hoops headache for this coach.

One of the greatest patriotic speeches in American history was given March 23, 1775, at St. John's Church in Richmond by Patrick Henry, who made this famous plea for the colonial cause: "Is life so dear or peace so sweet as to be purchased at the price of chains and slavery? Forbid it, Almighty God! I know not what course others might take, but as for me, *give me liberty or give me death.*" Some coaches might take that speech to mean the difference between winning and losing.

James Madison, Thomas Jefferson, and other Virginians led the fight to create the Constitution of the United States. Madison called the shots, like a head coach, thereby receiving his fatherly distinction. But it was his good buddy, Jefferson, who wrote the Declaration of Independence in 1776 and the Virginia Statute for Religious Freedom in 1788.

Madison, Jefferson, and Monroe formed the "Virginia Dynasty"; all three strengthened this nation and added new territory to it during their presidencies. Another Virginian, John Marshall, served as Chief Justice of the United States from 1801 to 1835, thus becoming America's first referee.

Madison was our country's fourth President, immediately after Jefferson, and he served two terms, from 1809 to 1817—or forty-four years before basketball creator James Naismith was born. I link those two, Madison and Naismith, both important men in my life.

Madison was born in Port Conway, Virginia, the eldest of twelve children. At eighteen, he entered the College of New Jersey, now Princeton University. He completed his studies in just two years, graduating in 1771. He contemplated the ministry, but he had a weak speaking voice, and so he entered politics.

In 1776, he was elected to Virginia's first legislative assembly, where he met Jefferson. Madison lost his re-election bid a year later, blaming the defeat, believe it or not, on his failure to provide enough refreshments for the electors. Thus, he assigned himself a political technical foul.

He rebounded in 1779 with his election to the Continental Congress. He then represented Virginia at the Constitutional Convention in 1787. Only thirty-six, he took a leading role in achieving Congressional approval of the Constitution. But his doing so displeased Virginians to the point they bonded within the state legislature in 1788 to stop his bid for the United States Senate. Madison, using a new offense, ran for the U.S. House of Representatives in 1789 and defeated Monroe in somewhat of an upset.

Madison and Jefferson organized the Democratic-Republican Party, the forerunner of today's Democratic Party. When Jefferson became President in 1801, he appointed Madison as Secretary of State. After Jefferson's second term, he handpicked Madison to succeed him as President in 1809. Madison received 122 electoral votes to forty-seven for the Federalist candidate, C. C. Pinckney. Madison was re-elected four years later, garnering 128 electoral votes to eighty-nine for former New York City Mayor DeWitt Clinton.

Madison recommended the War of 1812, and Congress approved it, which meant the United States would square off with Great Britain once again. The Federalists opposed the war, which they labeled "Mr. Madison's War." The Americans trailed early in the war, then threw a full-court press at the Brits and prevailed in 1814.

Madison married Dolley Payne Todd, a widow with two children, in 1779. Dolley Madison is immortalized as the definitive White House hostess with her stylish clothing and extravagant parties. She entertained important White House guests as the official hostess while serving two presidents. Jefferson was a widower at that time, so Dolley did his social planning and her husband's own social calendar. She held that hostess position for sixteen years and became the first person to serve ice cream in the White House.

Washington Irving, in a January 13, 1811 letter to Henry Brevoort, wrote about the presidential couple thusly: "Mrs. Madison is a fine, portly, buxom dame who has a smile and a pleasant word for everyone . . . as to Jeemy Madison—ah, poor Jeemy!—he is but a withered little apple-John." Top that commentary, CNN, MSNBC, or Fox News!

After her Jeemy passed away at Montpelier, their estate near Orange, Virginia, Dolley returned to Washington, DC, where she lived until her death in 1849. As for their epitaphs, James Madison had a university named after him, while his wife's name appears on packages of cupcakes.

And there were other notable "firsts" in Virginia, such as the 1862 sea battle between the Monitor and the Merrimack as the first fight between ironclad warships, the nation's first city manager form of government in Staunton in 1908, the implementation of *Brown vs. the Board of Education* in Prince Edward County and elsewhere in 1954, and the election of Douglas Wilder in 1990 as the first African-American governor of any state since Reconstruction. And while Virginia gave birth to this country, it also honored its dead. Both the Tomb of the Unknown Soldier and the gravesite of President John F. Kennedy are located at Arlington National Cemetery.

I learned a great deal about Virginia history after I moved there, seeing all of its Civil War battlefields. The Civil War wasn't exactly Mr. Madison's war, although most of its battles were fought in Virginia. Dawn and I took the kids to the New Market battlefield, where an annual Civil War re-enactment commemorates, especially, the valor of the youthful cadets of VMI (Virginia Military Institute), who marched from Lexington and fought and won there. It is a sight to see "soldiers" dressing up in the blue and the gray and engaging in a mock life and death struggle.

Virginia is a beautiful state, noted especially for its Blue Ridge Mountains and Shenandoah Valley. Living in that colonial state for thirteen years was an unforgettable experience for my family and me. Every time I hear that haunting song, "Shenandoah," I get goose bumps.

I wonder, in my wildest imagination, what it would have been like for me, the poor history student, to discuss early American politics with James Madison or to get the opportunity to explain the game of basketball to him. With his smallish 5-foot-4 frame, I would have to lift Mr. Madison up on my shoulders for him to dunk. Now that would be some shot for his namesake JMU Dukes!

Duke Dog, JMU's mascot, pals around with a lifesize staute of James Madison in a plaza in front of Varner House (not pictured) on pedestrian-only Madison Drive in the center of the 1908 campus. The bronze statue was created by Lee Leuning, of South Dakota, known for his attention to correct anatomy and exacting detail in representational works, and it was dedicated on September 17, 2002. Moody Hall (near right) and Maury Hall (far right) bestow the classic blue limestone facade that is a hallmark of JMU's original architecture. Photograph (original in color) courtesy of the James Madison University Marketing Photography Department.

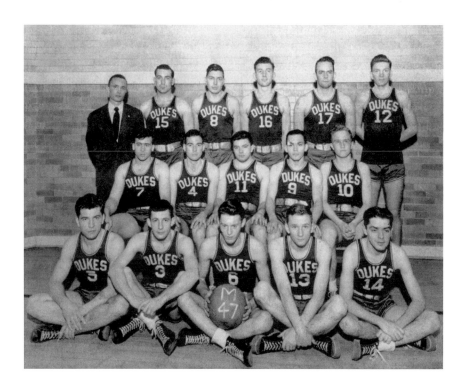

In 1946, men could enroll as day students to Madison College for the first time, and a few did. In 1947, Claude Warren, coach at Harrisonburg High School, started Madison College's first men's basketball team. The players named themselves the "Dukes," hoping Dr. Samuel Page Duke, the college's second president, would fund uniforms and equipment. It didn't work for the uniforms—the players bought their own—but the nickname stuck. The Dukes played home games in Reed (now Keezell) Hall and furnished their own transportation to away games. Back row: David Turner, Walter Eye, Tom Driver, Raymond Showalter, Bill Wolfe, and Beryl Snellings. Center: R. T. Bruce, Dick Spangler, Alvin Carter, Dale Sumption, and Ronald Burton. Front: Tom Garner, Bill Nash, J. B. Figgartt, Pete Corbin, and D. J. Driver. Photograph courtesy of the 1947 *Schoolma'am*, the school's yearbook.

ACKNOWLEDGMENTS

The authors wish to thank Dr. Ronald E. Carrier, a visionary and worker ant. He believed in this book so strongly that he wouldn't stop working until he personally saw that the manuscript became a reality.

To Dean Ehlers, a constant source of inspiration.

To those James Madison University Dukes—Pat Dosh, David Dupont, Joe Pfahler, Dan Ruland, and Linton Townes—whose return trip to their college campus in January 2014 provided this book a beginning and an ending.

To Jeff Bourne, James Madison's current athletic director and the president of the Dukes Club, who encouraged JMU alumni to assist in this book's funding. And long-standing gratitude goes to Dale and Nita Wegner, strong supporters of the JMU basketball program and hosts of numerous team functions.

Special thanks go to John A. Martin, JMU's Associate Athletic Director for Communications, and Jonathan Frame, of JMU Athletics, for their invaluable research and photographic skills. A ton of gratitude goes to Andy Jokelson and Ted Schroeder, for their conscientious editing of an earlier version of the manuscript. And thanks to Jon Wheeler and Morgan Pfaelzer, for their respective assistance and design of the six drawings that appear in the book.

Heartfelt appreciation is extended to publisher George F. Thompson, who was there from the start, supporting the authors' unique story concept, offering cogent comments on content, sequencing the illustrations, and overseeing the project; to Randy Jones and Mikki Soroczak, who skillfully edited the manuscript and assisted George with the photographs and drawings; and to David Skolkin and Tim Edeker, for their wonderful book design.

And, finally, thanks to Nancy Bondurant Jones, who chronicled the transformative history of James Madison University in her thoroughly researched and illustrated book, *Rooted on Blue Stone Hill: The History of James Madison University* (Center for American Places, 2004).

To all of the above, a hearty thank you and Go Dukes!

ABOUT THE AUTHORS

Lou Campanelli was head basketball coach at James Madison University from 1972–1985 and at the University of California, Berkeley, from 1986–1993. He took his teams to the NCAA tournament six times and to the NIT three times. He then became an advance scout for the Portland Trailblazers (1994–1995) and Cleveland Cavaliers (1996–1998) of the NBA before becoming Coordinator of Men's Basketball Officiating for the PAC-10 Conference from 2000–2006. Among his many honors, Coach Lou was inducted into the Colonial Athletic Conference Hall of Fame in 2007 and into the James Madison University Hall of Fame in 1999.

Dave Newhouse was, for more than fifty years, an award-winning sportswriter and columnist, predominantly at the *Oakland* (CA) *Tribune*, prior to his retirement in 2011. He is the author of eleven books, including *Founding 49ers: The Dark Days before the Dynasty* (2015), *Old Bears: The Class of 1956 Reaches Its Fiftieth Reunion, Reflecting on the Happy Days and Unhappy Days* (2007), *The Ultimate Oakland Raiders Trivia Book* (2001), *Jim Otto: The Pain of Glory* (2000), *Heismen: After the Glory* (1985), *The Jim Plunkett Story: The Saga of a Man Who Came Back* (1981), and (with Herb Michelson) *Rose Bowl Football since 1902* (1977). In 2014, Newhouse received the Media Award from the Multi-Ethnc Sports Hall of Fame.

ABOUT THE BOOK

Dare to Dream: How James Madison University Became Coed and Shocked the Basketball World was brought to publication in a limited hardcover edition of 500 copies and a softcover edition of 1,000 copies. The text was set in ITC New Baskerville, the paper is Huron Matte, 70 pound weight, and the book was professionally printed and bound by Thomson Shore in the United States of America.

Project Director and Publisher: George F. Thompson
Editorial and Research Assistant: Mikki Soroczak
Project Advisor: Randall B. Jones
Manuscript Editor: Purna Makaram
Book Design and Production: David Skolkin and Tim Edeker

Special Acknowledgments:
The publisher extends special thanks to Dr. Ronald E. Carrier; Jeff Bourne; Randall B. Jones; Gail Turnbull, Assistant Director of the Edith J. Carrier Arboretum; Holly Donahue, Assistant Photographer in the James Madison University Marketing Photography Department; and Kate Morris, Research and Technical Services Librarian in the Department of Special Collections of the James Madison University Libraries. Their support and assistance made this book possible.

Published 2015. First hardcover (limited) and softcover editions.
Printed in the United States of America on acid-free paper.

George F. Thompson Publishing, L.L.C.
217 Oak Ridge Circle
Staunton, VA 24401-3511, U.S.A
www.gftbooks.com

23 22 21 20 19 18 17 16 15   1 2 3 4 5

The Library of Congress Preassigned Control Number for both the
limited hardcover edition and the softcover edition is 2015950741.

ISBN: 978-1-938086-33-5 (limited hardcover edition)
ISBN: 978-1-938086-34-2 (softcover edition with flaps)